JESUIT AT LARGE

JESUIT AT LARGE

Essays and Reviews
by Paul V. Mankowski, S.J.

Edited with an Introduction
by George Weigel

IGNATIUS PRESS   SAN FRANCISCO

All previously published essays by Paul V. Mankowski, S.J.
have been reprinted with permission.

CONTENTS

Part Three
Of Many Things: Reviews, 1993–2019

INTRODUCTION

George Weigel

Father Paul V. Mankowski, S.J., would have scoffed at the claim that he was any sort of paradigmatic figure.

His sense of humor was too ironic, and Ignatian asceticism was too deeply embedded in his soul, for him to do anything but laugh at such a notion (before suggesting that the claimant had perhaps been too generously served). His likely disclaimers notwithstanding, however, Paul Mankowski's life, which ended suddenly on September 3, 2020, embodied the turmoil, at once creative and destructive, that characterized the Catholic Church and the Society of Jesus in the years immediately before, during, and after the Second Vatican Council. Father Mankowski made important contributions to the creativity of that period. And he suffered, more than many others, from the destructive forces that marred his time.

For those who never had the privilege of knowing him, a bit of biographical data may set the stage for meeting his mind, heart, and soul through his writing, some of the most emblematic examples of which are collected in this volume.

Paul Vincent Mankowski was born in South Bend, Indiana, on November 15, 1953, the second of five children of James Mankowski and Alice Otorepec Mankowski. South Bend, the longtime home of Studebaker, was a town dominated by heavy industry in those days. Jim Mankowski was a quality control inspector for Bendix, and his example left a decisive imprint on his intellectually incandescent son, for Paul Mankowski never lost his respect and affection for the working-class Catholicism in which he was raised. The future Oxford and Harvard graduate and Pontifical Biblical Institute professor was (in a word he might have mocked) rooted—in faith, family, and an ethic of hard work, responsibility, honesty, and self-sacrifice. Fidelity to those realities and virtues meant, for him, fidelity to the truth about himself. Thus throughout his life, Paul Mankowski displayed little sympathy, and indeed considerable disdain, for various clerisies: for those, that is, who imagined themselves superior to people who earned their livelihood and supported their families by the biblical sweat of their brow. It should come as no surprise, then, that Paul helped earn his undergraduate tuition at the University of Chicago by working in a U.S. Steel mill during the summer months.

He didn't imagine himself a model Catholic kid and "was never," as he once put it, "one of those little boys who always dreamed of being a priest." In college, he admitted, he "got up to most of the usual iniquities," but he regularly attended Sunday Mass, didn't go through any crisis of faith, and, as his undergraduate studies were about to end in 1976 with a degree in classics and philosophy, imagined that he had his life rather "neatly planned out." He would pursue doctoral work in ancient history at the University of Chicago and then become "a tweed-and-briar-pipe classics prof, sire a large Catholic family, and spend a comfortable life fishing and hunting and reading Horace and bringing home good wines and Mass-books to the wife and kiddies."

Then came the bolt from the blue: "In early May of 1976 I was clobbered, out of nowhere, by the very strong certainty that God was calling me to give up that future and become a Jesuit"—a religious community with which he had had minimal previous contact. He resisted the call, praying in response, "Thanks, but no thanks. I'll be a good Catholic family man, kick my share and more into the collection plate, fight my corner doctrinally, but please pick someone else for your priest." The answer was disconcerting, he later recalled: "No. You." After some weeks of this, he told God, "OK, you win." At the end of May he found the phone number of the Jesuit Seminary Association (which he correctly assumed to be a fundraising operation) and asked to speak to a vocation director. Years later, he remembered "how flustered the secretary was in scrambling to get the number for me, as if she [were] afraid I'd hang up and become a Dominican if she didn't find it in time."

He told his parents of this surprising development a few days before his baccalaureate graduation, and they, "as in every subsequent vicissitude ... handled it about as well as it could possibly be handled: 'It's your life, your decision; we wish you the best but will not interfere.'"

The more wrenching emotional challenge lay elsewhere: "Telling my girlfriend was harder. She was ... unsuspecting and unprepared ... and it was a real shock. Part of the difficulty is that a boyfriend and girlfriend carry on a life of intimacy that rarely includes an explicit statement of commitment. Yet the nature of the intimacy precludes a discussion of the boy's becoming a priest as a frank and objectively considered option; it's not the kind of thing the boy can hint at or bring gradually into the usual conversations ('You know, I've been wondering lately whether Roman history might not be more interesting than Greek, also whether I should become a priest or not')."

Paul Mankowski entered the Jesuit novitiate in Berkley, Michigan, near Detroit, in the fall of 1976. On completing that preparatory formation, he was assigned to studies at Oxford University, where he read philosophy and classics in "Mods and Greats" and earned an M.A. in 1983; during his free moments, he was the sparring partner of Tony Abbott, future prime minister of Australia. Returning to the United States, he was awarded master's and licentiate degrees in theology from the Jesuits' Weston School of Theology in Cambridge, Massachusetts, in 1987, and was ordained priest that same year at St. Francis Xavier Church in Cincinnati. His doctoral studies took him back to Cambridge, this time to Harvard; there he earned a Ph.D. in Comparative Semitic Philology with a dissertation on Akkadian loan words in biblical Hebrew that became a standard reference work.

As his doctoral studies were nearing completion, he was assigned to the Pontifical Biblical Institute in Rome, where he taught introductory, intermediate, and advanced Hebrew for fifteen years (often lecturing in the Italian he had mastered in a few months), while occasionally leading a popular seminar on translation techniques. During those years, he spent Christmas vacations as a chaplain to the Missionaries of Charity in various locales, including Albania and Haiti. After his tertianship in Australia (during which he was introduced by a friendly Catholic farmer to the methodology of bovine obstetrical examination), he was acting pastor of English-speaking Sacred Heart parish in Amman, Jordan, before returning to the United States to become Scholar-in-Residence at the Lumen Christi Institute at his alma mater, the University of Chicago. There, he engaged in a wide-ranging ministry that included intellectual work with scholars and other professionals in Great Books seminars and extensive spiritual direction and counseling—two activities that were bedrocks of his entire priesthood. He professed final vows on December 12, 2012. After his death from a burst cerebral aneurysm, he was buried from St. Thomas the Apostle Church in Chicago's Hyde Park neighborhood, near the Woodlawn Jesuit Community house, where he had lived for years.

Those are the mere facts, flavored by bits of autobiographical reminiscence in one of Paul Mankowski's many literary styles: droll wit. But the mere facts do not capture the essence of this man of extraordinary qualities, infrequently encountered in the same person.

He was off-the-charts brilliant, an extraordinary linguist and a scholar of international repute. But he wore his great learning lightly, was a serious and knowledgeable sports fan, and was always happy with a rod or gun in the outdoors, not least in company with his father.

He rarely expressed doubts about anything. But he displayed a great sensitivity to the doubts and confusions of those who had the humility to confess that they were at sea.

He could be as fierce as Jeremiah in denouncing injustice and dishonesty. But the compassion he displayed to spiritually wounded fellow priests and laity who sought healing through the workings of divine grace at his hands was just as notable a feature of his personality, if not, as is the nature of these things, as publicly visible.

His spiritual direction, which was characterized by a gift for listening, also combined erudite humor with a profound grasp of the essentials of living an integrated Catholic life. Thus, he would advise a penitent to pray the Liturgy of the Hours daily ("It's good to have Iron Age words in your mouth every day") and to take regular advantage of the practice of sacramental confession ("[which] will show you how to live with charity").

He was a true ascetic who took the religious vow of poverty seriously. His clothes were typically threadbare hand-me-downs from others. On making final vows, he received some monetary gifts— all of which he gave to a crisis pregnancy clinic. When friends picked up the tab for a meal together, he would donate whatever his share of the bill would have been to the Missionaries of Charity. He gave away the books he reviewed and was an academic without a personal library, thinking nearby university and public libraries sufficient.

Yet for all that he lived a rigorous life of evangelical poverty and material detachment, he was the best company imaginable in a seminar, at a party, or over a table, and his gift for comedy was legendary. For decades he sent friends send-ups—revised hymn texts, parodies of famous men's diaries, concocted news stories and press releases mocking some political or ecclesiastical fatuity—that were, in the vernacular of twenty-first-century text-messaging, LOL.

He was a writer of genius. As the selections from his essays and reviews collected here suggest, he could handle virtually any literary assignment with insight, analytic acuity, stylistic aplomb, and, more often than not, pungent wit. He had a gift for finding the precisely right word or image to make a striking point: a result, one expects, of his own wide-ranging reading in both non-fiction and fiction.

He loved the Church's tradition, including its liturgical tradition. But Paul Mankowski was no "Traddie" or Ultra-Traditionalist as that term came to be used in the last decade or so of his life. He knew that there were truths embedded in the Reformation maxim *ecclesia semper reformanda* (the Church always to be reformed). He understood what the great John Henry Newman meant by the development of doctrine. And he was under no illusions that the Church of the 1950s could be frozen in amber as some sort of once-for-all expression of Catholic life. At the same time, Paul Mankowski understood what too many others failed to grasp: that all authentic Catholic reform was a development, a "re-*form*," of the "form" that Christ had given the Church as its perennial constitution. Exasperated by activists who wanted to "take back our Church," Mankowski wrote to friends in 2002, "The Church is not ours to take back because it never belonged to us, and the instant we make it 'our own' we are damned. No merely human institution, no matter how perfectly pure and gutsy and dutiful its members, can take away even a venial sin. That is the point St. Paul takes sixteen chapters to get across to the Romans."

Paul Mankowski was, in a word, a man of Vatican II rightly understood: a man not of rupture or Catholic "paradigm shifts" but rather a man of reform and development in continuity with tradition.

Father Richard John Neuhaus, whom he befriended in the early 1990s, dubbed Father Mankowski one of the "Papal Bulls": Jesuits of a certain generation notable for their intellectually sophisticated and unwavering Catholic orthodoxy. Paul Mankowski was no bull (papal or otherwise) in a china shop, though. He relished debate and was courteous in it; what he found off-putting was the unwillingness of Catholic progressives to state their position frankly. This struck him as a form of hypocrisy. And while Father Mankowski often brought strays back to the Lord's flock with the kindness of a good shepherd, he was unsparingly candid about what he perceived as intellectual dishonesty, or what he deplored as "ignoble timidity" in facing clerical corruption and clerical sexual abuse, against which he was a prophetic campaigner.

Paul Mankowski was not a man of the subjunctive. And he paid the price for it—which brings us to the central drama of his life, his relationship with the Society of Jesus.

Paul Mankowski entered the Jesuits during what only the willfully obtuse will deny was an extremely difficult period in the history of one of Catholicism's most distinguished religious communities. The Society of Jesus had thirty-six thousand members at the close of the Second Vatican Council in 1965; Mankowski could count some fifteen thousand Jesuits throughout the world at his death. Jesuits abandoned the priesthood and religious life in droves in the decades after Vatican II; others redefined "religious life" and the exercise of the priesthood according to the cultural fashions of the moment rather than the wisdom of the Ignatian tradition. A religious community once known for its sophisticated defense of the settled truths of Catholic faith, and for its rigorous spirit of obedience to ecclesiastical authority, became a late twentieth-century bastion of the Western ideology of expressive individualism, in which the evangelical counsels of "poverty," "chastity," and "obedience" were often "reimagined" according to personal taste or predilection—which typically meant with their demanding edges rounded off. Those Jesuits who adhered to what St. Ignatius Loyola and St. Francis Xavier would have understood by poverty, chastity, and obedience were not infrequently outcasts—and persecuted outcasts—within the religious community to which they had committed themselves.

In the decades before Vatican II, the philosophical, theological, historical, and biblical creativity of Jesuit scholars made seminal contributions to the intellectual ferment that shaped the Second Vatican Council's teaching: its development of Catholic self-understanding about the nature of the Church as a communion of disciples in mission; its reform of Catholic worship; its understanding of divine revelation as expressed in both Scripture and Tradition; its approach to the quest for Christian unity and to the Catholic dialogue with Judaism and other world religions; its affirmation of religious freedom as one pillar of a free and virtuous society. In the decades after the Council, however, some Jesuit thinkers stretched the boundaries of orthodoxy to the breaking point and had to be called to order by the teaching authority of the Church—an exercise of ecclesiastical discipline in service to doctrinal coherence and intellectual integrity that was typically resented and on occasion actively resisted by the dominant forces in the Society. These patterns of doctrinal and theological dissent had a profound impact on what had long been regarded as among the jewels in the Society's crown, its institutions of higher learning—the most prestigious of which, in the twenty-first-century United States, could only be regarded as "Catholic" in a vestigial sense.

And then there were questions of lifestyle. Few if any religious communities throughout the world Church were immune to the tsunami of the sexual revolution. The Society of Jesus was no exception, and its own difficulties were exacerbated by the prominence of Jesuit theologians who publicly dissented from authoritative and biblically based Church teaching about the Catholic ethic of human love, on matters ranging from contraception to homosexuality. The linkage between a culture of dissent in the theologians' guild and the clerical sexual abuse of the young was denied by Jesuit thinkers, even as the Society's financial resources in the U.S. were severely depleted by abuse settlements.

This chaos and confusion seemed to some to exemplify the ancient Latin adage *corruptio optimi pessima* (the corruption of the best is worst). Yet there were Jesuits who strove to remain faithful to St. Ignatius' vision of the Society: to think with and for the Church, to set the world ablaze with the Gospel, and to live the consecrated life of the evangelical counsels in lives of radical commitment to the Gospel and the salvation of souls. Paul Mankowski was one of those men. And because of that, much of his Jesuit life was marked by suffering, on a vocational journey in which he was often berated, deplored, and rejected by his own.

He refused to be embittered, however. Almost thirty years after entering the Society of Jesus, Father Mankowski responded in 2004 to a young man's inquiry about the possibility of joining the Jesuits in terms that express both his stringent honesty and his love for the Jesuit charism and vocation:

Thanks for your letter. I'm pleased to try to answer your questions as best I can.

It is my conviction that, at present, the Society of Jesus is a corrupt order. This means that it has serious problems in all its endeavors at all levels of authority, and, more importantly, it has lost the capacity to mend itself by its own internal resources. Many Jesuit superiors of my acquaintance explicitly (if cagily) dissent from Church teaching on hot-button issues, and almost all superiors dissent at least tacitly.

It is also the case that the vows of religion are (in the aggregate) in a shambles. Poverty and obedience are stretched about as far as the terms can go without snapping, but the real scandal is chastity. No aspect of the Church's current scandals is without a Jesuit counterpart.... But more disruptive ... is the tolerance of attitudes and practices that seem to mock the earnestness of Jesuits trying to live the life with integrity....

In all candor I have to say that, at present, I see no indication whatever of the capacity or a willingness on the part of the Roman Jesuit leadership to address and remedy these problems. I believe those in command are, for the most part, frightened to stand up to the full extent of the rot. I believe a few positively desire the rot; they want religious life to disappear and want to be agents in its disappearance.

That said, if I had to do it all over again, knowing what I now know, I would enter the Jesuits tomorrow. Let me try to explain why.

All the ancient orders of the Church go through periodic cycles of corruption and reform, and the more deeply one reads in the history of the Church the more appalling the troughs of corruption appear. But while an order's charism is perpetual, the period into which you or I happen to be born is contingent. The Dominicans were healthy in the 13th and 19th centuries and rotten in the early 16th century. If a man has a vocation to the Dominicans, then it doesn't matter (i.e., with respect to the authenticity of his vocation) whether the order is healthy or corrupt at a given time. One man God wills to save by the challenges that come his way in a healthy order, another man God wills to save through the difficulties he'll face in a corrupt order....

So the only really important question is whether you ... have or don't have a vocation. If you do, your own desires, and the state of the order, become secondary—not without significance but secondary....

I also have to say that there are advantages to belonging to a corrupt and largely subversive order. First among these is that the orthodox men you meet are orthodox for the right reason: because they believe it's the truth, not because it's a shrewd career move. They are excellent men, better at any rate than I deserve to have as friends, and they are men who will not leave your side when it looks like you're fighting a losing battle. I see this as part of the grace of vocation. The Jesuit vow formula says, "And as You (God) have given me the desire to serve You, so also give me the grace to accomplish it." He does.

... By the way, I offered my Mass this morning for the intention that God might be with you in your vocational discernment.

Your brother in Christ,
Paul Mankowski, S.J.

That commitment to living the Jesuit life as St. Ignatius Loyola intended it to be lived, and to help reform the Society of Jesus by doing so, led Father Paul Mankowski into the conflict he describes in the memorandum that appears as the appendix of this volume. A word about that conflict and its place in the larger drama of post-conciliar Catholicism is in order.

In July 1996, the journal *Catholic World Report* published an article titled "The Strange Political Career of Father Drinan," written by the distinguished historian James Hitchcock, himself a longtime faculty member of Jesuit-led St. Louis University. The occasion for the article was the support given President Bill Clinton's veto of a bill banning partial-birth abortion by Father Robert Drinan, a Jesuit of the New England province who had served five terms in the U.S. House of Representatives before leaving public office by order of Pope John Paul II. During his congressional career, Father Drinan was a reliable vote in favor of the most extreme interpretations of the abortion license created by the 1973 Supreme Court decisions *Roe v. Wade* and *Doe v. Bolton*; in doing so, he helped provide political cover for numerous Catholic politicians who tacked to the prevailing cultural winds by taking a similar stand. Nonetheless, Drinan's support for Clinton's veto of the partial-birth abortion ban disturbed even Catholics of the theological and political left.

Hitchcock's article was intended to demonstrate that the "strange" political career of Robert Drinan involved more than a Catholic priest's relentless support of the abortion license as a matter of public policy. It involved clericalism of the rankest sort, in which a Jesuit superior informed the Society's Roman authorities that there was no layman in Massachusetts capable of replacing Drinan in Congress. It involved duplicity, dissembling, and prevarication within the Society of Jesus, and between some of the Society's senior American leaders and American bishops. It involved those same U.S. Jesuit leaders deceiving the Jesuit General in Rome, and it eventually involved the General's own weakness in bending to what he likely knew was wrong. And throughout, it involved years of cover-up.

The publication of Hitchcock's article unleashed a firestorm of criticism, but the hot blasts of opprobrium were not aimed at Father Drinan or his Jesuit enablers. They were aimed at Father Paul Mankowski, who had given materials he had gleaned from the archives of the New England Province of the Society of Jesus to Professor Hitchcock as documentation for his article. In a letter to fellow Jesuits denouncing Mankowski, the New England provincial of the time (who had not been involved in the Drinan affair before and during Drinan's congressional career) misrepresented both the nature of the archival materials cited and the circumstances under which Father Mankowski had obtained them. Those misrepresentations continue to dominate perceptions and discussion of this matter today.

The results of all this for Paul Mankowski were draconian. He was forbidden for years to publish in his own name. He was constrained in his pastoral work. He was often treated like a pariah. And while he was eventually permitted to take final religious vows and become a "spiritual coadjutor" within the Society of Jesus, Mankowski was refused "full incorporation" into the Society (which involves taking the famous Jesuit "fourth" vow of obedience to the pope with respect to mission).

The circumstances under which Father Mankowski obtained the Drinan archival materials and his intentions for their use are described in the memorandum found in the appendix. Mankowski entrusted the memorandum to several friends and it is published here, unedited, for the first time. It does not make for easy reading. But it is essential. It is essential for an accurate historical rendering of Father

Drinan's congressional career, which was and continues to be inaccurately described. It is essential to understanding the contemporary history of the Catholic Church in the United States. It is essential reading for those who would work for the reform of the Society of Jesus. And it is essential for the posthumous vindication of Father Paul Mankowski's honor.

In his homily at Paul Mankowski's funeral Mass on September 8, 2020, Father Kevin Flannery, S.J., a longtime friend, spoke of Mankowski's quiet but intense devotion to St. John Fisher. Fisher—the only member of the English hierarchy who refused to bend to Henry VIII's will in the matter of the king's divorce from Catherine of Aragon and subsequent marriage to Anne Boleyn—was the "prototypical, principled 'odd man out' "—and so, Father Flannery subtly suggested, was Paul Mankowski. And like Fisher, Paul Mankowski was an odd man out in the Society whose charism he cherished, the Society from and in which he suffered a great deal, because of his devotion to the truth.

Describing Evelyn Waugh's Catholic faith in one of the reviews included in this collection, Father Mankowski drew something of a self-portrait:

> The faith Waugh embraced could be called "impersonal," if by that term we mean not hostile to the person but indifferent to the cravings and pleas of the ego. C.S. Lewis wrote that the Real is that which says to us, "Your preferences have not been considered." So too for Waugh, it was the fact that the Church had not consulted him, or any other creature, on the formulation of her doctrines that made her claim plausible.

The same might be said of Paul Mankowski's description of Flannery O'Connor in an address given at St. Louis University's Catholic Studies Center less than a year before his death:

> Flannery O'Connor ... knew that she had to work to earn a hearing, and that she would be facing cultural headwind all her life. It was a challenge she took up with relish. Reviled, scorned, snubbed, and patronized by louts with a fifth of her intellectual horsepower, yet never answering a curse with a curse—she always returned to her own

work to polish, to make it clearer, to sharpen the edge of the blade, to make it accomplish the Lord's work even if it failed to accomplish her own.

Paul Mankowski concluded that lecture by calling Flannery O'Connor "a saint for our times"—an appellation he would have derided had anyone applied it to him. Yet if the essence of sanctity, as the Catholic Church understands it, is heroic virtue, then there were certainly elements of sanctity in the life and ministry of Paul V. Mankowski, S.J. He lived as a true man for others, unsparing of himself. He knew the meaning of obedient suffering and embraced it as a necessary feature of his consecrated life. He spent his remarkable intellectual gifts in service to evangelization and Christian formation.

The emergency personnel who tried to save him on the day of his death tore open his shirt to administer CPR, mistakenly thinking that he had suffered a heart attack. Later, a fellow Jesuit at the Woodlawn Jesuit House wrote to friends about one of Paul's meager personal effects—a small thing that captured the essence of this Jesuit at large as a radically converted Christian disciple:

> There was one other item in his right breast pocket (or what was left of it). A simple, yarn-stitched "Cross in My Pocket" with this verse: "I carry a cross in my pocket, a simple reminder to me of the fact that I am a Christian no matter where I may be; it reminds me to be thankful for the blessing day by day and to strive to serve him better in all that I do and say. So I carry a cross in my pocket reminding no one but me that Jesus Christ is the Lord of my life, if only I'll let him be."

Part One

CATHOLICISM IN THIS TIME:
ESSAYS, 1990–2019

Why the Immaculate Conception

Pure. Whole. Intact. Entire. Spotless. Stainless. Sinless. Unsoiled. Unsullied. Unblemished. Uncorrupted. Immaculate!

I live in an age, and a country, wherein the largest single cause of death of infants under one year of age is homicide. I live at a time when, according to those who claim to know these things, Ronald McDonald has surpassed Jesus Christ in popularity among children. I live at a time when the best known moral theologians have despaired of leading people to a more virtuous life, but are principally concerned to insulate the sinner from the consequences of his sin; logic has given way to latex as the preferred medium of instruction. I live in a country where, this very day, in the time between my rising and my standing here before you, four thousand of our fellow citizens, four thousand human beings with an eternal destiny, were summarily killed by abortion. I live at a time when most promises will be broken, most vows will be repudiated, most marriages will fail. I live at a time when it is virtually impossible to go through a day without using some commodity which, however innocent in itself, is not hawked in terms of some base or venal allure. I am promised prosperous and intriguing companions by the folks who brew my beer; and those who sell my shaving cream are at pains to assure me that it will provoke the women I encounter into sexual frenzy. (The last claim, I might add, is an exaggeration.)

It may seem pointless at such a time, in such a place, to hold up the Virgin Mary, and especially her Immaculate Conception, as a source of nourishment for our lives as Christians. For her perfection can appear so remote from the moral sweatiness and squalor in which our personal struggles occur that it recedes entirely into the background; it is swallowed up by our furious temptations and enthusiasms, and

Originally published in *Voices* 5, no. 1 (Winter 1990), online edition. Taken from a homily preached at Women for Faith & Family's Immaculate Conception Mass and festival, held at St. Roch's Church in St. Louis, December 8, 1989.

so is lost to us. This remoteness is widened, and not helped, by a way of speaking which would present the Virgin Mary to us as "the representation of an Ideal," that is, as an abstraction, or at best a personified Virtue, like the Roman goddesses of Wisdom or Moderation. Thus, she, who begins as a real flesh-and-blood woman, "a virgin, betrothed to a man named Joseph," as [Lk 1:27] has it, becomes at the end an abstract noun, a figure of speech.

And of course it's not hard to see why in and of itself a personified Ideal is of little consequence to the moral or spiritual life. To use an analogy from a more trivial world, we might imagine a mythological golfer who scored 18 in every round he ever played, yet few instructors would "hold up" such a figure as an example to his pupils, and even fewer players would tell themselves in preparing to make a treacherous shot, "Steady now. Remember that the Great McTavish always did the 530-yard fifth hole in one stroke ..." Ideals can be beacons to guide us, but they are seldom fires at which we can warm our hands; they may be necessary to our thinking, but they don't strengthen the will.... If you think about the two or three saints to whom you yourself have the deepest devotion, is it not the case that part of what attracts and fascinates you about these saints is that you can recognize a certain kinship in the kind of fragility they possess, a fragility against which their heroism blazes with particular glory in your eyes, in your heart? Isn't it the case that, since you can see God's work in their weakness, you can come to accept the possibility of God's working in your weakness too?

Perhaps then we're in a little better position to understand the unique complications this presents in terms of the Virgin Mary. She says, "My soul glorifies the Lord ... for He has looked with kindness on His lowly servant" [Lk 1:46, 48]. Now isn't there a voice in the back of our heads which whispers at this point, "Lowly? We should all be so lowly!" That is, we assume that Mary's perfection would have been as obvious to her as it is to us, and it seems a trifle stagy in such circumstances to pretend to true lowliness. Now I apologize to those of you who have never been vexed by this problem, but I think it is common enough to be worth trying to free ourselves from it.

It seems to me that in speaking of the Virgin Mary as sinless, as immaculate, we all too often mean that she was constitutionally *incapable* of sinning, that she was no more capable of sin than a man is capable of giving birth or an oyster is capable of flight. There are some difficulties here. First, we are told in the Letter to the Hebrews that "we have not [in Jesus] a high priest who is unable to sympathize with our weakness, but one who in every respect has been tempted as we are, but without sin" [4:15]. There is then a theological difficulty in attributing to Mary that freedom from temptation which her own Son did not cling to. Further, if we speak of the Virgin Mary as constitutionally incapable of sin, it is all the more difficult to discover in her the humanity which is by its very weakness transparent to God's power. Consequently, in an age like our own especially, she is all the more likely to be treated as precisely that sort of Ideal which cannot warm our affections or stir our courage.

One obvious, all-too-predictable solution is to deny the Immaculate Conception and the sinlessness of Mary, under the fatuous pretense that by doing so, she will become more "human," and so more accessible to the rest of us sinners. Wrong on all counts, the most obvious being that a human who sins is *less* human after he succumbs than he was before. Still, there is a persistent, though imbecile, way of speaking in which some public figure who has an adulterous affair or a personal foible come to light thereby reveals a "human side" of himself. In fact, it is in keeping his commitments and displaying evidence of virtue that a man is most fully human; in giving in to temptations, even trivial or petty ones, he becomes that much more bestial.

When we fall, we fall from a *human* dignity, not an angelic one; our skid may well end at a level of animal savagery, but we never "tumble down" into humanity—and not because pigs are of themselves wickeder than men, but because the elevator, so to speak, was already at that floor. There is no point, then, in exploring this avenue further. I think the way out is more direct. A friend of mine is fond of saying, "Whenever I hear the word 'dialogue,' I reach for my dogma." Let us, in the same spirit, reach for our dogma and see if it has anything to say to us.

Pope Pius IX's dogmatic definition of 1854 [*Ineffabilis Deus*] runs thus: "The Blessed Virgin Mary, at the first instant of her conception, by a singular privilege and grace of almighty God, in consideration of the merits of Jesus Christ, the Savior of mankind, was preserved free from all stain of original sin." First, it should be noticed that the grace given to the Virgin Mary was "in consideration of the merits of Jesus Christ." That is, in and of herself, she too was in need of salvation and was saved through the sacrifice of her Son, although it worked "retroactively," as it were, so as to affect her even at her conception.

A very partial analogy might be drawn with a woman afflicted from birth with a progressive terminal disease, whose own child grows up to be the scientist who discovers the cure for the disease, and so heals the mother. But let's not push that too far. The second point, and this is the one I want to stress, is that it is *original sin* from which Mary was preserved at her conception. The contamination which we all inherited from Adam, namely, estrangement from God with its consequent warping of our human appetites, as well as death itself, did not touch her. The fittingness of this "singular privilege and grace" was, to my mind, well expressed by the English bishop Langdon Fox, who asked, "How could Mary be said to have been made fit to stand in the relationship of Mother to the all pure God if the Devil could claim, and claim truly, that once, even if only for a moment, she had been in the state of original sin?"—that is, if the devil had her in his control even briefly. Be that as it may, it should be clear that freedom from original sin does not bring with it an incapacity for actual sin. After all, Adam and Eve were both created without original sin; it was in fact their first *actual* sin whose effect we call "original" in their descendants.

Now the upshot, it seems to me, is this. The Blessed Virgin Mary lived her life in the state in which Adam and Eve lived before their sin. She was as capable of sin as they were; her life, to this extent like ours, was a series of choices between good and bad, self and other, God's will and her own. Her glory, for which all generations will call her blessed, is that in every instance she said, "I am your servant. Let it be done to me in accordance with your word" [Lk 1:38]. She, who was full of grace, said, "Your will be done, not mine." When she praised God because he had looked on her in her lowliness, she was not feigning humility. She was uniquely aware that it was God's grace, and not her own merit, in virtue of which she had been set apart. And the consciousness of the gap between her humanity and God's power was uniquely acute in her case.

C. S. Lewis remarked somewhere [in *Mere Christianity*] that we are not to imagine that Jesus had an easier time with temptation than we.

In fact, he said, Jesus Christ was the only one who ever felt the full strength of temptation, because he was the only one who never gave in to it. He said by way of explanation something like this: "After all, you don't discover the true strength of the German Army by laying down and letting it roll over you; but only by standing up to it and fighting it at every turn." If I might extend (and correct) C. S. Lewis here, I would say that the Virgin Mary is, apart from her Son, the only one who really knew humility, since it was she who, in every instance, chose obedience, who let God's will trump her own, who refused to be duped into trusting in her own resources.

We might illustrate what this means from the Gospel: I once heard another Jesuit talk over coffee about a homily he had to give at a summer camp for retarded children. The Gospel text on which he was to preach was the account of the rich young man. Unsure how he was going to communicate the message to his congregation, this priest somewhat despairingly brought out a simple coffee cup after reading the Scripture. He said, "You see, the rich young man's cup was already full of all the things he had, and so Jesus couldn't give him anything; there was no room." I still think that to be one of the most striking exegeses of that passage I've ever heard. And, when it is reversed, the same image can be applied to Mary. Her cup alone was genuinely empty; she alone had room only for God, for herself, no element of possessiveness or self-will, which took up the space made for God's love. She alone was truly an earthen vessel, a repository, she whom the archangel Gabriel called "full of grace" [Lk 1:28].

Her humility, her lowliness, was not a sham. Alone of our race, she could point to her humility without an admixture of hypocrisy. The lowliness was hers; the glory was God's. Far from being aloof from the pain of decision, she is the only one of us who ever felt the full sting. If you think I am laying it on a bit thick here, I'd invite you to try living for ten minutes genuinely unconscious of your own dignity, genuinely reliant on God. It hurts like blazes.

There is a strain of feminist Mariology which feels repugnance at the dogma of the Immaculate Conception because it views the notion as demeaning to women. Orthodox theologians were so scandalized by the particularly feminine dimension of sinfulness (according to this school) that they found it necessary to cook up the idea of an immaculate conception in order to sanitize the event of the Incarnation. I hope I have shown that this way of thinking has got things exactly backward. In articulating its belief that Mary was free of original sin, the Church is thrusting the Blessed Virgin into the heart of the problematic struggle of temptation and grace; it is the opposite of insulation. It is not some angelic perfection, but her *humanity* which is vindicated by Pius IX's definition—her dependence on merits of Jesus Christ, her constant reenactment of the drama of Adam's choice, a drama which is no less dramatic for its happy ending, a drama which ultimately includes us all, in the vision of the woman clothed with the sun, crushing the serpent at the world's end.

Every true Christian instinct points to this; all orthodox devotion to Mary rejoices in her triumph, because she was conscious of that profound humility of which we have ourselves only the faintest inklings; whether she is pictured at the foot of the cross, or with a child at her breast, or as the queen and bride arrayed in splendor, the prefigured bride without spot or wrinkle, it is our fragility in which we give thanks for God's love, God's grace, God's fidelity to us in her.

Pure. Whole. Intact. Entire. Spotless. Stainless. Sinless. Unsoiled. Unsullied. Unblemished. Uncorrupted. Immaculate!

In Praise of Conformity:
Why Priests Should Stop Fooling
Around with the Liturgy

The theologian Brian Daley, S.J., has suggested that the Eucharist serves as an "icon" of the Church. That is, it both represents the Mystical Body of Christ in symbolic terms and re-enacts the central event of salvation history. In this view, there is no detail concerning the celebration of the Eucharist which can be termed trivial or unimportant, for there is no aspect of our gathering for Mass which cannot acquire a meaning larger than itself, and hence become a source of edification or corruption. It is idle to pretend that the Eucharist is not a battleground: every Christian disagreement—theological, ethical, or ecclesial—will be fought symbolically in the arena of liturgy as well as discursively in the arena of the academy. For a man to claim he is "indifferent" about liturgy is to admit he is indifferent about the faith.

In my experience, such indifference is rare among churchgoers, regardless of their level of theological awareness. For steamfitters as well as for the clerical professoriat, it matters whether or not a priest uses the *lavabo*; it matters whether or not he crosses himself when he begins Mass. In the diction he chooses, in the rubrics he follows or omits, in his gestures and dress, every celebrant connects himself doctrinally with some believers and signals a doctrinal distance with others. The degree of offense each worshiper takes when a distance is signaled varies in direct proportion to the seriousness with which he invests his own hopes for the Church.

I have lived in a house of religious where the "trivial obedience" of commingling water and wine at the Offertory would cause two contrary reactions: one man would go white with indignation and stiffen as the veins bulged on his forehead. His brother priest would nod in approval and satisfaction. These men were exact contemporaries.

Originally published in *Crisis Magazine*, February 1, 1991.

Of course, the lines are seldom drawn quite so sharply, and not all reactions are so blatant as a consequence. There is a great deal of pseudo-naiveté used to paper over the cracks in the integrity of the liturgy whereby expedience and not disagreement is proffered as the reason for innovation.

Is it ever convincing? Surely it is disingenuous to pretend that the reception of Communion by the people before the celebrant (to take an example at random) is a simple convenience and not also a doctrinal statement. No doubt it is possible, in theory, consciously to depart from approved liturgical usages without intending to give notice of some underlying doctrinal disparity, but in the real world it almost never happens that way.

I have often heard my seniors engage in wry reminiscence about the number of mortal sins a priest was liable to commit when saying Mass "in the old days" by the tiniest violation of a single rubric—and indeed it seems that a rather morbid imagination was at work in some of the theology then. On the other hand, it is beyond question today that a priest has 201 ways of saying "In yo' face!" to his brothers while celebrating the Eucharist. Perhaps the old count wasn't so far-fetched after all, even though the fulcrum of sinfulness is different from that envisioned by the manualists. The currents run deep.

Guitar Theology

A cultural anthropologist-turned-cartoonist might say that the prime emotive thrust which powered pre-Vatican II liturgical practice was a distrust of spontaneity. Mass was "by the book." The people stood, knelt, and genuflected on cue. Hymns had a somewhat exaggerated gravity. While the Latin of the liturgy was never so obscure to the people as later polemicists have made it out to be, it was still mysterious, remote, and formal. It's almost impossible to be "down to earth" in Latin. All the trappings of religion were invested with the same tidiness, the same relentless adulthood. If a magazine publisher needed to add an ecclesiastical tone to a headline, he printed it in elaborate "Old English" letters, since this most formal, most adult typeface became synonymous with things churchy. One can still find older churches today where the fire-signs over the doors are painted in large Latinate uncials. Behind this rigidity, perhaps, was the assumption that anything freer, anything more spontaneous, would somehow smirch the dignity of the Church; perhaps deeper still was the suspicion that if the shackles *were* taken off, the sentiments released would certainly be heterodox.

As a Church we are still eddying in the backwash from the wave of reaction precipitated by Vatican II—or better, from that picture of Vatican II which was given to us by the *apparatchiks* in the liturgical commissions, for it is quite clear that fraud was perpetrated in the "selling" of the Council to the laity. (Whether the fraud was benevolent or injurious depends on the value one assigns to continuity.) Mere allowances made by the Council were proclaimed to be directives; exceptions were said to be rules; chinks in the windows were taken to be doors. In Eucharistic practice, as in doctrine proper, there is more than a grain of truth in the joke that a "pre-Vatican II Catholic" is one who reads the Documents of Vatican II without a commentary.

Regardless of how one accounts for the changes, their impact can hardly be exaggerated. If the term "relentlessly adult" characterized the old Mass, the term "remorselessly infantile" might stand for the new. Spontaneity became the desideratum, and the place where Catholics chiefly chose to look for spontaneity was in the lives of children. The sugary hymns of Dan Schutte, Ray Repp, and Sebastian Temple are part of this legacy, and the general thrust of liturgical music reflects the change.

In the first place, "negative" feelings are almost wholly excluded from the modern corpus, or when they do appear are given such a banal and frothy treatment as to become unrecognizable. Whole portions of Scripture simply cannot make it into this genre because they can never be assimilated into the contrived bounciness and bonhomie through which its reality is filtered.

The use of the guitar is no less significant. It is primarily (in America) a teenager's instrument, the kind of thing that conjures up the beach bonfire and raggedy sweatshirts. It is, of course, the very antithesis of the concert organ, that grand and pompous engine of Johnsonian *pietas*. The guitar can be pawed by just about anybody. Obviously you can't *really* be spontaneous with it, but many people wished very much that you could, and we are still living, as a Church, with this fond daydream.

Nor is it an accident that contemporary Church music is scored in a high register. The new pretense is that ours is a *young persons'* Church; in the view of the major impresarios, there would be something fundamentally unwholesome, almost Republican, about introducing a choir of basses and baritones into a contemporary liturgy. Of course, you can sing "Yahweh, the Faithful One" in a baritone, just as you can sing "Old Man River" in a falsetto, but it's clear in each case that you'd be missing the point. And the point is that youth—spontaneous youth, uninhibited youth, bonhomous youth, joyous gregarious coyly androgynous youth—is the prime icon in the Catholic Church of Camelot. Some of the more sensitive liturgy coordinators will toss in a "traditional" hymn now and then as a kind of milk-bone for the rheumatoid faithful, but the picture is no less clear that such music belongs to the past.

Disenfranchised Believers

A side-effect of this emphasis is that Catholic culture has become much more haute-bourgeois, more suburban, than ever before. In effect the new liturgists disenfranchised working-class Catholics, and in particular working men, from reasonably wholehearted participation in the Mass. Say what you will, you cannot get a congregation of plumbers and foundry-workers to join in Ray Repp's hit "Allelu! Allelu! Evry'body sing Allelu!" and *mean* it. It might come off in Lake Forest but not in Gary. One of the main reasons the Church got fewer vocations from blue-collar families after the Council is the precious tone set by the parish liturgy. Few fathers who earn their living with their hands and shoulders are going to smile on the prospect of their sons' leading a congregation in "On Eagle's Wings."

What I say about liturgical music applies *a fortiori* to dance and "movement." Unless the Church consciously decides that it is in her best interests to further distance herself from humble working people, I cannot imagine why she continues to flirt with these diversions. I do not think it impossible that liturgical dance may have a limited place in certain peripheral, para-liturgical situations, but I would doubt the canniness or the sincerity of anyone who claimed that it should be part of the liturgical life of the conventional parish.

Once again this is more than simply a question of taste; a vision of the Church is at stake. One of the moments of most acute embarrassment for me as a religious occurred during a weekend gathering, as part of which we were formed in a circle and led in a Shaker "movement exercise." We bobbed and bowed and raised our hands like toy puppets as we sang:

> When true simplicity is gained
> To bend and to bow we won't be ashamed.
> So we'll turn to the left and turn to the right
> And turn and turn 'til we come 'round right.

I wince as I remember the sight of the faces of grown men—whom I had come to admire in office and classroom and chapel—freeze in obedience as they shuffled back and forth in their Docksiders. And for what? For "true simplicity"? Hardly. No authentic simplicity requires a man to lay aside the benign dignity of adulthood. No, it was for the image of a New Church.

The new liturgy has likewise decorated itself with the artistic concomitants appropriate to its status. Sister Corita taught us to expect bold daubs of bright sunny colors—again, we were to escape the stained-glass formalities of the past and trust in the naive good taste of the child and his paintbox. Corita's influence is palpable to this hour in nearly every banner, every embroidered vestment, every illustrated publication which finds its way into our churches. This involves a disservice to real children (by sentimentalizing their experience we render ourselves less able to attend to the darker questions they have), yet it did provide Catholics with a crude "alphabet" with which they might spell out those hopes so long petrified by the solemnity of the *ancien régime*.

Once I came upon a missalette (important word!) which featured on the cover a photo of a plump suburban child clutching a patently fraudulent watercolor which read, "Never underestimate the power of a rainbow." This was the philosophy, of course, not of the child, but of his tender-hearted schoolmarm; the image has remained with me. Real children are at once too canny and too cruel, too innocent and too wise, to come up with this Snoopy rendition of *Kraft durch Freude*, so the adult had to become the child herself: a synecdoche of American Catholicism.

I mentioned above the Latin uncials on the fire-signs; they need now to be replaced. We have moved from the unfree to the free, from the predictable to the impulsive. Signs once lettered needlessly in Gothic are now lettered needlessly in imitation of graffiti: it is the scrawl, the spray-painted splash, which is today's ecclesiastical type-face par excellence. We have come half circle.

Missing Gravitas

C. S. Lewis once wrote of Christian liturgy that even if the celebrant's vestments are not in fact heavy, they should look heavy. That is, they should make it clear to the worshipers that his part in the service is not an extension of his own personality but is a *munus*, a responsi-bility laid on his shoulders the way a chain-of-office was laid around the shoulders of a mayor.... This notion opens up into the wider question of the relation between obedience and freedom in liturgy. A deft treatment of this problem is found in Cardinal Ratzinger's book *Feast of Faith*:

> Liturgy has a cosmic and universal dimension. The community does not become a community by mutual interaction. It receives its being as a gift from an already existing completeness, totality.... This is why liturgy cannot be "made." This is why it has to be simply received as a given reality and continually revitalized. This is why its universality is expressed in a form binding on the whole Church, committed to the local congregation in the form of the "rite."
>
> ... It is a guarantee, testifying to the fact that something greater is taking place here than can be brought about by any individual com-munity or group of people. It expresses the gift of joy, the gift of participation in the cosmic drama of Christ's Resurrection, by which the liturgy stands or falls.
>
> Moreover, the obligatory character of the essential parts of the liturgy also guarantees the true freedom of the faithful: it makes sure that they are not victims of something fabricated by an individual or a group, that they are sharing in the same liturgy that binds the priest, the bishops, and the pope. In the liturgy, we are all given the freedom to appropriate, in our own personal way, the mystery which addresses us.

While admitting the need for constant revitalization, Ratzinger views the liturgy as imposing an obligatory form on priest and people—not to curtail their spiritual freedom, but to protect it.

It is doubtless the case that not all interpolations are equally bad, yet I hazard two generalizations concerning them: First, departure from the text or rubrics is almost never really necessary. Second, even the most innocent innovations upon more careful reflection turn out to be theologically obtuse and manifestly inferior to what is printed in the Sacramentary. Two examples should suffice.

"May almighty God have mercy on us, forgive us our weaknesses, and lead us to everlasting life." This is unlikely to have the faithful sprinting for the exits, but ultimately it's just plain dumb. It *makes sense* to ask God to forgive us our sins, for sins are voluntary and avoidable acts and we can feel genuine remorse for them. But our creative celebrant feels queasy at the mention of sin and so uses the gentler word "weaknesses." But weaknesses, like talents, are among those things for which we're not responsible. Weaknesses are part of the hand we were dealt—by God. What logic is there in asking God to "forgive" what he has granted or withheld? None whatsoever. The clumsy urge to innovate has replaced a solid with a surd.

"This is the Lamb of God, who takes away the sins of the world. Fortunate are those who are called to his supper." Once again, few garments will rend at these words, but they're entirely pointless. Theologically it is correct to say that they are truly blessed, *beati*, who are called to share in the meal of our redemption. But are they fortunate? "Fortunate" means aided by *fortuna*, that is, by sheer luck, by chance. Is this what we really want to say about those who receive the Eucharist, that they're lucky, that they've pulled the ace they needed out of the deck? Is there any room whatsoever in a theological view of the universe for "luck"? Can it ever be part of an alert theological vocabulary?

Both these turns of phrase would be quite venial if they were part of an impromptu address in which the speaker under the stress of the moment reached for the right term, missed it, and simply hit on an infelicitous expression. We all do it. But such changes are not of that sort. They are deliberate departures, conscious deviations from the text. With the best will in the world, it is difficult to see the point of substitution in the first place; it is doubly painful to have to rub one's temples and pretend not to have heard Father's "improvement." The examples cited above are among the blandest and most innocuous I could muster. The real-life situation is, I fear, much worse.

Fair Warning

I have yet to be in a situation where liturgical deviation was a matter laid before the whole of the "worshiping community." I have never, for example, seen a celebrant address the congregation in these terms: "Before we begin Mass, I thought it only fair to let you folks know that I will be introducing several departures from the Sacramentary into today's liturgy. I intend to omit the words 'Do this in memory of me' after the consecration; I intend not to genuflect; I intend to use gender-neutral language during the Preface. If anyone here might find any of these changes offensive, let me urge him or her to find a more comfortable occasion of worship than the present one."

It doesn't happen, does it? Precisely among those whom we might expect to be most alert to the notion of covenant, we find that liturgy is rarely "covenanted" between presider and faithful. Even in those situations (such as weddings) where the preferences of a large number of people are consulted, the ordinary member of the congregation has little idea about what variations will actually take place when he walks through the church doors.

Liturgical deviation is essentially manipulative. It trades on the docility of the community of the faithful (who, it must be remembered, have come primarily to worship) by assuming that in almost every case considerations of good will and respect for the clergy will overcome any bafflement or uneasiness occasioned by novelty. The game is to present the Church with a *fait accompli*, and then wait for doctrine and practice to catch up at their own pace. Now it occasionally happens in a given setting that a certain set of innovations are employed so consistently as to acquire (for that particular setting) the status of a "received liturgy" in Ratzinger's sense. This may be the case in certain monastic houses. Spiritual freedom might thus be regained for the happy few. But it is precisely this kind of freedom which, it seems to me, most dissenters are out to destroy.

Liturgical conformity, by its very nature, tends to *build up* the Church, the Body of Christ. It is essentially edifying. The obedience of the universal Christian community to the rite committed to it strengthens the Church, and—this is the point—it strengthens the Church as the Church understands herself. However, it is news to no one that there are groups even within the Church who find her self-understanding extremely offensive. For these, the very notion of the Church as an "edifice" is repellent. Their (often explicit) aim is to deconstruct the Church, that is, to "disedify" her. They speak of Church "structures" as inherently and irredeemably oppressive. It stands to reason, then, that manipulation of the liturgy will be a prime tactic of these groups, since there is surely no more effective way to "disedify" the faithful.

Am I therefore claiming that every priest who omits the *lavabo* is in league with [Catholic feminist] Rosemary Ruether to bring the institutional Church to her knees? I am not. On the other hand, it is hardly news that the Catholics who are most anxious for liturgical variation have very deep sympathies with dissenting movements. Personally, I know of no priest who would style himself a "dissenter" who is not also a deviationist as a celebrant.

What about Vatican II?

I anticipate an objection to my remarks along the following lines: You give a picture of liturgical conformity with minimal allowance for change, but this runs counter to the intention of the Second Vatican Council that the Mass be adapted to the needs of different regions and peoples. This objection involves a red herring which must be disposed of.

Liturgy "embodies" doctrine. Even in its non-verbal aspects, Eucharistic celebration proclaims those beliefs which we as a Church hold to be true. Now by "adapting" the liturgy to different regions it seems to me beyond dispute that the Council Fathers meant that there are occasions in which we must adapt in order to proclaim the same truth. They did not intend adaptation to mean acknowledgment of the particular doctrinal convictions voiced by some part of the Church. To speak of "the tensions of unity and diversity in the Church" is to obscure the real point. The tension is that between *doctrinal* unity amid *cultural* diversity. Inasmuch as a given celebration of the Eucharist acknowledges some conviction not held by the

Universal Church, it is not a liturgy at all but an imposture, a *coup de theatre*.

For example, a priest may find himself chaplain to a university community where many members are offended by any reference to God as "Father." Yet the acknowledgment of God as Father is an essential part of Christian *kerygma*; it is unarguably the belief of the Catholic Church. The priest may responsibly take prudent measures not to give casual offense, but if he "adapts" the wording to "Parent" or "Mother/Father," he has forsaken that very doctrine which he was entrusted to pass on in the liturgy. He blesses a fissure in the Church; he promotes disunity.

It is a common rebuke leveled at those who plead for the Book in preference to liturgical innovation that they are guilty of exclusivity, whereas a truly inclusive Church would adapt her rites and usages so as to embrace the largest possible number. There is a truth here, but it is obscured by a widespread confusion.

I say in effect, "Let's worship as one because our faith is one. If you believe x, y, and z, let us sit at the table of the one Lord." *De facto* this is enormously inclusive. I take my stand with objective forms of worship (or, to be more precise, with "received liturgy" in Ratzinger's phrase) because doctrinal exclusivism is most truly catholic, most color-blind to differences of culture, race, social class, and political conviction.

On the other hand, if one is willing to "temper the wind to the shorn lamb" by anticipating occasions of offense in the liturgy and altering it accordingly, he is obliged to face three consequences: (1) He has given feelings of *ressentiment* a theological status with the Christian community. (2) He makes himself and his fellows prey to the more articulate, better educated, and more influential part of the community, and so opens the door to manipulation of the liturgy by those whose purposes are not shared by the Church Universal and whose principles are least likely to be those of the "little ones" toward whom the Church has special guardianship. (3) He encourages a kind of congregationalism by which vague notions of "comfort" or "feeling at home" are given primacy over the more truly catholic esteem for the bedrock of shared faith.

The paradox is that liturgical and doctrinal "openness" (by which I mean a flexibility born of the desire not to exclude) inevitably allies itself with the attitudes and aspirations of one particular part of the

Church community. By gradual degrees the congregation separates itself from the larger body of Christians—not because it closes its doors to anyone, but because its own style of openness will necessarily appeal to an ever smaller and more inward-looking population. The "exclusivity" of the Roman Rite is joyfully embraced by Christians all over the world; the "openness" of the Church of Joliet won't even play in Peoria; in ten years, it won't play in Joliet.

The liturgy belongs to the Church—to all of us, living and dead—as the emblem of our common faith and the enactment of that sacrifice once-for-all by which we are redeemed. No one has any license to rob us of our rightful patrimony. Taken together, all the visions of the deconstructionist, all the resentments of the disaffected, all the personal quirks and daydreams of the individual minister, all the globally contextualized inclusivities of the professorial hierophant, do not add up to a single reason to deprive the faithful of the Mass, the Mass in its full integrity. Those who come into our midst mouthing the sweet words of compassion and openness are, very often, trying to wheedle us out of our birthright. Perhaps the time has come to resist.

Of Rome and Runnymede

Curious. Why should the *New York Times*, the *Washington Post*, and the *Boston Globe* all see fit to carry the [1990] story of the promulgation of *Ex Corde Ecclesiae*, the papal [John Paul II] declaration on the mission of Catholic universities? On the face of it, Vatican norms for higher education hardly seem to have national "news value," especially from the perspective of those papers that have frequently strained the bounds of responsible journalism to the breaking point in order to reinforce the notion that the Vatican view of *anything* is hopelessly inapplicable to our contemporary situation. Could it be that they protest just a little too much, that this is yet another instance in which the power brokers of a militant secularism see more clearly than Christians themselves how the teaching Church cuts too close to the bone for anyone's comfort?

Earlier drafts of this document had caused consternation among the Catholic educational elite, who interpreted Vatican insistence on the integrity of Catholic truth as a threat to the autonomy deemed necessary to an *American* university. The party line was, the Congregation for Education (then headed by Cardinal William Baum) doesn't understand our unique responsibilities in a pluralist democratic society. This reasoning prompted a Jesuit scholar of my acquaintance to murmur, "If the 109 U.S. Catholic college presidents are such poor communicators that they are unable to convey to an American cardinal the purpose and status of their own institutions, then we're in deeper trouble than I thought." Of course, Rome understood only too well what the Americanists wanted to accomplish, and the Congregation's misgivings were targeted accordingly; there was much wry amusement to be had from the "How can this possibly apply to us?" routine, when almost every bullet in the draft had a patently recognizable name on it.

With the appearance of the final document, the predictable *volte-face* has occurred, and now we are meant to find the prime significance

Originally published in *First Things*, March 1991.

of *Ex Corde Ecclesiae* in its recognition of institutional autonomy and norms that are "few, general, and applied at the local level." The prestige media has rallied 'round to help put out the word that Catholic educators who take their values from the surrounding culture have nothing to fear from the latest foray. A premature judgment.

In his preface to the text [no. 8], the pope says, "I felt obliged to propose a ... document for Catholic universities as a sort of *magna carta*, enriched by the long and fruitful experience of the Church in the realm of universities and open to the promise of future achievements that will require courageous creativity and rigorous fidelity." The words "*magna carta*" ought to make the drowsy reader start. The implications of the historical analogy are astonishing, since we are obliged to find a sense in which *Ex Corde Ecclesiae* is intended as a gesture of defiance, as a declaration *from below*, as a rebuke to the encroachment of tyranny upon the rightful prerogatives of a long-oppressed order. The rhetoric of emancipation has been used for so long by the academy against the teaching Church that it is a commonplace; all the more interesting then that the pope should take it for his own.

"What is at stake," writes the pope, "is the very meaning of the human person" [no. 7]. This meaning has to be vindicated in every age and in every culture with respect to the threats posed by constantly changing circumstances. This vindication "requires a clear awareness that by its Catholic character a university is made more capable of conducting an impartial search for truth, a search that is neither subordinated to nor conditioned by particular interests of any kind." There is a neat inversion here of the standard anti-hierarchical polemic in which every insubordinate scholar is a martyr to truth, David set upon by Goliath, Galileo besieged by a Grand Inquisitor. How can the pope, this late in the twentieth century, pretend to a reverence both for dogma and for an impartial search for truth?

Perhaps the pope is on to something overlooked by others, that the secular academy in our century has abetted partisan attempts to discredit methods proper to science and scholarship, and this with a vigor unparalleled in the history of the West. We have seen Marxists condemn Mendelian genetics as a counterrevolutionary intrigue, Nazis reject the theory of relativity as a Jewish fabrication, feminists dismiss propositional logic as a white male conspiracy—all with the (rather uneasy) connivance of the university authorities. Would an impartial observer find more political contamination in Renaissance scholarship than in our own, or less intellectual independence among the orthodox churchmen than among the dissenters of our time? Is Scaliger more a child of his age than Stanley Fish? Charles Curran less a product of politics than Henri de Lubac? Is there doubt any longer that the proper distinction is not between dogmatists and free inquirers, but between those who are aware of their dogmas (and to this extent free) and those who are unaware that they hold any dogmas at all (and thus their unwitting slaves)?

The terms of the *magna carta* are these: (1) that genuine scholarship and scientific independence are in grave danger of forfeiting their rightful prerogatives to an increasingly tyrannous politicization of knowledge, a tyranny that has made itself felt by placing ideological constraints on nearly every field of enquiry; and (2) that Catholic scholars have in this document a charter of their duty "to speak uncomfortable truths which do not please public opinion, but which are necessary to safeguard the authentic good of society" [no. 32], and their freedom "to preserve the sense of the human person over the world and of God over the human person."

John Finnis recently reminded us what was at stake in an earlier *Kulturkampf* wherein worldly power felt threatened by teaching authority. After the declaration of papal infallibility in 1870, Reich Chancellor Bismarck wrote that Vatican I had established a "papal totalitarianism" over Catholics. In a response that must be seen as uncomfortably prescient in terms of subsequent European history, the German bishops said, "It is not the Catholic Church that has accepted the immoral and despotic principle that superior orders release one unconditionally from personal responsibility." The bishops' position was vindicated some seventy years later—ironically, at Nuremberg.

The reception given to *Ex Corde Ecclesiae* must be understood in light of the fact that it is in the Catholic faculties themselves in which virulent anti-Roman sentiment is to be found, and not merely in the Bismarcks of our time; indeed, the faculty *apparatchiks* of the Catholic left have found an ally in Big Government in their project to insulate themselves from the magisterium, whence the (often disingenuous) claims that the "state-approved charters" of American colleges are jeopardized by an "extrinsic ecclesiastical authority."

The professoriate is extremely uneasy with the notion of evangelization as a task of the Catholic university, precisely because a true Gospel freedom runs counter to that politicization of knowledge, and especially of theology, which the professoriate has been at such pains to advance. The authority by which evangelical liberty is safeguarded is the enemy of every Goliath, and most commentators have chosen to ignore the central place this document gives to evangelization in the university's mission, for reasons that are not hard to find. For if the message of *Ex Corde Ecclesiae* is taken seriously by Catholic scholars, it is all too likely that the tyranny of ideology over the search for truth—a tyranny so long complacent, so long indulged—will have met, if not its Waterloo, then at least its Runnymede.

Voices of Wrath:
When Words Become Weapons

Remember the white boots scam? It happened in the late 1960s, at the height of the Black Power movement. One of the movement theorists, it seems, came up with the idea that the reason white people conventionally wore black and brown shoes was to effect a symbolic degradation of the Negro. By wrapping its feet in dark hides, the race of exploitation and oppression signaled at some profound subliminal level its collective will to keep black people underfoot. Justice, of course, demanded a reversal of past terms of inequity, and a number of black radicals wore white boots as a sign of political awareness and defiance.

And not only radical blacks. White liberals anxious to advertise their sympathy with the cause of freedom and to do penance for the sins of their fathers wrapped Indian headbands around their brows and pulled white boots over their own socks. For a brief shining moment (in faculty lounges and bohemian cafes, at least) it looked as if the imposture were going to work.

It didn't. At this distance it is impossible to determine whether the deciding factor in the collapse of the hoax was a residual sense of embarrassment or a restored sense of humor, but someone woke to the realization that complicity in historical fraud, no matter how good-willed its motive, failed to diminish but added to the indignity of those he was trying to help.

Demagogues who combine a revolutionary social program with a totalitarian disposition have frequently made use of pseudo-scientific histories to awaken and fuel resentments in the class they wish to emancipate and to shame the rest of the population into passive acquiescence. Typically such histories are esoteric and mystical, in that they seek to explain purported inequities by reference to motives hidden deep within the human psyche—too deep, in fact, to be discovered

Originally published in *Crisis Magazine*, December 1, 1992.

in the ordinary, exoteric business of historical cause and effect. Only an Enlightened Spirit can have the vision and courage to bring out into the open the *real* malice latent in the humdrum operations of human existence, operations that the rest of us would be inclined to regard as neutral or innocent. For the demagogue, this ploy has two great advantages: it is, strictly speaking, not falsifiable (Who can prove that Tom Jefferson's choice of footwear was *not* predicated on a desire to dehumanize his slaves?) and it keeps the interpretive key to the past firmly in the palm of the demagogue himself; only the oppressed, when properly coached by their liberators, have the magic spectacles that make visible the evidence of their oppression.

It is clear, then, why language, which is part of the ordinary business of life—and yet whose history, for most of its users, is at once opaque and evocative—has always proved a rich mine for this kind of demagoguery. A particularly instructive example, offered by the sociologist Peter Berger, deserves to be quoted at length:

My mother was from Italy and my father was Austrian. As a child I spent a lot of time in Italy. This was in the 1930s, when Italy was of course under Mussolini. Sometime during that period, I forget which year it was, Mussolini made a speech in which he called for a reform of the Italian language.

In modern Italian—as in most Western languages, with the interesting exception of English—there are two forms of address, depending on whether you are talking to an intimate or to a stranger. For example, *tu* and *usted* are used in Spanish. In modern Italian *tu* is the intimate form of address, *lei* is the formal address. *Lei* happens to be [a feminine form]. I do not know the history of this, but it has been a pattern of modern Italian for, I would imagine, some two hundred years. No one paid any attention to this. Even as a child, I knew what one said in Italian. It meant nothing.

But Mussolini made a speech in which he said that the use of *lei* is a sign of effeminacy, a degenerate way of speaking Italian. Since the purpose of the fascist revolution was to restore Roman virility to the Italian people, the good fascist did not say *lei*; the good fascist said *voi*—from the Latin *vos*, which is the second person plural. From that point on, everyone who used *lei* or *voi* was conscious of being engaged in a political act.

Now in terms of the empirical facts of the Italian language, what Mussolini said was nonsense. But the effect of that speech meant an awful lot, and it was intended to mean an awful lot. Because from that moment on, every time you said *lei* in Italy you were making an anti-fascist gesture, consciously or unconsciously—and people made you conscious of it if you were unconscious. And every time you said *voi* you were making the linguistic equivalent of the fascist salute.

Mussolini's genius here deserves its full due. His self-appointed task was to take the vague feelings of defeatism and unhappiness of the Italian people and sharpen their focus until they hardened into deep, seething resentments, resentments strong enough to provide the sense of "empowerment" that would allow them (again, properly coached) to seize power for themselves. His mystical insight allowed him to see and expose the degenerate effeminacy hidden in one use of the pronoun *lei*. The choice was a deft one, not only because it helped explain national feelings of weakness while increasing para-noia about the influence of the malefactors—our very speech has been corrupted!—but because any genuinely scholarly attempt to put the record straight was bound to appear as the precise kind of effete and devious subterfuge that the Maximum Leader had warned against. Remember too that Mussolini could not on strictly logical grounds be *proven* wrong, a fact that tame Fascist professors would be sure to exploit.

Would the Italian bishops have done well to rewrite the Scriptures in Fascist language? Would we be proud of our own episcopacy if, in the late '60s, it had required priests to celebrate Mass in white boots? Such questions are not vacuous, for the Church in the United States is currently faced with the prospect of a new lectionary—the cycle of biblical readings that comprise the Liturgy of the Word at Mass— whose principal change from the earlier lectionary concerns the revi-sion of biblical readings into inclusive language.

"Inclusive language" does not, in the bishops' parlance, refer to vocabulary or imagery concerning God or the Divine Persons; God will still be "our Father." According to the steering committee responsible for the revision [the bishops' Committee on the Liturgy], "English vocabulary has changed so that words which once referred to all human beings are increasingly taken as gender-specific and, consequently, exclusive." Further, we are told that "urgent pastoral needs override the demand for strict literalism"—the literalism, that is, of translating the masculine pronoun of Greek or Hebrew by its English equivalent. Just what these needs are, or in what sense they are pastoral, is not disclosed.

The truth of the matter is that there is no such thing as inclusive language or exclusive language, any more than there is such a thing as an "effeminate" pronoun system. These categories have no linguistic meaning whatsoever, but betray a fundamental misunderstanding about the nature of language. The fact that "man" (along with "he" and "his") refers sometimes to a human being and sometimes to a male human is not, as some believe, a feature specific to English—such as would be avoided by Latin *homo* or Greek *anthropos*. The explanation belongs to the structure of logic itself; it is pre-grammatical, more fundamental than any tongue, laid down in the keel of the human brain. It has nothing to do with gender.

If set A is so treated that subset B is distinguished within it, the label or name given to A will have two meanings (or two uses): first, the general or universal meaning, and second, that of all non-B members of A. Linguists refer to the use of B as "marked" and that of A as "unmarked." For example, if next to the word "pig" we introduce the word "piglet," piglet is marked (for size) and pig is the unmarked form. Because it is unmarked, pig has (along this axis) two meanings: pig *in se*, and adult pig. In the sentence "I have one pig and eight piglets" the word "pig" refers to the adult; in the sentence "I bought three goats and six pigs" we can't know how many adults and how many piglets made up the purchase. The second example is not an instance of "exclusive language"; no potential piglet is left out of the discourse; "pig" is simply unmarked for size.

Gender contrasts are treated linguistically the same way. When a form marked for gender is introduced, its correlative assumes two uses: the gender alternate to the marked form, and the usage non-specific as to gender (*not* the same as neuter). Thus, we have "poet-ess," which is marked for gender, next to "poet," unmarked. There is a general tendency—not a law—in language gender contrast for the marked form to be the feminine. It is important to stress that the marked/unmarked distinction is entirely independent of the sex or social status of the speaker and even of the surface grammar of the language. The feminine is the marked form in languages whose only adult speakers are women, such as several South Arabian dialects. The feminine is the marked form in Sumerian, the oldest of all written languages, which has no *grammatical* gender whatsoever; yet it has unmarked *dumu*, son or child, versus marked *dumu-munus*, daughter. On the other hand, examples of the reverse treatment are not lacking. For English, think of "duck" (unmarked) versus "drake" (marked), or even "nurse" (unmarked) versus "male nurse" (marked). The point of all the foregoing pedantry is this: regardless of the language, regardless of the speaker, regardless of the pertinent semantic axis, the marked/unmarked contrast is ineradicable. To stigmatize one particular operation of this contrast as sexist is useless—as useless as damning second person *lei* as un-Fascist or natural leather tones as racist.

Or as useful. For if your goal is to sow resentment where none previously existed, and to expose otherwise undetectable heresy, such anathemas are very handy indeed. They are, in a peculiarly apt sense of the word, shibboleths (see Judg 12:6). They are passwords designed to distinguish the men of Gilead from the Ephraimites, so that the sins of the latter may be made plain. Thus, Peter Berger was very perceptive in his remark that to use *voi* in the Mussolini era was the linguistic equivalent of a Fascist salute. Once conscious of the alternatives, even if he knew the reason for the innovation to be nonsense, the speaker had to make a choice, had to decide whose side to take. The utility of a shibboleth is that it provides no middle ground, no *tertium quid*; it demands an either/or: complicity or defiance.

There is no such thing as exclusive language, but there are such persons as feminist women, and they have many sympathizers and allies of convenience in positions of great influence. Like the members of the Black Power movement, they are able to point to obvious and undeniable instances of discrimination in society, resentment for which is almost universally agreed to be justified. Like the members of the Black Power movement, they have also had to be *coached*, through relentless repetition, into spying injustice in places no sane person ever dreamed it existed. Indeed, for the revolutionary leader, the more cryptic the purported oppression the better, since the psychic disruption of the follower (resulting from the mental contortions necessary to convince himself of the truth of the leader's vision) makes him less resistant to other parts of the revolutionary program— innovations to which common sense might suggest doubts or hesitations. And, of course, the more arcane the supposed injustice, the more elaborate and unconvincing its refutation. All scholarly defenses of common sense seem pompous and contrived; all are bound to increase the very hostility they seek to allay. For feminists, the exclusive language hoax is an agit-prop bonanza.

As [philosopher] Karl Popper has demonstrated, one of the signs of the explanatory bankruptcy of any theory is a situation in which any and all possible states of affairs provide evidence *for* the truth of said theory. Such a hypothesis will not correspond to reality but will simply reflect the private obsessions of the theorist. Few of us, perhaps, will doubt that, if *voi* had been the ordinary second-person pronoun in his time, Mussolini would have found traces of degeneracy in this very word or in some other aspect of the language. It is rage in the face of the status quo that matters; its source is of secondary import. By the same token, does anyone believe that if the reverse of the actual situation obtained in English—if "woman" were the unmarked generic and "man" the marked form—that feminists would not find injustice in this too? The ground-breaking article would be called "A Word of Her Own," and I could write it myself.

The claim is sometimes made that the imposition of inclusive language is justified by the fact that language changes over time; words shift their meanings, and the proposed diction is simply a tardy recognition of what has already occurred. Well, it is true that the semantic range of a given word is susceptible of change, and words referring to males and females are as susceptible as any other. Yet this only points up the futility of performing the kind of surgery on living language that is demanded by the inclusivist project. (This demand is hard to understand on its own terms; why so much effort to direct us where we can't help going? A surgeon might alter a child's arm so that it attained its adult length, but we would hardly call the operation *growth*.) As new words and new applications continue to be dumped into the active lexicon of a language, they will continue to bud and fructify according to linguistic laws of nature, not according to the strictures of inclusivism. You can see this on any playground, and even in places where political gender-awareness has reached its highest pitch—even, say, in the student lounges of Wellesley College, where a dyed-in-the-wool feminist will run into a room full of women, or women and men, and say, "D'you *guys* want to order out for a pizza?" The unmarked form can no more be pruned from language than can semantic change itself.

The stock objection to this argument is, "But some women really do feel left out by the word 'men.'" No doubt. So too, there are freshmen every autumn who really do buy a copy of *The Apology of Socrates* and wonder, Why did Socrates have to say he's sorry? Yet we don't conclude that Plato had two meanings here; we say some students don't know what Plato meant: usage *is* meaning, and to privilege the hearer's semantics over the speaker's is madness. For example, the bishops' committee quoted above says, "The Word of God proclaimed to all nations is by nature inclusive, that is, addressed to all peoples, men and women." Yet, by their own reasoning, "men and women" won't quite do, for it excludes children and hermaphrodites, who are themselves entirely human, in need of redemption, and addressees of the Word. Even "men, women, children, and those of indeterminate gender" is inadequate, because someone, sometime, might well hear "children" and infer that it excludes infants. Notice: this proliferation is stark nonsense, but the only objection that can be tendered by the champions of inclusive language—namely, that the unmarked locution includes the various marked forms—is one that precisely invalidates their own claim. They can't have it both ways; the dilemma is fatal.

Recasting the lectionary into inclusive language does not open the Scriptures to those for whom they had been previously closed. It is a curtsy in the direction of feminism, a small genuflection meant to signal ideological sympathy and nothing else; it is way of announcing, "We too are Gileadites in good standing." On the other hand, perhaps it is proper that bishops do bend the knee to the regnant ideology of the era, or at least of the *beau monde* of each epoch. Perhaps there was an Italian Fascist who sincerely found the Church's language insufficiently virile, and who would have allowed himself to be evangelized if the episcopacy had indulged him in the matter of pronouns. Perhaps such a minor act of complicity, even if one is innocent of the accusation in virtue of which it is demanded, would have gained a soul that was otherwise lost.

I, for one, am not convinced. I remain an Ephraimite. Confessing to injustices we have not committed can only deaden us to those we have. Surely there is enough genuine wickedness of which we are guilty, and which deserves to be remedied, without feigning remorse for sins we can't see, even after reflection. *Deus non eget meo mendacio*, said Augustine, "God does not need my lie," and this is preeminently true of the Church's pastoral effort. If I can only appease my accuser by an act of dishonesty or a soothing falsehood, I have failed in my pastoral responsibility. I have, moreover, blinded myself to my brother's real need. Isn't it odd, to put it mildly, that those who hunger and thirst for justice should cry more loudly for proper pronouns than proper health care? Isn't it striking that they seem fuelled more by hatred of the status quo than by love of neighbor? And isn't it plausible, in the last analysis, that what they really want from the Church is not reparation, but revolution?

The Prayer of Lady Macbeth:
How the Contraceptive Mentality
Has Neutered Religious Life

"Unsex me here!" Lady Macbeth's prayer, significantly, was made to the gods of death—"you spirits / That tend on mortal thoughts"—and we remember with a shudder how completely and vividly her plea was answered. She was, largely though not entirely, a contrivance of fiction, and yet Shakespeare's powerful and gruesome anti-heroine was a forerunner of a species of Christian for whom the conjunction of prayer, personal resolve, and the negation of life produced a radically new thing, a third order of sexuality—a way of being human that is neither authentically male nor recognizably female, neither inceptive nor receptive of life, neither ordered to creation nor designed to nurture: "Unsex me here!"

It is important to notice that when Lady Macbeth prays that she be unsexed, she is pleading not for a diminishment of libido but for a freedom from compassion. The juices of sexual frenzy may flow unchecked; it is the promptings of motherhood that must be ripped clean away.

> Come to my woman's breasts
> And take my milk for gall, you murd'ring ministers,
> Wherever in your sightless substances
> You wait on nature's mischief!

The upshot is that it is not lust but life that must be alienated from the votaries of this Third Order of the Unsexed.

The question I have been asked to address is, "Has the contraceptive mentality affected religious life?" The short answer is, "Yes, emphatically." I want to use the prayer of Lady Macbeth to discuss

Originally published in *Faith & Reason* 19, no. 1 (Spring 1993) and adapted from an address to the national meeting of the Institute on Religious Life held in Chicago, April 16–18, 1993.

the paradox of celibate men and women re-centering their lives on a contraceptive worldview. The contraceptive mentality is more than the conviction that artificial birth control is morally licit. It comprises an extensive fabric of attitudes about sin, religious authority, and human fulfillment, as well as sexuality—attitudes that are determinative of choices central to every human life, including those for whom personal fertility and infertility are utterly irrelevant issues.

Contraceptive acts, and their moral condemnation, are equally ancient. As is well known, the contraceptive crisis was brought into being with the development and marketing of orally administered anovulants. The Pill (or, as it is irreverently known in Britain, the Tablet) focused the moral issues and polarized the champions of rival solutions decisively and irrevocably. This is not simply, or even primarily, the consequence of what is misleadingly called the Sexual Revolution brought on by the Pill. The sexual revolution was no revolution at all but the normal operation of social laws of gravity. "Folks done more of what they done before" simply because one constraint—fear of unwanted pregnancy—was eased. The water of sexual libido ran downhill after a sluicegate was opened: no surprise there. No, the real revolution occasioned by the Pill was not sexual but religious.

Contraception has traditionally been censured as an instance of sexual misdemeanor, and sexual sins have generally been treated by moralists of all traditions as sins of the weakness of will. Pagan, Christian, Muslim, and Jew knew equally well that it's wrong for the head of the household to sport with the dairy maid but recognized that in a moment of weakness a man generally resolved to live uprightly could succumb to temptation. The understanding of remorse, penance, and reconciliation varied widely, but all acknowledged the phenomenon of lust mastering the moment. The Pill changed all that. To contracept by this method involved not a surrender to the urgent passions of an instant but an action—better, a series of actions—clearly foreseen and assented to in cold blood, passionlessly, with deliberation and resolve. The majority report of Pope Paul VI's commission on birth control clumsily attempted to assimilate use of the Pill to the class of human actions undertaken impulsively, but this concession was rightly rejected with scorn by Catholic couples who insisted that they embarked on contraception as a consciously (and, in their view,

conscientiously) studied choice. To those who had made their peace
with the Pill in the early '60s, the shock delivered by *Humanae Vitae*
[in 1968] was staggering. It still is.

> "Unsex me here!" begged Lady Macbeth.
> Make thick my blood.
> Stop up th' access and passage to remorse
> That no compunctious visitings of nature
> Shake my fell purpose, nor keep peace between
> Th' effect and it.

This is not a person trying to justify the ill means to a contemplated
good end, or someone asking for pardon after the fact for an acknowledged wrongdoing. She prays to be rid of the access to remorse, to
get beyond questions of conscience entirely. She resolves to be fixed
on her purpose and on it alone, to the exclusion of all other considerations. Once the Church included the choice to contracept by means
of the Pill in the class of morally condemned actions, no Catholic
could leave the confessional in doubt about his capacity to "sin no
more" in this respect (as, say, a penitent might doubt his strength to
avoid the sins of fornication or blasphemy). Contraception involves
no temptation at all in the sense of pressure to yield to an impulse
(Was Lady Macbeth to murder Duncan?) but rather the resolution
to lead one's life in defiance of the Church. To contracept while
attempting to remain a Catholic accordingly required the development of an entirely novel religious stance, a stance founded on two
beliefs: first, the conviction that the teaching Church is wrong in an
area in which she explicitly claims authority; and second, the conviction that a Catholic can coherently hold that the Church is wrong
in one place and right (or right enough) in others such that Church
membership remains a conscientious and meaningful choice.[1]

Even on the pastoral level, very few religious were directly
affected by the face-value content of *Humanae Vitae*. Yet the religious stance that emerged in the rejection of *Humanae Vitae* was of

---

[1] I have unlikely (and unsympathetic) support for these claims from Charles Curran,
who admitted that proponents of contraception hugely underestimated the negation of the
Church's doctrinal authority entailed by reversal of past teaching. See "Ten Years After,"
Commonweal, July 7, 1978, pp. 426–30.

paramount importance to their lives. For it involves the belief that there is a higher, or deeper, or at any rate more reliable mediator of God's will than the teaching Church. This point cannot be stressed too much. If the Church is wrong in *Humanae Vitae*, the judgment that it is wrong can only be made with reference to some standard. That standard, obviously, cannot be the Church herself; some contend that it is moral intuition, others a more academically respectable reading of Scripture or of the history of doctrine, still others some comprehensive system of ethics or logic. But the crucial point is that whatever standard is taken as fundamentally reliable, this standard judges the Church and is not judged by her. Here is the real revolution incited by the Pill; next to it the rise in promiscuity is a mere flutter. As did their lay married counterparts, religious men and women instinctively perceived (and in many cases, rushed toward) the breach in the dam of doctrine and discipline caused by adoption of this new standard. Keep in mind that this new crisis is of an entirely different order than the classical moral controversies in Church history, which involved the laxity and rigor of the Church's treatment of what all parties to the dispute agreed to be sins. Dissenters from *Humanae Vitae* are about something else entirely, for they maintain that an action specifically and categorically condemned by the Church may be contemplated and chosen in good will as a licit option by a conscientious Catholic.

Suppose for a moment that a Catholic comes to believe that the teaching Church is wrong in condemning contraception but right about everything else. How does he judge the Church wrong in the one case? As we have seen, by reference to some standard that is more reliable than the Church. But how does he judge the Church to be right in the other million-and-one instances? Obviously, only in virtue of the same standard by which he found her defective. It is absurd, not to say insane, to claim that one obeys, or is faithful to, the Church in those areas in which he happens to agree with her—because "happens to agree" is the operative phrase. If my pocket calculator has proved unreliable in one calculation, I might still maintain that it "gives true answers" for other calculations, but not others: only, in fact, those which I have some reason to believe to be true. And my basis for judging the instrument accurate in these other computations be the calculator itself—but rather some norm (a mathematical table, my own longhand reckonings) that I take to be fundamentally sound. Consequently, it is absurd to say that I can depend on my calculator where it gives me true answers, since my use of the word "depend" expresses nothing more than a simple convergence between the calculator's answer and the true one.[2] And it is important to stress that once I have found a more reliable instrument, the less reliable one is superfluous—worthless, in fact. I can only hold on to it for sentimental reasons. By the same token, once my paramount theory of ethics or my personal religious intuition has proved more reliable than the Church, my continued association with the Church can never be more profound than a "Catholic" aestheticism. I can only pretend to let myself be taught by the Church the way I "depend" on my faulty calculator: my loyalty will be an act of sentimental affection, not an act of discipleship.

The contracepting Catholic who, for example, claims to be faithful to the Church on social doctrine is in the position of the Briton who is summoned by the queen to be her prime minister: his selection is in reality a matter of democratic political machinations, ceremonially tricked-out as an act of the royal will. Is he obeying his monarch in answering her summons? Only in the vacuous sense that a person says "Yes" to his own invitation. Institutionalized Catholic dissent on contraception makes the hierarchical Church into something like the British monarchy: it is a consciously antiquated ceremonial instrument for injecting a certain pomp into the solemnization of decisions made on grounds wholly unrelated to her logic, purposes, and history.

For the vowed religious, the first casualty of the contraceptive mentality is the Church as the focus of religious authority. The realization, perhaps, was gradual, but when prominent theologians, bishops, and entire episcopal conferences distanced themselves from *Humanae Vitae* without severing themselves from the Church, the logic of their dissent could hardly be confined to a single issue. In an astonishingly brief

---

[2] Of course my analogy is crippled by the fact that no one pretends that a calculator is an ultimate [guarantor] of reliability (as is claimed for the Church), nor does the calculator (as the Church does) make this claim for itself. The parallelism is based on the fact that for both Church and calculator, dependability is entirely conditional on the [consistency] of its operations and decisions, since these are not open to direct inspection. If one answer be suspect, all are.

span of years, the Church has been transformed from the measuring rod to the thing measured; no longer the guarantor of authentic religious life, she is everywhere under suspicion. In liturgy, Scripture, pastoral efforts, theology, and sacrament, the Church is regarded by entire congregations as guilty until proven innocent, and proof of this innocence is (in these circles) seldom forthcoming.

In the days when contraception was an unreliable affair, and pregnancy was a common consequence of sexual relations, extra-marital sex involved a clear offense against charity, and the Church's teachings forbidding adultery and fornication were easily defended on this ground—too easily, in fact. Moreover, the crude mechanical instrumentation of the older contraceptive devices lent weight (though a specious one) to the argument of preachers that artificial birth control is contrary to nature.[3] Once again, the advent of the Pill obliterated both defenses, and the Church's teachings on the spiritual significance of marriage, the body, and sexuality were put into the hands of pastors who were, for the most part, wholly unprepared to understand or communicate them.

Dissenters, on the other hand, pounced on this opportunity and placed enormous rhetorical stress on the primacy of charity in the Church's moral tradition. No one could deny the centrality of charity in this tradition, but on the level of popular controversy, it resulted in the illegitimate derivation of two erroneous propositions: first, that an act that is not a sin against charity is no sin at all; second, that any act done with a charitable intention is for that reason justified. The application to married life virtually wrote itself: contraception involves no obvious sin against charity (for neither husband nor wife is wounded) and therefore involved no sin at all. Or again, if contraception be employed with a charitable intention (making life easier for one's spouse; ensuring more advantages for one's children) it is morally praiseworthy. The theological justification for these arguments, however, necessitated a reformulation

---

[3] It is, of course; but not because latex and nonoxynol-9 are themselves "un-natural." An aesthetic and physical repugnance to contraceptive appliances has led to an interest in NFP [natural family planning] on the part of the Green Party and environmental enthusiasts who would embrace it as a kind of vegetarian ("no added preservatives or artificial sweeteners") birth control. Where the authentic discipline of married love is absent, NFP is no more un-natural than the Pill.

of the Christian imperative of charity and of traditional Catholic moral reasoning. In this new scheme, the morally preferable option is not one that conforms to a relevant principle of conduct but the one that results in more good (i.e., more "pre-moral good") than its rivals. It takes little imagination to devise scenarios in which contraception will result in more pre-moral bounty than other options, and therefore contraception was handily offered to Catholic couples as a licit moral choice.

The chasm that separates those dissenters from *Humanae Vitae* who employ this new scheme from orthodox Catholics has been described with felicity and precision by John Finnis,[4] who argues that, while it was the traditional belief of Christians that they were to serve the good, the dissenters hold that our duty is to the good.[5] Now whereas the belief that our Christian duty is to effect the good has been used by Catholic theologians to justify instances of abortion, euthanasia, threatened destruction of civilian populations as a deterrent, and so forth, it is contraception that provided the real impulse behind the advancement of this theory, and indeed it is the justification of contraception that continues to provided the rallying point of dissent in the Church.[6]

Consider once again all that is consequent upon the change from serving the good to effecting the good. Call to mind the direction of change in religious communities in their apostolic involvement over the past twenty-five years, the de-emphasis on Adoration, catechesis, spiritual works of mercy (even the term has become comically antiquated); the new stress on consciousness raising, political action, community organizing, world peace, environmental awareness. I want to stress that none of these latter activities need be pursued in

[4] In *Moral Absolutes: Tradition, Revision, and Truth* (Washington, D.C.: Catholic University of America Press, 1991), p. 49.

[5] If my first duty is to serve the good, I will refuse to violate an exceptionless moral norm, no matter what consequences threaten. For example, even if I will lose my job and my family will be deprived of material support unless I perjure myself on a police report, I must tell the truth and deal with the consequences as best I can. However, if my duty is to effect the good, I will choose whatever means produces the greatest aggregate of good results, irrespective of the moral norms that may be violated in doing so. If I have to lie so that my children can eat, and the lie will produce no countervailing harm to other people, I will choose the advantageous lie.

[6] In this opinion I am following Finnis, *Moral Absolutes*, p. 85.

a manner incompatible with traditional moral reasoning, but the fact that this reasoning plays small part in the motivations of religious men and women who champion these causes is evidenced by the rationale commonly given for the moral compromises these tasks ask of them. Call to mind the excuses and justifications frequently offered by priests and nuns acting as university officials or appointed agents of state for their complicity in scandals of political and public life, for their actions that are contrary to Church teaching. Is it not the case, almost without exception, that their plea is to a higher responsibility to effect the good rather than to serve it? Is it not the case that those whose aim is to cause a certain effect regard their more scrupulous brothers and sisters with Lady Macbeth's exasperation?

> Yet I do fear thy nature. It is too full o' the milk of human kindness
> To catch the nearest way. Thou wouldst be great
> Art not without ambition, but without
> The illness should attend it. What thou wouldst highly,
> That wouldst thou holily; wouldst not play false,
> And yet wouldst wrongly win.
> Thou'dst have, great Glamis, That which cries,
> 'Thus thou must do, if thou have it';
> And that which rather thou dost fear to do Than wishest should
>   be undone.

Translated into contemporary terms, the message runs thus: "Only weaklings let moral principles stand in the way of social change. You can accomplish nothing great if you let yourself be trapped by the snare of holiness. If you're going to succeed, you have to regard success itself as the only gauge of morality. True charity, after all, is not serving the good, but delivering the goods."

And so it goes, step-by-step, on a gentle downslope in the lives of religious: faith in a provident God gives way to the Faith That Does Justice, which in turns gives way to the Justice That Brings Itself into Being, which turns out, in practical terms, to mean an ideologized justice that must dispense with faith when faith would hinder its full realization. Thus in the space of twenty-five years the voices that urged us to follow the patriarch Moses in his exodus of liberation now urge us to believe that patriarchy—indeed the very Law by which Moses vindicated himself—constitutes the final and most formidable obstacle to true human freedom. The God of the Patriarchs is worse than the bondage of Pharaoh.

I have pointed to two revolutions in Catholic religious life that were precipitated by the rise of the contraceptive mentality. The first was doctrinal: what Vincentian Father Patrick Collins has called (approvingly) the change from "the experience of religious author- ity to the authority of religious experience," the demotion of the Church from judge to defendant. The second revolution was moral: the change from serving to effecting the good. The third revolution might broadly be termed spiritual.

From the earliest days of the Church, Christian life has involved asceticism: a regimen of spiritual discipline whereby forgoing the comforts and consolations of bodily life was regarded as training for holiness leading to fuller communion with God. We can distinguish two strands within this tradition: what we might call the asceti- cism of acceptance or patience, and the asceticism of renunciation. Asceticism of patience asks us to accept with tranquil resolve the unavoidable hardships of life, those from which there is no escape, as a sharing in the blessedness of the world's poor and as a way of perfection: physical deformity or illness, the hardships of war, the pain of an infertile marriage are examples of these austerities. Asceti- cism of renunciation involves those hardships that are not inevitable but are undertaken either in conformity to moral principle or as a wholly gratuitous means of discipline aimed at holiness. Now the meaningfulness of the discipline of renunciation is a precarious thing, because it flies in the face of humanistic theories of self-actualization and personal fulfillment, theories which see voluntary renunciation of a human good as not only absurd but pathological. Noble acceptance of unavoidable suffering (the early death of one's child, say) can be prized as a "growth experience" in this scheme, but to court pain or diminishment is depraved.

Before the availability of reliable contraception Catholic couples could plausibly be urged to accept the various disciplines of married love as part of an asceticism of patience. With the Pill, the ground changed almost overnight. Now couples were required to make the asceticism of renunciation a part of their married lives, because the twin hardships of sexual abstinence and provision for large families became easily, eminently avoidable. For a while the question hung precariously in the balance: Would Catholic couples accept the Church's discipline and the new invitation to an asceticism of renunciation, or would they opt for the techno-fix and push voluntary asceticism to the margins of their lives? Not for the first time, they looked to their clergy and religious—those set apart and coached in asceticism—for their clues on how to respond to these two new offers. Even at this date I find it impossible to believe that a spirited and joyful embrace of *Humanae Vitae* by clergy and religious, combined with sound instruction and spiritual aid to the laity, would not have resulted in a general Catholic adherence to the new mode of asceticism.

It didn't happen that way. With a vehemence that outdid the most truculent layman, Catholic clergy and religious led the charge,[7] and I would wager that given an equal number of randomly selected priests or religious and married laymen, one would find greater support for the Church's teaching in the latter group than the former—by far. Re-enter Lady Macbeth:

> Nought's had, all's spent
> Where our desire is got, without content.
> 'Tis safer to be that which we destroy,
> Than by destruction dwell in doubtful joy.

Was it merely coincidence that the massive dissent from *Humanae Vitae* marched with a near total abandonment of the asceticism of renunciation in religious life? I can't offer proof for my hunch, but I doubt it. Even in the crises of the Reformation there was no sea change in the religious discipline of communities that remained Roman Catholic comparable to the disappearance of fasting, vigils, corporal mortification, penitential labor, and even time set aside for prayer, from the lives of all but a few contemporary religious. Certainly there was a variety of forces set in motion in the aftermath of Vatican II that contributed to the re-fashioning of religious life, and it would be simplistic to point to the rejection of *Humane Vitae* as the source of every ill, but once human sexuality became assimilated to the number of satisfactions whose exercise belonged to the prerogative

[7] For a candid account of the clerical-academic orchestration of the assault on *Humanae Vitae*, see Charles Curran's contribution in *Journeys*, Gregory Baum, ed. (New York: Paulist Press, 1975).

of the self-constituting individual, and was consequently emancipated from any larger system of meaning and responsibility, the denial to the self of any and all satisfactions, pleasures, and consolations seemed precariously close to irrational. The notion of rigorous training (the idea from which the classical idea of asceticism is derived) vanished in favor of a number of developmental schemes of monitored growth in which the underlying anthropological assumptions were contrary to those undergirding the older. In the new scheme, all men are born good, naturally holy, and their chief requirement is opportunities for education, self-expression, and enrichment of experience in order to become godlike, that is to say, fully human. The banisters and railings and fences and other "boundary safeguards" of religious life were discarded, inasmuch as their existence implied notions of trespass and constraint and an innate human tendency to sin. Gone is the rule of tactus,[8] the stricture that sent nuns out of the house in pairs, the early curfews, mandatory and distinctive religious garb, the manifold impediments of cloister. Gone are the multitudes of requisite permissions; gone is all but minimum responsibility for the use of time and money—both of which used to be viewed as the common property of the community, not perquisites doled out to the individual for his discretionary employment.[9] Gone is an entire fabric of sexual discipline.

"Unsex me here!" It is not, I believe, tendentious to maintain that the consequence of the obliteration of asceticism in religious life has been sexual anarchy. The evidence for this is, regrettably, overwhelmingly abundant. It is a curious paradox, but even though, generally speaking, priests were never less masculine and sisters less feminine than today, the libido is at the same time all but out of control. Few religious, however, seem willing to countenance a restoration of the former discipline. I recently attended a day-long workshop on clergy sexual misconduct that dealt with the problem entirely in terms of "professional boundaries." Do you see the irony? Having cast away the framework of prayerful asceticism assembled by

[8] It forbade a religious to touch another person.

[9] I do not mean to imply that these strictures were equally valuable, or even that some were not harmful and in need of replacement. I simply want to call attention to (1) their earlier comprehensiveness and complexity; (2) the suddenness and thoroughness of their disappearance; and (3) the change in anthropology that occasioned their fall.

countless monks, priests, and nuns over seventeen centuries, human nature "actualized" itself in horrifying ways, and we now have to improvise hastily by tacking in place the boundaries appropriate to dentists and high school guidance counselors.

We are frequently invited, sometimes by fellow Catholics, to view the scandal of priestly and religious pedophilia (and other sexual abuses) as an occasion to despair, as an assault on our faith. Now I believe as firmly as anyone that clergy pedophilia is an abomination and a horror—but it certainly doesn't rattle my faith: after all, when the prayer of Lady Macbeth goes up, when we trade in the multiform protections and incentives of a responsible tradition of asceticism for the wisdom of Abraham Maslow and Carl Rogers, one would expect it to breed maggots. Personally my faith would be more shaken if the contrary were true, if those who had thrown over the cautions urged by Benedict and Francis and Ignatius and Teresa found a surfeit of joy and energy in their apostolic lives, a radiant and unshakeable chastity, an enviable psychic and sexual tranquility; if they attracted an abundance of new vocations from the brightest and most vital of Catholic youth; if their prayer out-shone their forebears in its vigor, profundity and fruitfulness—*that* would unsettle my faith, for it would mean that the wisdom of this world had proved wiser than the inheritance we have from the martyrs. True, all the results aren't in yet, but I believe this turn of events ... unlikely.

Has religious life remained unaffected by the contraceptive mentality? The answer may be forthcoming if we rephrase the question: Have Catholic religious been successful at transmitting and multiplying the abundance of life they enjoyed before the crisis of contraception made itself felt in their lives? The only religious who can say "Yes" without duplicity are those who failed to "unsex" themselves doctrinally, morally, and spiritually in the time of struggle. On the other hand, those Third Orders of the Unsexed are heading remorselessly down the course marked out by their ancient, and so-very-contemporary, patroness.

> She should have died hereafter;
> There would have been time for such a word.

"Tames" in Clerical Life

The profound problems that beset priestly life today have been discussed for the most part by means of categories that reflect the preoccupations of our time and the way in which the problems have come to our attention. Because sexual scandal has figured so largely in the contemporary crisis, the now conventional division of male populations into gays and straights has, not surprisingly, played a large part in these discussions. But the reality is considerably more complex than the standard vocabulary of "sexual orientation" would suggest. Though it seems contradictory, even the battles over issues of sexuality among priests[1] may have their basis in personal factors in which sexuality itself plays a relatively minor role.

What is here proposed is that the contemporary priesthood exhibits a disturbingly high number of one particular sociopsychological type, to be designated by the neologism "tame," and what follows is a first attempt to sketch a profile of the tame priest. The author is innocent of training in psychology, and the data have been neither collected nor analyzed systematically; they are simply the result of twenty years of observing the subject at close hand. The description is addressed to the experience of those familiar with the current condition of clerical life, and to the common-sense intuitions of others.

Perhaps the most universal and distinctive characteristic of tames is their paradoxical combination of great sociability with an incapacity for true friendship. Tames are great mixers at parties and all social functions, and they have the ability to join in almost all conversations and project friendly interest. In the jargon of the M.B.A. they are abundantly endowed with "people skills." Yet their friendliness itself makes them unfit for friendship. They exist on the level of superficial companionability and lack the depth of personality and character

Originally published in *The Latin Mass* 5, no. 33 (Summer 1996), under the pseudonym "Fr. X."

[1] To be understood as clerics in the broad popular sense, including seminarians, religious brothers, diocesan and religious priests, bishops, and others.

necessary to make and keep a friend. Whereas most men in their late twenties unconsciously begin to narrow the number and deepen the quality of their friendships, tames preserve a kind of adolescent gregariousness and live on in the world of the fraternity or freshman dorm. While they tend to be cheerful on social occasions, the mask occasionally slips to show a characteristic expression of apprehension, hunger, and puzzlement. Strong friendships draw one apart from the crowd, and being out of the mainstream, on the margins, is something a tame cannot tolerate. Tames prefer instead to exercise their talent in the public arena, where they can flit from buddy to buddy, chatting, telling jokes, fetching drinks, and collecting from as many as possible the external tokens of friendship.

Being tame is not itself a sexual orientation, yet within the clerical life tames tend to behave politically, socially, and morally in a manner as uniform as that of gays.[2] It is part of the syndrome that tames are not conscious of themselves as tames; there is no question of their forming a caucus as do gays. Yet because their responses to concrete crises and problems are so uniform tames comprise a block *de facto*, and have an influence in the Church disproportionate to their number. In fact, the defeats and frustrations visited upon straights in the clergy are primarily due not to gays but to tames.

It is usually very hard to know whether a particular tame priest is heterosexual or homosexual. They are seldom obviously effeminate; most laymen will assume, in default of indications to the contrary, that they are straight. But they wear their masculinity as a businessman might wear a baseball cap at a picnic; his support for his team is not necessarily insincere, but you get the feeling that it is *displayed* as an emblem of good will—"I'm an easy-to-get-along-with kind of guy"—and not as a constitutive part of who he is. Tames never seem entirely at peace with this aspect of their lives and, in situations where gays and straights are clearly at odds, live in a kind of emotional No Man's Land. This is not because tames waver between competing appetites like bisexuals, but because *any* definitive involvement risks isolation, and isolation terrifies them.

---

[2] I use the term "homosexual" to refer to someone whose libido is directed at members of his own sex. By "gay" I mean a homosexual male who has made a definitive personal decision to allow himself to be known as homosexual at least semi-publicly, and who is tolerant of sodomy; in this scheme all gays are homosexual, but not all homosexuals are gay.

One external indication of the tame seminarian or priest is the changes of dress to which he will subject himself. Sometimes he will change clothes four or five times a day, depending on the activity planned and (more importantly) on who will be in the company. Tames will own the full array of clerical gear, but are also outfitted as laymen for a wide range of formal and informal occasions. Tames live in the present, in the "now"; they are extraordinarily sensitive to the people in the same room with them; they intuitively grasp the balance of power, the divisions of opinion, the dominant party or ethos. Their over-adaptability in clothing is symptomatic of their over-adaptability generally. Tames are capable of astonishing changes of opinion depending on the composition of their company-of-the-moment; it is not quite accurate to say they are chameleons, because in a sharply contrasted environment they will not adapt themselves to the majority if the minority clearly has greater power and prestige. Always and everywhere, tames will go with a winner.

Tames lack strong personal opinions and highly individual tastes in authors, music, films, and so forth. They may buy many books and be great concert- and moviegoers, but such interest stems either from the nexus of sociability provided by these activities, or from the negative consideration that ignorance of the current issues or artists might isolate them from those who count. This may be disguised by the fact that in certain communities at certain times it becomes fashionable to have a bizarre hobby or cultivate an esoteric composer, and a tame will play along by affecting an unconventional interest; usually these are abandoned with relief as soon as possible. On the other hand, tames are pathetically envious of the flesh-and-blood solidity of the unfeigned enthusiasms of others, envious of the spiritual freedom to enjoy something, anything, purely in and for itself and without regard to what others think or say. Like ghosts that must feed on the blood of the living, tames are often emotional parasites who draw their satisfactions at second hand; they may be incapable of taking a real interest in fly-fishing or Palestrina or astronomy, but they are fascinated by the single-hearted devotion of those who do, and like to mimic the motions of the enthusiast.

Tame priests are without exception worldly. Their worldliness, however, is always a nervous worldliness, and they never allow themselves to wallow in pleasures as do gays or simple hedonists. Tames dress better, dine better, drink better Scotch, take more expensive vacations, and generally entertain themselves at a higher level than their fellows, but their enjoyment is poisoned by constant reference to what others may think of their acquisitions and recreations. They are always on guard against equal and apposite dangers: censure for unbecoming profligacy or for unbecoming rusticity. Even at his favorite restaurant a tame is seldom at ease, not knowing who may walk through the door and see him: Is the wine too common or too extravagant, his dress too clerical or too casual?

A "giveaway" characteristic of a tame is panic. Tames live in terror of being caught out of being discovered on the wrong side of an argument, hacking the wrong horse, having committed too deeply to reverse course with grace. As a consequence a tame will often register a momentary flash of panic when something occurs to make him unsure of his surroundings—for example, the entrance of an unknown party into a conversation in which he has prematurely taken a stand, or the friendly approach of a pariah at a public function. Tames see failure and unpopularity as contagious, and will oil their way out of contact with either as soon as possible. In their dealings with equals tames often make them feel used—not because they deliberately and cynically set out to manipulate, but because they are virtually incapable of exchanging a human (or supernatural) good with another person.

Tames have a morbid *lack* of curiosity about the first principles of things: metaphysics, the grounding of moral arguments, dogma. This does not come from any lack of brain-power but is simply a reflex of their concern for the here-and-now. The functional/pragmatic/political is supreme. A tame may hold an office that obliges him to defend some moral or dogmatic principle as inviolable and he may do it competently, but always with an eye to the occasion; even defense of principle, for a tame, is itself not principled but simply a means to realize some practical good. In general, tames have a distaste for confrontation and avoid situations where they are forced into conflict. In most controversial situations tames hedge their bets by showing mild support for both sides as long as possible, only declaring allegiance when it is clearly to their advantage to do so. Tames are capable of professing directly contrary opinions within a matter of hours, and frequently shock others by their apostasies. Because they adapt so spontaneously to the environment they are sometimes unconscious of inconsistency and puzzled when it is brought to their attention. Tames are rarely capable of loyalty in the strict sense, but only the kind of loyalty salesmen show to their products or lawyers to their clients-of-the-moment; they are Company Men, spirited defenders of the institution in which they wish to advance.

Tames tend to be dutiful in the same way that they are loyal. They are "responsible citizens" in the places where they live and work. They are team players and willing to work long hours; they are eager not to give others cause for complaint, and they tend to make themselves—if not indispensable—important worker bees in the machinery of the chancery or seminary or office of religious education. In addition to the energy that comes with ambition, tames have the sort of managerial affability that attracts favorable notice in any bureaucracy. They are relatively unlikely to leave the priesthood; thus, if tames make up only 30 percent of a seminary entrance class, they may well compose 70 percent of those still working as priests ten years after ordination.

The religious convictions of tames are tailored to conform to those of the environment, especially to the most influential forces in the environment. Tames are liberal in liberal dioceses, and conservative in conservative ones, but are willing to sing the same song as whatever group they find themselves part of, whether it be a carload of fellow priests on the way to a beach house or a dozen older women at a communion breakfast. Neither as liberals nor as conservatives do they display any depth of concern for their spiritual life; their personal Bibles and breviaries rarely show the telltale damage of daily use; neither do tames themselves react to the crises in the life of the Church as if their principal import were spiritual. Yet their religiosity also contains unpredictable sentimental attachments to the worship of their youth: a man of conventional secular outlook may on occasion display a sugary Marian devotion or passionately object to the rewording of a favorite hymn from the past. Parallel to the envy tames have for genuine friendship is this attitude of lovelorn regret for their own childhood, when perhaps affections were still pristine and not warped by the need to have a concrete practical advantage. Even when their theology is up to date and deftly articulated, tames give the impression that they "stopped listening" spiritually at about the age of nine or ten; they seem stunted, and unaware of the lack.

In the contemporary Church, tames serve the agenda of gays in the long run, even though they sometimes find themselves forced to take a contrary stance. Tames are extremely susceptible to emotional blackmail of all kinds, and gays are adept at putting a thumb on the emotional windpipe of weak men in order to manipulate them.[3] Of course this takes many forms; one of the simplest (playing on the tame avoidance of conflict) is to engender a stormy atmosphere in a room in which the gay agenda is under discussion, with the threat of outrage and vengeance if the correct conclusion is not reached. Tames will often sell the pass to avoid the risk of having to fight for it before a wider public.

Gays have also pulled the tames into their service by the gambit of discussing chastity and sexuality in terms of "affective maturity." This is how it works: first, one wins the admission that "affective maturity" is the principal gauge of authentic celibacy. Once this is conceded, it is stipulated that the condition *sine qua non* of affective maturity is "comfort" with one's own sexuality (mature men are comfortable being themselves), and this in turn is seen to preclude disgust or moral censure directed at a "sexuality other than one's own." A Caucasian at peace with his racial dignity does not derogate blacks; by the same token a straight at peace with himself does not look askance at gays. Whoever objects to the presence or influence of gays in priestly life is *ipso facto* convicted of affective immaturity and his opinion thereby disqualified. Tames are without exception pushed into emotional checkmate by this maneuver, and invariably side with gays in showdowns, intuitively (and correctly) realizing that this tactic will prevail at any ecclesiastical institution that surfaces the issue in these terms.[4] By this ploy, and variations on the theme, gay priests have been able to leverage their clout three or four times out

---

[3] Some gays have themselves "emerged" from the condition of tames and are able to exploit the insecurities of tames from their own experience; they know the psychological pressure points from inside.

[4] Examples of these controversies might be whether to admit homosexuals to the seminary, or whether to allow a gay-rights group on a Catholic campus; whether to make condom education part of a workshop on sexuality; whether pastoral care of AIDS patients should have a moral component; etc.

of proportion to their numbers. The paradoxical truth is that tames are more effective agents of the gay agenda than gays themselves; on one hand they are more presentable advocates (uneffeminate, good at reassurance, good at string-pulling); on the other they are motivated by a terror of the either/or and of being thrust to the margins of the institution—a terror stronger even than the hopes and anxieties of gays. The tame commitment to be noncommittal is the engine that powers gay progress in the Church.[5]

It will be clear that tames tend to be ambitious (generally) and careerist (specifically) to an extent unhealthy in any institution and particularly so in the Church. Yet they are not purely cynical climbers of the type met more frequently in business or politics. They are not cynical because they lack the psychological detachment necessary for cynicism—the ability to put a distance between themselves and their own tactics. They enter into the role demanded by the moment so deeply that they really believe they are "witnesses for renewal" at nine o'clock and really believe they are guardians of orthodoxy at eleven. When a tame succeeds in reaching a position of authority—as a bishop, rector, provincial superior—the increase in the amount of stress combined with the decrease in places to hide causes highly erratic behavior and reveals his radical emotional instability. Once in power, tames are ravenous for personal loyalty. It might be said that their demand for personal fealty is in proportion to their own incapacity for adherence to principle, that the oilier they were to superiors the more peremptory they are in their dealings with underlings. Their uses of authority and failures to use authority seem equally arbitrary, and the "management style" typical of tames includes long periods of seeming paralysis broken by sudden quixotic sorties.

---

[5] It should be stressed that the ecclesial landscape in which tames feel safest is largely congruent with the current clerical gay agendas: what gays view as a tactical advantage tames require as a psychological necessity. Both want the Church's moral and doctrinal terrain to be as fuzzy as possible; both like to live in the "high grass" and rejoice in bureaucratic vagueness and ambiguity. The strongest emotion tames ever show is their hatred of those who try to force them off the fence or put things in black-and-white terms; most younger priests can attest that the highest-voltage diatribes against homophobia they have encountered were delivered not by gays but by tames.

Concern for appearance, distaste for conflict, and fondness for the advantageous lie are the main factors contributing to this tame style of management—two styles, actually, depending on whether they are dealing in private or in the public sphere. In one-on-one situations, for example, tames in positions of authority will rarely deny the validity of a complaint of corruption lodged by a subordinate. More often they will admit the reality and seriousness of the problem raised, and then pretend to take the appellant into their confidence, assuring him that those in charge are fully aware of the crisis and that steps are being taken, quietly, behind the scenes, to remedy it. Thus, the burden of discretion is shifted onto the subordinate in the name of concern for the good of the institution and personal loyalty to the administrator: he must not go public with his evidence of malfeasance lest he disrupt the process—invariably hidden from view—by which it is being put right. This ruse has been called the Secret Santa maneuver: "There are no presents underneath the tree for you, but that's because Daddy is down in the basement making you something special. It's supposed to be a surprise, so don't breathe a word or you'll spoil everything." And, of course, Christmas never comes. Perhaps most of the well-intentioned efforts for reform of the past quarter-century have been tabled indefinitely by high-ranking tames using this ploy to buy their way out of tough situations for which they are temperamentally unsuited.

The public arena brings forth from tames another side of their personality. Tames lack the resources of character needed to remain indifferent to hostile news media; moreover, the techniques of evasion and equivocation refined earlier in their lives are largely useless as bishops, when the media (and general public) reflexively attribute to them as their own the positions of the Catholic Church. A few tames are able to charm the media into a kind of truce: good ink in exchange for a blind eye toward heterodoxy; several others can be seen to engage in a disastrous cycle of appeasement and recrimination. They sue for the favor of the press by taking pains to portray themselves as moderates and by lashing out at more aggressive conservatives, causing dismay to many of the Church's friends and giving delight to her enemies. Then an occasion arises when they are forced to defend some unpopular teaching, and the press turns against them with glee. Then comes the bishops' predictable sputter of indignation, their predictable semi-retraction and statement of regret, and the long, long process of buying their way back into the state of (editorial) grace by undercutting less diffident Catholics.[6]

From this provisional attempt at description it will be clear that the distinguishing characteristics of tames are for the most part destructive of what the Church needs to accomplish through her clergy. The U.S. Church may be especially instructive in this regard. Seventeen years into the pontificate of a "conservative" pope, concerned to appoint dutiful and orthodox bishops, the problems of clerical homosexuality and pedophilia, doctrinal dissent of the professorate, liturgical abuses, acceptance of contraception, etc., have improved in no respect and worsened in many. It is reasonable to assume that there is not a single cause for this strange paralysis, but it is worth asking whether the prevalence of the tame priest does not go far to explain the combination of outward managerial competence and personal moral cowardice that has examined these problems so often, so "professionally," and never lit on the obvious steps toward their solution.

[6] It is noteworthy that bishops who are tames almost always have a number of gays as advisers or high officials in the chancery; once in office they are virtually powerless to prevent gays from collecting around them, and as a consequence any pressures for reform are effectively neutralized.

What Went Wrong?

What went wrong, and why? Everyone in the room will rightly understand the question to refer to The Crisis, the daily revelation over the past eighteen months of numberless instances of priestly turpitude, episcopal mendacity, and the resultant bewilderment and fury of the laity. My own take on the problem, which I offer for your consideration, is that The Crisis is chiefly surprising in how unsurprising it is. No one who has been fighting the culture wars within the Church over the past twenty years can fail to recognize his own struggles with a hostile bureaucracy and conflicted hierarchy in the struggles of those pleading for relief from sexual abuse—notwithstanding the disparity in the attendant journalistic drama. In fact, I'd contend that the single important difference in the Church's failure regarding abusive clergy and the failures regarding liturgy, catechesis, pro-life politics, doctrinal dissent, and biblical translation is this: that in the case of the sex-abuse scandal, we've been allowed a look over the bishops' shoulders at their own memos. Deviant sexual assault has accomplished what liturgical abuse never could: it has generated secular media pressure and secular legal constraints so overwhelming that the apparat was forced to make its files public.

What we read in those files was shocking, true, but to most of us it was shocking in its sense of *déjà vu*. In the years following the Second Vatican Council, the housewife who complained that Father skipped the Creed at Mass and the housewife who complained that Father groped her son had remarkably similar experiences of being made to feel that they themselves were somehow in the wrong; that they had impugned the honor of virtuous men; that their complaints were an unwelcome interruption of more important business; that the true situation was fully known to the chancery and completely under control; that the wider and more complete knowledge of

Adapted from an address delivered to the Confraternity of Catholic Clergy on July 15, 2003. Available at CatholicCulture.org.

higher ecclesiastics justified their apparent inaction; that to criticize the curate was to criticize the pastor was to criticize the regional vicar was to criticize the bishop; that to publicize one's dissatisfaction was to give scandal and would positively harm discreet efforts at remedying the ills; that one's duty was to maintain silence and trust that those officially charged with the pertinent responsibilities would execute them in their own time; that delayed correction of problems was sometimes necessary for the universal good of the Church.

This picture was meant to describe the faithful's dealing with the normally operating bureaucracy, in which the higher-ups are largely insulated. Occasionally someone manages to break through the insulation and deal with the responsible churchman himself. In this case another maneuver is typically employed, one I tried to sketch eight years ago in an essay called " 'Tames' in Clerical Life":

> In one-on-one situations, tames in positions of authority will rarely flatly deny the validity of a complaint of corruption lodged by a subordinate. More often they will admit the reality and seriousness of the problem raised, and then pretend to take the appellant into their confidence, assuring him that those in charge are fully aware of the crisis and that steps are being taken, quietly, behind the scenes, to remedy it. Thus, the burden of discretion is shifted onto the subordinate in the name of concern for the good of the institution and personal loyalty to the administrator: he must not go public with his evidence of malfeasance lest he disrupt the process—invariably hidden from view—by which it is being put right. This ruse has been called the Secret Santa maneuver: "There are no presents underneath the tree for you, but that's because Daddy is down in the basement making you something special. It's supposed to be a surprise, so don't breathe a word or you'll spoil everything." And, of course, Christmas never comes. Perhaps most of the well-intentioned efforts for reform in the past quarter century have been tabled indefinitely by high-ranking tames using this ploy to buy their way out of tough situations for which they are temperamentally unsuited.[1]

What I've put before you are two scenarios in which complaints of abuses are brought to those in authority and in which they seem to vanish—the complaints, I mean, not the abuses. One hoped that

---

[1] "Tames in Clerical Life," *The Latin Mass* 5, no. 33 (Summer 1996).

something was being done behind the scenes, of course, but whatever happened always remained behind the scenes. As the weeks went by without observable changes in the abuse and without feedback from the bureaucracy, one was torn between two contradictory surmises: that one's complaint had been passed upstairs to so high a level that even the bishop (or superior) was forbidden to discuss it; alternatively, that once one's silence had been secured and the problem of unwelcome publicity was past, nothing whatsoever was being done.

Now the remarkable thing about The Crisis is how fully it confirmed the second suspicion. In thousands and thousands of pages of records one scarcely, if ever, is edified by a pleasant surprise, by discovering that a bishop's or superior's concern for the victim or for the faith was greater than that known to the public, that the engines of justice were geared up and running at full throttle, but in a manner invisible to those outside the circle of discretion. Didn't happen.

I think this goes far to explain the fact that when the scandals broke it was the conservative Catholics who were the first and the most vociferous in calling for episcopal resignations, and only later did the left-liberals manage to find their voices. Part of our outrage concerned the staggering insouciance of bishops toward the abuse itself; but part, I would argue, was the exasperation attendant on the realization that, for the same reasons, all our efforts in the culture wars on behalf of Catholic positions had gone up in the same bureaucratic smoke.

I take issue, then, with commentators who refer to The Crisis as an ecclesial "meltdown" or "the Church's 9/11" or who use some similarly cataclysmic metaphor. Whatever there was to melt down had already done so for years, and that across the board, not just in priestly misconduct. Therefore, in addressing the question "What went wrong, and why?" I need to try to explain not simply the sex-abuse scandals but the larger ecclesial failure as well, weaknesses that existed even before the Second Vatican Council.

Paradoxically, one of the major factors in the corruption of clerical life at the end of the twentieth century was its strength at the beginning of it. Here I quote from James Hitchcock:

A gloomy fact about clerical life is that, with the possible exception of the very early centuries, there was no time in the Church's history when such life was idyllic. The Middle Ages had their share of misbehaving priests, and the ordinary parish clergy were uneducated and part of a peasant culture which was in some ways still pagan. The Counter-Reformation made strenuous efforts to improve the state of the clergy, not least through the establishment of that institution which ought to have been obvious but for some reason had not been—the seminary. Even despite these efforts, clerical scandals and various kinds of clerical incompetence long continued, amidst occasional saintly priests and many others of solid piety and zeal. In the United States the period c. 1900–1960 can be considered a golden age of the priesthood, not merely in modern times but throughout all the Catholic centuries. (This golden age was not confined to America but existed in other countries as well.) While priests of that era certainly had their faults, by all measurable standards there was less ignorance, less immorality, less neglect of duty, and less disobedience than at almost any time in the history of the Church. More positively, priests of that era were generally pious and zealous, and those who were not at least had to pretend to be.[2]

Not only was the reality of priestly character in good shape, but the reputation of Catholic clergymen was likewise high. This brought with it several problems. First, being an honorable station in society, the clerical life provided high grass in which many villains and disturbed individuals could seek cover. I would estimate that between 50 and 60 percent of the men who entered religious life with me in the mid-1970s were homosexuals who had no particular interest in the Church, but who were using the celibacy requirement of the priesthood as a way of camouflaging the real reason for the fact that they would never marry. It should be noted in this connection that the military has its own smaller but irreducible share of crypto-gays, as do roughnecks on offshore drilling rigs and merchant mariners ("I never got married because I move around so much it wouldn't be fair on the girl ..."). Perhaps a certain percentage of homosexuals in these professions can never be eliminated. I further believe that the most convincing explanation of the disproportionately high number of pedophiles in the priesthood is not the famous Abstinence Makes the Church Grow Fondlers[3] Theory but its reverse, proposed to me by a

[2] James F. Hitchcock, "Thirty Years of Blight," *Catholic Dossier*, July/August 1998.
[3] The phrase comes from the subtitle of an article by William Saletan, "Booty and the Priest," in the online magazine *Slate*, March 6, 2002.

correctional officer at a Canadian prison. He suggested that in years past, Catholic men who recognized the pederastic tendency in themselves and hated it would try to put it to death by entering a seminary or a monastery, where they naively believed the sexual dimension of life simply disappeared. It doesn't disappear, and many of these men, by the time they found out they were wrong, had already become addicted. This suggestion has the advantage of accounting for the fact that most priests who are true pedophiles appear to be men in their sixties and older and belong to a generation of Catholics with, on the one hand, a strong sense of sexual mortal sin and, on the other, strong convictions about the asceticism and sexual integrity of priestly life. To homosexuals and pedophiles I would add a third group, those I call "tames"—men who are incapable of facing the normally unpleasant situations presented by adulthood and who find refuge, and indeed success, in a system that rewards concern for appearance, distaste for conflict, and fondness for the advantageous lie. In sum, the social prestige and high reputation that attached to the post-World War II priesthood made it attractive to men of low character and provided them with excellent cover.

A second key factor in the present corruption is loss of the bishops' ability for self-correction. This problem has institutional and personal dimensions. The model of episcopal collegiality in place since the Council has not increased the mutual good will of the bishops but has, paradoxically, made the *appearance* of good will obligatory in nearly all situations. Once more I turn to James Hitchcock. Speaking of the Church's necessary recourse to diplomacy in dealing with militarily superior nation-states, Hitchcock says:

> It is ironic and discouraging that in the modern democratic era, when the Church enjoys the blessings of complete independence from political control, diplomacy still seems necessary, now often concentrated on internal ecclesiastical matters. It appears, for example, that the Pope is not free simply to appoint bishops as he sees fit, but that an elaborate process of consultation, of checks and balances, takes place, after which successful candidates are often people who have no highly placed enemies. The Holy See now appears to treat national episcopal conferences, and the numerous religious orders, almost as foreign powers. Scrupulous correctness is observed at all times, formal verbiage masks barely hidden disagreements, and above all potential "incidents" are

avoided.... This endemic practice of diplomacy within the Church has yielded small results. Abuses have been tolerated not for the sake of unity but merely for the appearance of unity, which itself soon becomes an over-riding concern.[4]

Because what matters most in this mindset is perception, the appearance of unity, it has become virtually impossible to remove a bad bishop without prior public scandal—"public" here meaning notorious in the secular sphere, diffused through the mass media. When the scandal is sexual or financial, it seems the Holy See can move quickly to remove the offender. When the scandal is in the arena of heresy or administrative irregularity or liturgical abuse, there is almost never enough secular interest generated to force the Holy See's hand. Bishops Milingo and Ziemann and Roddy Wright have many brethren; Bishop Gaillot has few. Intermediate reform measures like seminary visitations are doomed to failure for the same reason; there simply is no possibility in the present disposition for a hostile inspection, where the visitors try to "get behind" the administration and find the facts for themselves. To do such a thing would be to imply lack of trust in the administration and hence in the bishop responsible for it, and such an imputation is utterly impossible. The same is true in bishops' dealings with universities, learned societies, and religious congregations. The only permissible inspections are friendly inspections, where the visitors ask the institution under scrutiny for a self-evaluation, which, of course, will be overwhelmingly positive and which will render the chances of reform almost nil.

A third answer to "What went wrong?" concerns a factor that is at once a result of earlier failures and a cause of many subsequent ones: I mean sexual blackmail. Most of the men who are bishops and superiors today were in the seminary or graduate school in the 1960s and 1970s. In most countries of the Western world these places were in a kind of disciplinary free-fall for ten or fifteen years. A very high percentage of churchmen who are now in positions of authority were sexually compromised during that period. Perhaps they had a homosexual encounter with a fellow seminarian; perhaps they had a brief

[4]James F. Hitchcock, "Conservative Bishops, Liberal Results," *Catholic World Report*, May 1995.

heterosexual affair with a fellow theology student. Provided they did not cause grave scandal, such men were frequently promoted, according to their talents and ambition. Many are competent administrators, but they have a time-bomb in their past, and they have very little appetite for reform measures of any sort—even doctrinal reforms—and they have zero appetite for reform proposals that entail cleaning up sexual mischief. In some cases perhaps, there is out-and-out blackmail, where a bishop moves to discipline a priest and priest threatens to report the bishop's homosexual affair in the seminary to the Nuncio or to the press, and so the bishop backs off. More often I suspect the blackmail is indirect. No overt threat is made by anyone, but the responsible ecclesiastic is troubled by the ghost of his past and has no stomach for taking a hard line. Even if personally uneasy with homosexuality, he will not impede the admission and promotion of gays. He will almost always treat sexuality in psychological terms, as a matter of human maturation, and is chary of the language of morality and asceticism. He will act only when it is impossible not to act, as when a case of a priest's or seminarian's sexual misconduct is known to the police or the media. He will characteristically require of the offender no discipline but will send him to counseling, usually for as brief a period as possible, and will restore him to the best position that diocesan procedures and public opinion will allow him to.

Note: sexual blackmail operates far beyond the arena of sexual misconduct. When your Aunt Margaret complains about the pro-abortion teachers at the Catholic high school, or the Sisters of St. Jude worshiping the Eight Winds, or Father's home-made Eucharistic Prayer, and nothing is done, it is eminently likely that the bishop's reluctance to intervene stems from the consciousness that he is living on borrowed time. In short, many bishops and superiors, lacking integrity, lack moral courage. Lacking moral courage, they can never be reformers, can never uproot a problem, but can only plead for tolerance and healing and reconciliation. I am here sketching only the best-case scenario, where the bishop's adventures were brief, without issue, and twenty years in his past. In cases where the man continues his sexual exploits as a bishop, he is of course wholly compromised and the blackmail proportionately disastrous.

A fourth element in the present corruption is the strange separation of the Church from blue-collar working people. Before the

Council every Catholic community could point to families who lived on hourly wages and who were unapologetically pious, in some cases praying a daily family rosary and attending daily Mass. Such families were a major source of religious vocations and provided the Church with many priests as well. These families were good for the Church, calling forth bishops and priests who were able to speak to their spiritual needs and to work to protect them from social and political harms. Devout working-class families characteristically inclined to a somewhat sugary piety, but they also characteristically required manly priests to communicate it to them: that was the culture that gave us the big-shouldered baritone in a lace surplice. Except for newly arrived immigrants from Mexico, Vietnam, and the Philippines, the devout working-class family has disappeared in the U.S. and in western Europe. The beneficial symbiosis between the clerical culture and the working class has disappeared as well. In most parishes of which I'm aware the priests know how to talk to the professionals and the professionals know how to talk to the priests, but the welders and roofers and sheet-metal workers, if they come to church at all, seem more and more out of the picture. I think this affects the Church in two ways: on the one hand, the Catholic seminary and university culture has been freed of any responsibility to explain itself to the working class, and notions of scriptural inspiration and sexual propriety have become progressively detached from the terms in which they would be comprehensible by ordinary people; on the other hand, few priests if any really depend on working people for their support. In a mixed parish, they are supported by the professionals; in a totally working-class parish, they're supported by the diocese—that is, by professionals who live elsewhere. That means not only does Father not have to account for his bizarre view of the Johannine community, but he doesn't have to account for the three evenings a week he spends in lay clothes away from the parish.

A related but distinct factor contributing to The Crisis is money. The clergy as a whole is enormously more prosperous than it was a century ago. That means the clergyman is independent of the disapproval of the faithful in a way his predecessors were not, and it also means he has the opportunities and the wherewithal to sin, and sin boldly, very often without detection. Unless he makes unusual efforts to the contrary, a priest today finds himself part of a culture of pleasure-seeking bachelordom, and the way he recreates and entertains himself overlaps to a great extent that of the young professional bronco. Too often, regrettably, the overlap is total. But even when a priest is chaste, by collecting boy-toys and living the good life he finds himself somewhat compromised. He may suspect a brother priest is up to no good by his frequent escapes to a time-share condo, but if he feels uneasy about his own indulgences he is unlikely to phone his brother to remonstrate with him. My own experience of religious life is that community discussion of "poverty issues" is exceptionlessly ugly—partly because almost everyone feels vulnerable to criticism in some aspect or other of his life, partly because there's an unspoken recognition that poverty and chastity issues are not entirely unrelated. As a consequence, only the most trivial and cosmetic adjustments are made, and the integrity of community life continues to worsen.

One more point, perhaps more fanciful than the others. I believe that one of the worst things to happen to the Church and one of the most important factors in the current corruption of the clergy is the Mertonization of monastic life. I may be unfair to Thomas Merton in laying the blame at his feet and I don't insist on the name, but I think you all can recognize what I mean: the sea change in the model of contemplative life, once aimed at mortification—a death to self through asceticism—now aimed at self-actualization: the Self has taken center stage. This change is important because, in spite of fifty-plus years of propaganda to the contrary, the monastic ideal remains a potent icon in any priest's self-understanding. Obedience, simplicity of life, and fidelity to prayer have different orientations in the case of a canon, a friar, and a diocesan priest, obviously, but they are all monastic in transmission and all essential to the clerical life. Where monastic life is healthy, it builds up even non-monastic parts of the Church, including and in particular the lives of priests in the active apostolate; where it is corrupt or lax, the loss extends to the larger Church as well—it's as if a railing were missing on one side of a balcony. When I was preparing for priesthood my teachers lamented what they called the "monastic" character of pre-conciliar seminaries and houses of formation (fixed times for common prayer, silence, reading at meals, etc.), complaining that such disciplines were ill-suited to their lives because they were destined not to be monks but pastors, missionaries, and scholars. But looking at the lives of my contemporaries one of the things I find most obviously lacking is an appetite for prayer created by good habits of prayer—habits which are usually the product of a discipline we never had. The same is true of asceticism and self-denial generally. When laypeople enter priests' quarters today, they rarely seem to be impressed by how sparse and severe our living arrangements are. They rarely walk away with the impression that the man who lives here is good at saying "No" to himself. Yet monks are, or used to be, our masters at saying "No" to the Self. Something went wrong. Putting the same idea in another perspective, it's wryly amusing to read commentators on the sexual-abuse problem recommend that priests be sent to a monastery for penance. What penance? Is there a single monastic house in the United States where the abbot would have the authority, much less the inclination, to keep a man at hard labor for twenty months or on bread and water for twenty days?

Let me sum up. I believe the sexual-abuse crisis represents no isolated phenomenon and no new failure, but rather illustrates a state of slowly worsening clerical and episcopal corruption with its roots well back into the 1940s. Its principal tributaries include a critical mass of morally depraved and psychologically defective clergymen who entered the service of [the] Church seeking emoluments and advantages unrelated to her spiritual mission, in addition to leaders constitutionally unsuited to the exercise of the virtues of truthfulness and fortitude. The old-fashioned vices of lust, pride, and sloth have erected an administrative apparatus effective at transmitting the consolations of the faith but powerless at correction and problem-solving. The result is a situation unamenable to reform, wherein the leaders continue to project an upbeat and positive message of ecclesial well-being to an overwhelmingly good-willed laity, a message which both speaker and hearer find more gratifying than convincing. I believe that The Crisis will deepen, though undramatically, in the foreseeable future; I believe that the policies suggested to remedy the situation will help only tangentially, and that the whole idea of an administrative programmatic approach—a "software solution," if I may put it that way—is an example of the disease for which it purports to be the cure. I believe that reform will come, though, in a future generation, and that the reformers whom God raises up will spill their blood in imitation of Christ. In short, to pilfer a line of Wilfrid Sheed, I find absolutely no grounds for optimism, and I have every reason for hope.

Liberal Jesuits and the Late Pope

May the Lord preserve our pontiff and give him life
and make him blessed upon the earth
and deliver him not to the will of his enemies.

[—Prayer based on Ps 41:2]

Sinéad O'Connor, during a 1992 appearance on Saturday Night Live, ended her performance of a Bob Marley song by ripping a photo of Pope John Paul II top to bottom while chanting, "Fight the *real* enemy!" Most people who heard of the incident were shocked by the display of hatred. I wasn't. I'm a Jesuit, you see.

Over the course of twenty-eight years in the Society of Jesus, I've watched Wojtyła-[Pope John Paul II-] hatred turn into one of the principal subthemes of Jesuit life. I say "theme" and not "policy." The official documents have never departed from the language of deference to the pope. I'm talking about the informal expectations of day-to-day existence, the culture transmitted not by the printed word but by oblique rewards and punishments, by the smiles and scowls of the men who count. Viewed from within this culture of Jesuitry, Sinéad's pontiff-shredding was almost sacramental: an outward sign of an interior reality.

How widespread was this hatred? It's hard to say. Certainly John Paul II always had a staunch minority of admirers and defenders among Jesuits, nor were all superiors inimical to him. The prominence of the theme was a function both of the intensity of the pope-haters and of the tolerance shown this hatred by their brethren—that is, it was as much a matter of what was left unspoken as what was actually said.

Diogenes has cited a remark made by a Jesuit on the day of the attempt on the pope's life in May 1981. Father Cyril Barrett, S.J. ("in a bellow that filled a London restaurant"), said of the failed assassin

Originally published in *Catholic Culture*, April 4, 2005.

Mehmet Ali Agca, "The only thing wrong with that bloody Turk was that he couldn't shoot straight!" Note that this is not the language of passionate disagreement; this is hatred, pure and simple. But the key point is not Barrett's malice, nor even his Sinéad-ish ferocity in expressing it. The really telling fact is that the episode was recounted in Barrett's obituary, in a Jesuit publication, in a tone that, if short of endorsement, suggested nothing worse than a venial lapse of good taste on his part. Classic Cyril!

Before ordination I'd heard my Jesuit professors pray that Wojtyła come to an early death—and go unrebuked, or rebuked in that jocular vein that signals sympathy. It was the absence of contradiction that spoke loudest. Of course you can come up with many examples of pro-papal utterances by Jesuits, but try to find (comparably public, self-initiated) examples of remonstrance or correction of influential papal detractors by their superiors. You won't. Take the remarks quoted by McDonough and Bianchi in their book (*Passionate Uncertainty*) on the U.S. Jesuits. From a Jesuit academic: "The Society has not sold its soul to the 'Restoration' of John Paul II." From a Jesuit church historian: "[He's] probably the worst pope of all times" (referring to Wojtyła), and adding, "He's not one of the worst popes; he's *the* worst. Don't misquote me." They didn't.

The reason for these Jesuits' Wojtyła-hatred is no mystery. His fiercest adversaries have always been liberal-apostate Catholics: those who, in flat contradiction to the logic of doctrine, press for that doctrine to change. Women may become priests, and approval may be given to contraception, but the institution that enacts these innovations *ipso facto* has ceased to be part of the Catholic Church. The venom of liberals toward Karol Wojtyła was bitterest, ironically, in precisely that area in which he differed least from his predecessors and in which his successor will differ least from him: in repeating the truism that doctrine, being unchangeable, will not be changed.

Men's hatred for the one who has been unjust to them is trifling compared to their hatred for the one they have treated unjustly; every reminder of him brings a fresh twinge of pain. Liberal-apostates know that their stance is irrational, that they do the pope an injustice in pretending he is free to un-pope himself by altering the deposit of faith. The dreams that progressivists surfaced during Paul VI's pontificate—of a congregational, sexually emancipated, anti-sacral "picnic" Catholicism—were frankly infantile. Yet Catholics over fifty will remember the emotional mist of auto-suggestion that "the next pope" would move with the times and make these dreams come true. Not all Jesuits got smitten by this vision, but the majority did, and was stunned when Wojtyła failed to act out its fantasy. Many left the Society to seethe outside it; others remained, and seethe within.

I don't want to overstate the case. Several Jesuits around the world have a profound interest in the late pope and have been careful and articulate expounders of his work. But their endeavors are nearly always made to seem marginal: at best, philosophical hobbyism; at worst, deviationist crankery. When a group of us put together a conference on *The Thought of Karol Wojtyła* fifteen years ago, we asked the U.S. provinces to distribute a flyer to all Jesuit houses. One socius (second-in-command) sent off the flyer with the accompanying note, "This item is being passed on to you without comment"—which was more than a comment; it was a sneer plus a veiled threat: you may, if you wish, affect to treat Wojtyła with respect, but understand that you have demoted yourself to the second class. We all knew the score.

John Paul is dead, and his despisers must find other bones to gnaw. A younger, less rancorous, and (thanks, in part, to a quarter-century of choler) markedly smaller generation of Jesuits is presently in formation. No one knows which man, as pope, the new Jesuits will be called to serve, but the deposit of faith he inherits at the outset of his papacy will be intact at its end. We've come to a fork in the road: Jesuits can continue to serve a make-believe Church and rage in impotence against the pope who ignores it, or they can reconnect with a tradition of martyrs, more concerned with the conversion of Turks than in improving their marksmanship. "Deliver him not," reads the prayer *Pro Pontifice*, "to the will of his enemies." It would be good to speak these words once again, pleading for the success of the Society's endeavors instead of their frustration.

Thou Art a Priest Forever

"Abolish the Priesthood," reads the provocative title of the latest *Atlantic* cover story, penned by James Carroll. Is it the Brahmin priesthood that has to go? The Shinto *kannushi*? Ordained Anglican women? (Spoiler alert: No, no, and no.) It is the Roman Catholic Church that must do the right thing and drop her connection with the whole priest business.

This is a puzzling imperative. One can understand a call to fill a need, to address a deficiency by supplying a want. But there are thousands upon thousands of priestless institutions already out there, from Camp Fire Girls to plumbers' unions to Kiwanis clubs; why should the Catholic Church add to their number? On this matter Carroll is as confused as we are. He can point to a diseased and depraved priesthood, but he has no awareness of its healthy state, no comprehension of its authentic purpose.

There is no possibility, as Carroll imagines, of treating the Catholic priesthood like the Beefeaters at the Tower of London, which might be reconfigured as ushers or guides or eliminated altogether, as the exigencies of the moment direct. The theologian Donald Keefe, S.J., put it this way: "It should be kept in mind that the Church has no authority over her sacraments: they cause her; she does not cause them." Abolish the priesthood and, by entailment, not only the sacraments but the Church herself pop like a soap bubble and cease to exist.

In positive terms, what does Carroll give us by way of a theology of the Church? What does he reckon the Church is *for*?

> The Church is the largest nongovernmental organization on the planet, through which selfless women and men care for the poor, teach the unlettered, heal the sick, and work to preserve minimal standards of the common good. The world needs the Church of these legions to be rational, historically minded, pluralistic, committed to peace, a champion of the equality of women, and a tribune of justice.

Originally published as a *First Things* web article, May 20, 2019.

That Carroll views his church as an NGO tells us all we need to know about his Christology—and his fix for Catholicism. The good works he mentions have no need of priests but—in the historically precise sense—of clerics, persons expressly educated and motivated toward specific this-worldly ends. A cleric, whence English *clerk*, is a man who can read and write in ways his neighbors can't. All the more perplexing that Carroll of all people should single out *clericalism* as the Church's besetting sin:

> Clericalism, with its cult of secrecy, its theological misogyny, its sexual repressiveness, and its hierarchical power based on threats of a doom-laden afterlife, is at the root of Roman Catholic dysfunction.

Here Carroll's antipathies have ridden out in front of the hounds so far as to lose the hunt. Doctrines the apostles preached on the day of Pentecost are mixed up with ideological allergies common to *soixante-huitards*, heathen and non-, and made subject to the same condemnation. We are still no closer to grasping why men who offer the Eucharist should exit the stage and why, post-purge, the dysfunction he laments would be remedied. More to the point, the NGO that embodies Carroll's own dreams is itself not clergyless, but has a clerisy in the service of recreations "beyond the binary":

> Equality for women as officeholders in the Church has been resisted precisely because it, like an end to priestly celibacy, would bring with it a broad transformation of the entire Catholic ethos: Yes to female sexual autonomy; yes to love and pleasure, not just reproduction, as a purpose of sex; yes to married clergy; yes to contraception; and, indeed, yes to full acceptance of homosexuals. No to male dominance; no to the sovereign authority of clerics; no to double standards.

Carroll's ill-focused ardor is fueled not only by the prospect of sexual emancipation but by justified disgust at the sexual abuse perpetrated by priests and denied, disguised, and sometimes abetted by their superiors. Here his indignation will be shared by most Catholic readers. He reviews, in disjointed fashion, the last half-century of enormities. In Robespierrian mode he calls for an uprising of the masses, in defiance of self-serving Toryism: "The Church conservatives know better than most that the opposite of the clericalism they aim to protect is not some vague elevation of laypeople to a global altar guild but democracy—a robust overthrow of power that would unseat them and their ilk." It is perfectly understandable that outrage at gross and prolonged injustice might demand to see the last liturgy coordinator hanged with the guts of the last priest. In terms of dispensing even short-term justice, however, the historical precedents are not reassuring.

Is there a clue as to why Carroll should round up the usual suspects but send only the massing priests to the guillotine? There is. Carroll was himself a priest for five years. From his own account it does not appear that the spiritual side of the job interfered greatly with more important business.

> Ironically, the Church, which sponsored my civil-rights work and prompted my engagement in the antiwar movement, made me a radical. I was the Catholic chaplain at Boston University, working with draft resisters and protesters, and soon enough I found myself in conflict with the conservative Catholic hierarchy. It only gradually dawned on me that there was a tragic flaw deep inside the institution to which I'd given my life, and that it had to do with the priesthood itself.

The priesthood Carroll would abolish he once committed himself to, and once relinquished. Carroll's demands should, in fairness, be viewed against this background. If a lawyer advises a particular woman to file for bankruptcy, it's important to know that she was once his boss, more important to know that she was once his wife. Is he acting in service of her good or of his own vindictiveness? Here we have reasons for doubt. Consider that Carroll's roster of villains (Burke, Ratzinger, Viganò, and others) are despised not for their failings but their strengths, not for promises they failed to keep but promises on which they deliver. Chesterton once wrote that in the eyes of the world, a priest is reckoned a knave for breaking his vows and a fool for keeping them. Ditto for Carroll's NGO.

Carroll's proposal is an example of the disease for which it purports to be the cure. The model of priestly life he found valuable is dismaying not only for its preening 1970s-style Radical Chic but in the extent to which it viewed the sacramental character and duty of priesthood as an add-on: extraneous, detachable, and dispensable.

In sum, a kind of fanny-pack one might put aside when it inter-
feres with—what's the word?—invitations to intimacy. It was in large
measure this disintegration of the ritual and the pastoral, this reduc-
tive instrumentalizing of the sacred at the expense of praxis, which
permitted the Jekyll and Hyde lifestyle we find in [Theodore] Mc-
Carrick and in the great majority of abusers and enablers.

But what about Carroll's valid concerns for the world outside
the sanctuary? Would the re-sacralization of the priesthood pull the
Church back from her work with the poor and the friendless? Would
we become a house of self-regarding bourgeois pietism? Well, seek
out for yourself a slum among slums. Go to the convent of Mother
Teresa's sisters you will find there. Ask those sisters whether they
believe the priesthood should be abolished. Ask them whether, in
furthering their own work, the priest as scoutmaster or priest as con-
fector of sacraments is more valuable. You may have to wait until
Adoration ends for your answer.

Part Two

RELIGION AND THE CULTURE WARS:
ESSAYS, 1990–1993

Feminist Pilgrims

In one of the finest specimens of biblical narrative, we are told how David, fleeing from Saul, finds himself at the court of Achish, king of Gath, and how the servants of Achish blow David's cover by spreading the word of his military success:

> And David laid up these words in his heart and was sore afraid of Achish the king of Gath. And he changed his behavior before them, and feigned himself mad in their hands, and scrabbled on the doors of the gate, and let his spittle fall down upon his beard. Then said Achish unto his servants, Lo ye see the man is mad: wherefore then have ye brought him to me? Do I lack madmen, that ye have brought this fellow to play the madman in my presence? [1 Sam 21:12–15]

"Do I lack madmen?" We can picture poor Achish with perfect vividness: an up-country Palestinian chief trying his best to keep the clan together by giving jobs to his in-laws and jailing his rivals—what most men in comparable circumstances have done in every age. We see him, perhaps, rubbing his temples with his fingertips while dealing with the day's roster of petty crises bungled by his deadweight subordinates. A drooling and gibbering David is the last thing he wants in his IN tray. With his shaft of wry exasperation King Achish would win the instant sympathy of any administrator—indeed, of anybody with any responsibilities—who has ever had one problem too many walk through his door. Across a chasm of three millennia our hearts go out to him.

Perhaps, then, it is not too harsh a transition to refocus on another minor-league commandant in another region off the main trade routes, former president Daniel Ortega of Nicaragua. Ronald Reagan once called him "a dictator in designer glasses," but I prefer to see him as an example of something humbler and more likable: a modest and serious man doing what he could to keep afloat the family

Originally published in *Commentary*, June 1990.

business, which in this case was the business of riding herd on a Marxist revolution. Not so much a creator of contemporary politics as their product, he hitched his wagon to the Red Star while it was in the ascendant, only to find himself in charge of a country which, like Neutralia in Evelyn Waugh's novel *Scott-King's Modern Europe*, was "a typical modern state, governed by a single party, acclaiming a dominant Marshal, supporting a vast ill-paid bureaucracy whose work is humanized and tempered by corruption." And then came the elections of March 1990....

Now that the FSLN [Spanish for the Sandinista National Liberation Front] has huffed off with an ill grace to squat and pout in the Museum of World Leninism, we can look back with a kind of detachment at the curious fascination which it held for so many earnest Northerners in the past decade. A wide array of enthusiasts, hungry for evidence with which to vindicate their own schemes for a classless state, have wanted to view Nicaragua as the nation on the cutting edge of history, the crucible of politics, the laboratory in which the latest experiments in social engineering were the business not simply of the academy but of a real government with a real police force. Just as in the '30s most leftist intellectuals looked to the Soviet Union for a preview of the future shape of education or public health, so—half a century later—it was the Sandinistas who were seen to be building the New Jerusalem. Accordingly, it was to Managua and Esteli that the pilgrims trekked, clutching their Nikons and their dissertations, anxious for a cure or an imprimatur. A number of ingenious arguments have been advanced to address the painful question, how could so many have been so wrong? A look at the grasp of reality enjoyed by the votaries themselves will make the answer only too obvious.

It is hardly surprising, for example, that Western feminists should have mounted their own fact-finding tours to assess the progress of the Daughters of the Revolution. In May 1988 Maxine Molyneux published an article in the *Feminist Review*, "The Politics of Abortion in Nicaragua: Revolutionary Pragmatism—or Feminism in the Realm of Necessity?" Molyneux was grieved to learn that "Nicaragua is an anomaly among socialist states. Its comparatively advanced record on general political issues—pluralism, democracy, abolition of the death penalty—contrasts with a surprisingly conservative position on reproductive rights."

The chief villain was, of course, the Catholic Church, and particularly its hierarchy, which exercised a kind of mind control even over emancipated Sandinistas which Molyneux was at a loss to account for. But a second factor was the rather embarrassing one that the National Directorate of Nicaragua—though a splendid thing in itself—was overwhelmingly composed of *Latino* males, with predictable consequences: "The cults of *machismo* and *hombria* [manliness] place considerable store on being able to father large numbers of children, biologically if not socially."

It is interesting that leftists constitutionally averse to negative stereotypes of "ethnic minorities" find their scruples only too vincible when the ethnics in question fail to measure up. Nor is it only Nicaraguan men who are at fault. As Molyneux laments, "In Catholic countries where women's identification with motherhood is positive and particularly strong," even the sisters themselves can fall short of full enlightenment. One Nicaraguan feminist told the author:

> The losses of war have strengthened rather than diminished the emotional significance of motherhood. There are 11,000 women in Managua alone who are mothers of soldiers who have died in the fighting. Abortion in such a context is associated with more death; for some women it's unthinkable.

Our researcher does not explicitly draw the conclusion, but we are meant to feel that not the least of the tragedies of war is that it robs a young woman of her normal, wholesome urge for the surgical termination of pregnancy.

Yet true blame for Sandinista recalcitrance in the cause of reproductive rights may have reached even higher. Molyneux does not flinch from the suggestion that, at least in part, the president himself was responsible. She has come upon damaging excerpts from a 1987 speech:

> "One way of depleting our youth is to promote the sterilization of women in Nicaragua ... or to promote a policy of abortion"; "The problem is that the woman is the one who reproduces. The man can't play that role." [Ortega] said that some women, "aspiring to be liberated," decide not to bear children. Such a woman "negates her own continuity, the continuity of the human species."

The author is prepared to be somewhat lenient toward the heterodoxy of such opinions. She explains, "Ortega is a man who lives the war every day, and his off-the-cuff remarks reflect a pragmatic, political attitude toward what he sees." At the same time, though,

> some have seen a suggestion of moralism in his formulations in the implication that women have been bystanders in the revolutionary process and must now therefore discharge their debt to the nation by having babies.... What annoyed many women was the fact that Ortega saw fit to use the authority and discourse of the revolution and the war against the *contras* to attack and demobilize the campaigners and supporters of women's reproductive choice.

We are, in short, left with the clear impression by Molyneux that, while her idol may wear designer glasses, he has trotters of clay.

There was worse yet in store for Daniel Ortega. *Revolutionary Forgiveness: Feminist Reflections on Nicaragua* [Orbis Books, 1987] is the travel diary of the Amanecida Collective, a group of thirteen persons of advanced ideas from the Harvard Divinity School and the Episcopal Divinity School of Cambridge, Massachusetts. The book is principally the account of a one-month visit to Nicaragua made by eleven members of the collective. Even by the standards of the Managua photo-op, they were an imposing group:

> Diversity looms large in our spiritualities, as we represent different ecclesial backgrounds and foregrounds. Carol is Moravian. Flo is a Unitarian Universalist minister. Margarita and Kirsten belong to the United Church of Christ, and Susan is a United Church of Christ minister. Six of us are Episcopalians: Laura, Anne, Carter, Virginia, Laurie, and Jane; Carter and Jane are Episcopal priests. Pat is a musician in an Episcopal Church. Like several of us, Elaine is a former Roman Catholic. She is now post-christian and also is wrestling with the possibility of joining the Episcopal Church.

Even a Sandinista steeled to the ravages of Claymore mines and fragmentation bombs must have swallowed once or twice at the prospect of hosting the Amanecida Collective for a few weeks. Like missionaries clutching their Bibles in a white-knuckle grip, these troopers came with a robust faith: conventional militant feminism, but with a notably Sapphic twist:

Our commitment to the liberation of lesbians and gay men requires that we confront those people and those policies which proclaim sexual relationships between men and women, heterosexual marriage, and nuclear family constellations as normative for the health of society.... The problems of heterosexism and homophobia cannot be separated from those of gender, racial, and class oppression. To try to do so is to underestimate the systemic nature of the forces of oppression in the world and to miss altogether the key questions in any adequate analysis of injustice: who controls whom? ... Our christian/ postchristian faith becomes increasingly an advocacy posture for the self-determination of all people who have been objectified and damaged by the imperialistic, racist, sexist, heterosexist, classist, and anti-Semitic deeds done "in the name of Christ."

Clear, I hope? Less zealous reformers than the Amanecidanas might have noticed that the personal and social enthusiasms expressed in their manifesto did not dovetail especially well with the urgencies of the Sandinista revolution; yet they were not to be put off. The purpose of their trip was not so much to learn as to teach—or when they would learn, it was only to confirm by example what they had already grasped by faith (I mean, by their advocacy posture).

Thus, the official justification they were offered for the continued detention of political prisoners did not seem to trouble any of the visitors, yet it was noted by them with approval that in Nicaragua, "advertising that exploits women's bodies is now illegal." Certainly they were not about to let conventional barriers to understanding frustrate their plans to inspire and be inspired. One Nicaraguan woman at a rally for Ortega, noticing that the *gringas* had a tape recorder, asked if she could recite a poem. Our informant readily assented, and tells us, "I could not understand the words but listened to the tone of her voice, which rose and fell in a passionate lament." Even ignorance of the language is chalked up not to personal unpreparedness but to the wholesale blindness of European civilization:

We regretted that so few of us knew enough Spanish during our visits to be able to converse easily with Nicaraguans. Having a translator inhibited spontaneous communication. It also served as an uneasy reminder ... of the distance between North and South and of the cultural myopia in which most U.S. citizens of Northern European descent have been raised.

However, it all comes right in the end:

Non-verbal sounds in the night, as well as what we saw, tasted, touched, and smelled, were as important to our meeting Nicaragua and its people as any words we were able to understand.

No nineteenth-century sahib, no blasé son of the manse, no Church Mission Society zealot was ever so confident as the Amanecida Collective that you can get the Wog to tell you everything you need to know if you handle him properly. The absence of Spanish *is* regretted, but we come to suspect that this is largely because the good sisters had sermons of their own they were anxious to give. U.S. cultural myopia did not, it seems, impair their vision of the horrors of lingering sexism. The predictable enemies are scored, including Cardinal Miguel Obando y Bravo and especially the pope, "whose contempt for both women and the Sandinista regime" was seen as strikingly pernicious. But the "deeply rooted *machismo*" is also deplored and it is noticed with pique that there was "a *nine-man* ruling junta."

Inevitably, the focus comes around to the sad fact of Nicaraguan homophobia. What seems most to have unsettled the ladies of the divinity schools of Cambridge is that no one much cared about the problem. They asked insistently about gay rights, but were shrugged off. People gave unhelpful answers like, "The revolution is more important than these things." "Homosexuality doesn't exist in Nicaragua." "There are more important things to worry about." Like the true believers they are, the Amanecidanas were able at least to find a reassuring explanation: "Confusion over these issues results in a linking of homosexuality with prostitution and coercion, because that was a common male homosexual experience under Somoza's National Guard."

The faith was rattled, then, but still intact. One member of the collective burst into a long and agonized *cri du coeur*, of which I give not the twentieth part:

I am what I am and I am a North American.... I am what I am *una lesbiana norte-americana*.... How do I embrace this brokenness? Is it madness that I feel? Is it passion, the passion of thousands like me who know no other life? How do I convince Fidel? or Daniel? or Tomás? Or Ernesto? Why won't they see our struggles as connected? I am not the enemy. The white man is our enemy.... We must find a different God. A God beyond Father, beyond the jealous patriarchal role model we have been subjected to.... The white man will never give us power, we must find our own. We must take our power.

A stern moralist might argue that the Amanecida Collective was Daniel Ortega's just comeuppance for having succumbed in the first place to the temptations of the Left. Politics makes strange bedfellows (to use a spectacularly inappropriate cliché), and the enthusiasms of feminists are after all no more than the stock principles of Marxism extended beyond the bounds of sanity.

All this is admitted. But let's be fair. Here we had a man operating well within the tradition of the backwoods thane, keeping his brothers employed and his enemies in prison by a combination of wit, bluster, and *very* dangerous liaisons. Like that of Achish, king of Gath, his average day must have been a nightmare: intrigues, pronunciamentos, jailbreaks, agricultural disasters following upon each other thick as fleas. Think of what a free half-hour in the afternoon must have meant to the man. Think of the relief, the chance for a cigar enjoyed in solitude. And consider then the effect when his door was thrown open, the Amanecida Collective shuffled in for an audience ... and he *had* to think of something nice to say. If we can, after lo! these many years, commiserate with Achish, can we not spare a twinge of sympathy for Daniel?

What I Saw at the American Academy of Religion

The American Academy of Religion [AAR], in its statement of purpose, calls itself "an inclusive learned society and professional association in the field of the study of religion. The Academy [we are told] fosters teaching, research, scholarship, and critical awareness about the study of religion as a humanistic field of learning." The AAR was formed in 1964, grafted onto the stock of an organization called the National Association of Biblical Instructors [NABI], which had its own beginnings in 1909. Curious about the treatment of religion in the university and about the functioning of this learned society, I decided to attend its Annual Meeting, to be held in November of 1991 in Kansas City. Never having been a member of the organization, I came not as a participant but simply to observe and (as will be seen) to take notes.

I made no preparations for the convention beyond a perfunctory attempt to gain some historical perspective by paging through Volume One (1933) of the *Journal of the National Association of Biblical Instructors* [JNABI]. A report on the Twenty-third Annual Meeting, held in 1932, showed that it was a modest two-day affair, including half-a-dozen addresses with such titles as "Recent Excavations in Palestine," "The Bible and Modern Education," "A School Principal's Reactions to the Problems of Biblical Instruction," and so forth. From the treasurer's report I learned that the entire budget for NABI in the preceding fiscal year was $376. A note in the same issue from *JNABI*'s editor Ismar Peritz announced, "We do not share the views of those who hold, openly or tacitly, that the Bible and the religion it reveals are antiquated; we believe that biblical religion as culminating in the life, teachings, and regenerative power of Jesus is the only solution of the problems of universal citizenship."

Sixty years, it is fair to say, have wrought some changes in the association. The 1991 meeting was attended by more than five thousand

Originally published in *First Things*, March 1992.

professors and graduate students; a 184-page program listed over four hundred presentations in fifty-nine program units; an $850,000 capital campaign is underway. Yet the ways in which the AAR has expanded from its taproot are not simply a matter of size and structure. If we may take Mr. Peritz's opinions as a benchmark, there has been some shifting of deeper allegiances as well.

On arrival at the Kansas City Convention Center, I was issued a thick book containing abstracts of the papers to be presented at the meeting. These abstracts served to guide one's choice of session (as each time-slot offered as many as eighteen separate options), to help identify the speaker's principal interest in the problem at hand, and in more than a few instances to corroborate the evidence of one's ears. As might be expected at a conference of scholars, not all arguments were equally easy to follow.

In the first afternoon of the conference, I attended a session on the theme of "Violence, Victimization, and Social Control." The notion of religion as an instrument of social coercion was hardly restricted to this group; indeed, it served as one of the *leitmotifs* of the meeting: in its overt realizations, as in the paper titled "Exorcism as a Means of Christian Social Control," and in its covert forms, as discussed in "HIV-Antibody Testing as an Exercise of Socio-political Power." At the present session my attention was arrested by the thesis of James McBride of Fordham, which he epitomized as follows:

War, Battering, and Sports: The Gulf Between American Men and the "Other"

Abstract

The outbreak of armed conflict in the Middle East coincided with a marked increase in the cases of battering of women. As the day on which the number of such cases annually reach their peak, Super Bowl Sunday witnessed a great outpouring of "renewed patriotism," befitting the culmination of the first week of war. The purpose of this paper is to explore the relationship between the virile asceticism of character ethics and the psychic economy of the androcentric social order manifest in war, battering, and territorial games. In particular the analysis will demonstrate the intimate bond between the renewal of totemic identity and the ritual sacrifice of the "other," be they women, people of color, or religious "fanatics," by drawing upon the theoretical work of Theodor Adorno, René Girard, and Georges Bataille.

Our male-dominant culture, according to Dr. McBride, has a bone-deep terror of the "other," all that which is not itself, which it must destroy in fact or symbolically sacrifice by means of ritual. The terms "enemy" and "woman" are interchangeable: "The enemy must be female or must be made so," we were told. Women are battered; male enemies must be gelded first. The speaker confessed that in listening to reports on the Gulf War he noticed that "castration images" were so common that it could not be a coincidence. He passed around a political cartoon showing Saddam Hussein waist deep in a pool of oil ("Or feces?" he conjectured): evidence that the legless Hussein was castrated, and thus feminized, in the eyes of our political culture. The connection of war with sports was adduced through an analysis of the vocabulary by which the leaders of Operation Desert Storm explained their craft; General Schwarzkopf, for example, referred to his Kuwait invasion plan as a variation on the "Hail Mary pass play" in football. Dr. Naomi Goldenberg's insights into the totemic structure of this sport were presented to convince the skeptical that there's more to it than meets the eye. Each football play begins with a birthing ritual in which the quarterback puts his hands between the splayed legs of the center, directly beneath the anus. When the pigskin is delivered through the center's legs into the player-midwife's arms it becomes "live." (At this point there were bums of astonishment and assent from the audience.) The key in this exercise of male narcissism is "ball possession." One tries to penetrate the opponents' defense; to fail is to fumble is to become "ball-less," to be gelded. Football, like patriarchal culture generally, "creates women" so as to annihilate them as the enemy: like war itself, it is a ritualized realization of the male need for an "incestual relationship to the castrated mother." Applause for McBride was long and ardent.

More explicit in her religious concerns was Dr. Anne Hunter, who spoke in the same session. She identified herself as "coming from the battered woman movement," and admitted that she had "clawed her way out of an abusive marriage." Heterosexual gender norms enshrine male privacy and female publicity, it was argued; nurses tend to be in full view all day while doctors work behind closed doors. Male scrutiny of the female abets and justifies violence against women and strips the abused of defenses. Dr. Hunter discussed Jeremy Bentham's panopticon, a prison design in which back-lit cells are arranged in a circle around a darkened hub or core, from which the guards can see their prisoners' every movement at each instant, while the captives never know whether or not the hostile eye is trained on them. The Judeo-Christian doctrine of the all-seeing male God is a barrier to women's freedom, she explained, for it makes women into prisoners of Bentham's panopticon; they languish in cells on whose walls the threat "GOD SEES YOU" is permanently painted. Far from being consoling, biblical expressions such as "the hairs of your head are numbered," "from my mother's womb you know me," "he holds me as the apple of his eye," extend the normative male gaze into the most private part of women's lives. How did this come to pass? "When we live away from our internal erotic movements, we become prey to external constraint"—an elegant inversion of the Western moral imagination. Hunter's remarks also found an enthusiastic reception.

So did another presentation:

An Exploration of Quilt Design as a Reasoning Process

Abstract

This paper explores the idea that quilt pattern designs are one way women reason about life, quilting a way women communicate their thoughts to one another and arrive at communal consensus regarding an understanding of the world, and quilts themselves the sustaining, functional way women convey their consensus to others.

Quilt design is a method of moral reasoning created by women in a survival-adaptive response to sexist culture that discourages them from culture-recognized intellectual achievement, and quilting itself is a process by which women come to a consensus regarding truth—a way which, though often dismissed as "craft," offers the intriguing possibility of serving as a door to deep levels of communication and covenant not normally accessed in the contemporary world.

This address, given by Brenda Brasher of the University of Southern California in the section devoted to Arts, Literature, and Religion, left at least one listener somewhat unpersuaded. Yet it could hardly be categorized as eccentric by AAR standards. The imagery of loom and needle was much in evidence in Kansas City in the discourse of feminists, and as roughly a quarter (ninety-three, by my count) of all the papers were feminist in approach, this made for a palpable impact.

The language of the "web" forks into the token of the subversive female webster/weaver and that of the female spider/spinner, both potent icons for contemporary feminists.

Not that the use of the term "feminist" is without problems. At the same conference, I learned that feminism has identified itself too closely with the concerns of white middle-class women. Black women have already erected womanist, and Hispanic women "mujerista," theologies of their own. It seems not to be clear where this declamation of feminism is to end, but I noticed that most speakers used three adjectives (feminist/womanist/mujerista) to avoid the charge of exclusivism. It was in fact during a panel discussion on Teaching the Womanist Idea that Dr. Toinette Eugene identified "African-American quilting" as a distinct and valuable enterprise and source of self-definition, presumably in an effort to resist the hegemony of Anglo-feminist quilting theorists. Eugene was concerned to describe a "practical praxis circle" in which the personal experience of black women can be used as a ground of their spiritual empowerment.

Eugene's co-panelist Katie Cannon expressed her intention to depict "one small part of the *tabula rasa* of inclusivity" in the womanist mode, insisting that true liberation is based on the conviction that "orthodox truth not be the norm of our daily lives." Religion has a central place in Cannon's scheme, although she distanced herself from "our dominating and chauvinistic Christian heritage" (it was, as it happened, the Feast of Christ the King that day) and vowed to "deconstruct this ideology which led us into complicity with our own oppression." It was noticeable that Cannon and Eugene both showed a lively sense of humor with regard to their own theorizing—a feature that was not greatly to the fore in other sections of the meeting. Cannon was especially successful at evoking audience reaction, drawing several "Amens!" from her listeners. She attributed this response to the effect of *erons*, a term coined by her Episcopal Divinity School colleague Carter Heyward and explained as "particles of passion generated whenever we do our pedagogy."

Feeling the need for a walk and for coffee, I skipped the later presentations in this section and made my way through the Convention Center to the refreshment area. As with any large convention, there was an exhibition hall filled with vendor displays, belonging in this case to publishing houses and software companies. As with any large convention, there was an air of professional chirpiness exuded by the salespeople and one of cautious bonhomie by their customers. While almost everyone was dressed in business attire, the number of beards and thick glasses made it obvious that this was an academic gathering. I was amused to see two Shriners passing through the lobby, complete with fezzes, clearly having strayed from some Kansas City conclave of their own. Viewed through the AAR lens, they might have arrived from Andromeda. As it happened I bumped into an acquaintance, an Old Testament scholar, who was attending sessions of the Society of Biblical Literature [SBL], which meets concurrently with the AAR each year. He assumed I too was in town for the SBL and when told otherwise rolled his eyes and sighed. The SBL made an injudicious alliance with the AAR some years ago, he explained, and for financial reasons can't go its own way—much like a woman trapped in an unhappy marriage for fear of starving on her own. When I related the gist of the papers I had heard earlier he showed no surprise, but pointed out that there were subgroups within the AAR that had managed to insulate themselves from the general enthusiasms and preserve more traditional standards of scholarship; the sections dealing with Asian and North American religions were given as examples, as was a group concerned with Roman Catholic modernism.

It was to a session of the last-mentioned group that I went next, where a discussion of a paper by Joseph Komonchak of the Catholic University of America was underway. Aside from diction of a rather exquisite political correctness and some tittering at the mention of the name "Ratzinger" (whom Father Komonchak invoked respectfully), there was little to distinguish this section from a faculty seminar in a conventional university setting. A sober debate took place about the impact of Vatican II on Catholic perceptions of ecclesial continuity. Interesting arguments were advanced regarding a side issue, the origin of popular Marian piety in the nineteenth century: was it a "grassroots" phenomenon, or the market creation of European religious publishing houses, or (as one scholar argued) a stratagem of the hierarchy to reinforce the submissive role of women? No consensus was reached.

One of the less exotic-sounding listings in the meeting program was the Theology and Religious Reflection section. The paper titles, however, suggested that these words too were spoken with a distinct

AAR accent: "Existentialism and Feminist Liberation Theology," "Postmodern Multiplicity and Feminist Responsibility," "Developing a Feminist Rule of Faith." More abstruse, perhaps, was the offering of Diane MacDonald of the Iliff School of Theology:

Body as (Ex)tension or (Re)tension: From "Serpentine Wanderer" to "La Mère qui jouit"

Abstract

Although Mark C. Taylor's "body" metaphor of "serpentine wanderer" avoids the closure of the Cartesian and Husserlian selves booked to a "transcendental signified," Taylor's "wanderer" reverses the prioritizing of spirit over flesh in modern theologies, valorizing a flesh devoid of spirit, thereby collapsing the tensions of an irreducible "other." His metaphorical "body," then, is an (ex)tension of the phallocentric and phallocratic technology of modern theology, now confined to a two-dimensional wordplay indifferent to the cries and joys of a richly signed wor(l)d.

In contrast, Julia Kristeva's "body" metaphor of "la mère qui jouit" retains a fluid identity responsive to the irreducible "other" within both her internal and external relations. This "body" of (re)tension unleashes the powers of a heterogeneous semiotic into the ordering processes of symbolic language, thereby transgressing modern dualistic thinking, and leading to an ontology of relatedness infused with a praxis of "care."

It must be confessed that I found MacDonald's own explication more serpentine than *jouissante*. Were I forced to decode her thesis in monosyllables, I would render it thus: gay men see things in more black-and-white terms than do "bi" girls. The broader theological implications of her proposal continued to elude me even as she spoke, but the project of gender-based deconstruction was hardly unfamiliar by this time. Across the board at the AAR, for the speakers I heard address the issue, the notion of sexuality as an essentially plastic phenomenon, an artifact of culture rather than an endowment of nature, was a *datum* and not a *demonstrandum*. Little sympathy was shown Camille Paglia's dictum that "nature has tyrannically designed our bodies for procreation." The inference commonly drawn was that, lacking natural realities on which to base his thinking, the individual makes his own sexual proclivities into a personal project, and "morality" is simply an index of the authenticity with which he has embraced this project.

In a paper titled "From Gendered Subjects to Gender as a Liberating Performance," Mary Fulkerson of the Duke Divinity School did combat with the thesis of Simone de Beauvoir that while gender is a acculturation process, sex isn't. "Both sex and gender are done to one," she insisted. Compulsory heterosexuality is one of the current dominant power realities that deform human consciousness. Emancipation from hierarchies and dualisms is effected by defining gender as "a performative practice in relation to multiply constructed subjects." Thus, the figure of speech by which a nun is said to be married to the Church might be reconceived in terms of a "butch-femme relationship." A proof-text was found in Galatians 3:28. "We are all *performing* our sex," Dr. Fulkerson insisted, "there *really is* no male or female in Christ."

This point was made in stronger, if less Christological, terms by Ann Pellegrini of Harvard:

Sexual Alterities: Otherwise Put

Abstract

The practices of gender-fuck,* so much on display in lesbian and gay subcultures, might seem to challenge the hegemony of the sex-gender system. In displacing the purportedly "natural" symmetry of biological sex and social gender, practices of self-stylization, such as butch-femme, S/M, or cross-dressing, lay open gender as masquerade. A feminist-informed, queerly placed interrogation is offered here of the representational matrices within which the stabilizing terms of gender may be opened up and overturned. Drawing on recent work in gay and lesbian critical cultural studies, I attempt to outline the possibilities of sexual and desiderative alterities. And here the resort to the plural "alterities" is meant to resist the reificationist impostures of gender and sexual dualisms. It is also intended to suggest the instabilities of desire, the potential pleasures and dangers of moving beyond the number two.

Cheerfully announcing that "you can't tell a butch by her cover," Pellegrini presented a vigorous case, somewhat in the manner of James

---

* We reluctantly report the scatological language, but it seems necessary to conveying the substance and tone of discussions at the more elevated levels of religious studies in the contemporary academy.—The Editors

Joyce, for the "interstructuration of class and race" with contemporary paradigms of sexuality. The so-called natural symmetry of sex is a fiction of heterosexual males fraudulently elevated to a biological truism in order to reserve power exclusively to themselves. The myth of normality exists to brand dissidents as deviants so as to rob them of a political voice. When women gather to talk about oppression, she reminded us, they're called "dyke, queer, man-hater." When men assemble to do the same thing, they're called "senator, congressman, cardinal." No argument was offered—and, to judge from the question period that followed, no argument was deemed necessary—to establish a factual historical basis for malign male oppression. Nor was there any explicit or implicit protest on moral grounds to the erection of this system of coercion. It seems that earlier critics of patriarchy and its attendant sexual ethic complained that what the patriarchs advertised as morality turned out, on inspection, to be political self-interest, disguised; human liberation thus entailed a depoliticization of inherited sexual norms and attitudes. Pellegrini, by contrast, claimed such depoliticization to be illusory.

"There is no 'outside' of politics," she insisted. Every human endeavor, every theory, every activity, every work of art or occasion of leisure, every affection or antipathy, is at bottom a political gesture. This point was reinforced in rather stark terms by a detailed discussion of Robert Mapplethorpe's photography exhibit titled "The Perfect Moment." Pellegrini described the various combinations of unconventional coupling that the artist depicted, and drew particular attention to the fact that, in virtue of the height at which the photographs were displayed, the viewer himself was obliged to bend over to study each specimen, thus making himself willy-nilly complicit in its political purpose. What Mapplethorpe demonstrated in his work, we were told, is the truth that *"All relations are essentially relations of power."*

No exceptions were tendered to the rule stipulated above. Were we to interpret, I wondered, not only the relation of husband and wife but also those of mother and child, toddler and playmate, priest and penitent, healer and healed, as in the last analysis power ploys? There is no "outside" of politics. Pellegrini's own proposal, as I understood it, is simply to multiply sexual options, which are ultimately political choices, which are ways of exercising power: whence the invocation of "alterities." Gender is masquerade; we "put on gender" like a costume or a political badge. "Lesbians," she said, "are not always women." We were reminded that cross-dressing, voguing, and gender-fuck are occasions of heightened political consciousness in which the actor makes use of cultural counterdiscourses to free himself from tyrannous dualisms. I was unable to discover from the presentation itself what the practices mentioned above actually were; in view of the somewhat arcane academic enthusiasms of the audience, the question period that concluded the session did not seem the best occasion to ask.

Throughout the conference there was a curious discrepancy between the nature of the rhetoric employed and the overall demeanor of the participants. One would be hard-pressed to find a more unabashed, unvarnished, purely Nietzschean exaltation of power. "Power *produces* truth," we were told by one speaker, herself quoting theologian Sharon Welch. "There are no standards outside history to which one might appeal for adjudication." On the other hand there was little of the Nuremberg-style rapture one might expect to accompany such radical sentiments. Most presenters received vigorous applause, and it was patent that most listeners were in full sympathy with what they were told; yet they appeared to have heard it all before. The sessions were typically attended by 100–125 people, many of whom sat in apparent contentment throughout the talks, snacking on raisins and nuts they carried in clear plastic bags. Few took notes. No one, in my hearing, asked a question expressive of fundamental skepticism about the value of the deconstructionist or postmodernist project. Nor was any speaker called on to make clear how his paper contributed to the study of religion, according to the terms of the AAR. Of course it's pointless to dwell on the obvious; what was puzzling to an outsider seemed perfectly clear, even banal, to the initiated.

Lest it be suspected that by singular luck or uncommon industry I managed to capture the most exotic specimens of intellectual life at the AAR, I should point out that this was not the case. It is true that I avoided the highly technical sections on Hindu theology or Nag Hammadi Gnosticism or the thought of Ernst Troeltsch, and it is true that this more conventional scholarship accounts for a sizable portion of the AAR's business. On the other hand, if a paper might be judged by its title (or the rubric under which it was presented), I was coasting quite comfortably in the midstream. I

omitted a roundtable discussion on "A Comparison of the Counseling Techniques of Christ and Carl Rogers" and, with less regret,
a discussion of "Shit, God, and Kitsch: The Role of the Body in
Kundera's *The Unbearable Lightness of Being*." I declined to accept
John Simmon's offering, "Woman's Spirit Rising: The Introductory Class in Women and Religion Challenges Rural Midwestern
Values in a Live PBS Teleclass Format," which was presented in the
section on the Academic Teaching and Study of Religion. I ducked
a panel convened on the topic "Appropriation and Reciprocity in
Womanist/Mujerista/Feminist Work."

Many of the papers I happened to hear displayed a pronounced
interest in unconventional sexual appetites; yet this interest was diffused across the boundaries of many disciplines and many sections of
the Annual Meeting. There was, indeed, a session given over entirely
to the Lesbian Feminist Issues in Religion Group. Let one synopsis
(of a paper by Kathleen Sands of the University of Massachusetts,
Boston) stand for all:

Powers, Pleasures, and Goods: An Invitation to Conversation
on Lesbian Sex

Abstract

Using the S/M debate as a starting point, I suggest guidelines for a lesbian feminist discourse on sex. Anti-S/M writings, I observe, approach
sex with predominantly moral language, while pro-S/M literature
brackets moral concerns and, instead, approaches sex with interests
such as power, pleasure, and intensity of experience. These discourses
represent areas of concern generally characteristic of religious experience and communities: the moral, the mystical, the aesthetic, and
the somatic. Since these areas of concern are relatively autonomous,
conflicts arise about their respective roles within a life or a community. For example, tensions over lesbian S/M parallel the tensions religious communities often experience between mystical experience and
moral or doctrinal commitments. Lesbian feminist theologians ought
to offer moral strategies for bringing diverse concerns into moral har-
mony within the sexual lives of lesbians and our communities.

Already glutted with the metaphysics of sexual anguish (and quea-
sily mindful of the fate of Pentheus in Euripides' *Bacchae*), I decided
to skip this section. So too with the Gay Men's Issues in Religion

Group, which offered "The Gay Community as Wounded Healers," "Making Love as Making Justice: Toward a New Jewish Ethic of Sexuality," and "The Compatibility of Reason and Orgasm in Tibetan Buddhism: Reflections on Sexual Violence and Homophobia." A man can handle only so much religion, after all.

In the third (and, for me, final) afternoon of the Annual Meeting a session was listed of the Theology and Science Group on the [following] theme: The Natural and Moral Origins of Sin and Evil. I was looking forward to this forum with particular interest, inasmuch as the topic promised a change of intellectual diet and because Langdon Gilkey of the University of Chicago—a scholar of considerable influence—was scheduled to speak. To my disappointment, Prof. Gilkey was unable to attend. I did hear Mary Hunt, of the Women's Alliance for Theology, Ethics, and Ritual (WATER).

In a paper titled "If Biology Isn't Destiny, What Is?" Hunt deplored the "dangerous hegemony of the U.S. in the construction of a New World Order," and spoke hopefully of the contributions to be made by "feminist/womanist/mujerista advances in theology" in refocusing our energies for social change, as such theology provides "a critique of power through a hermeneutics of suspicion." Hunt expressed satisfaction that "the myth of objectivity has been put to rest in science as well as theology," and applauded the paradigm shifts in virtue of which both have moved "from value-free to advocacy-based priorities." Orthodox Christian theology has worked to encourage violence; for example, the story of "God sacrificing 'his' Son legitimizes child abuse." Chaos theory in contemporary physics can help lead us to a reassessment of the category of sin. Through the prompting of feminism, Hunt suggested, we are invited "to move from Chaos (capital 'C') to chaos (small 'c'), from ethics to ecology." If we are respectful of the insights from chaos, it was argued, the concept of sin may fall away.

While it was not made explicit, Hunt's reasoning seemed to follow this course: sin belongs to a structure of natural morality, which in turn requires that nature be fundamentally rational. But if nature is ultimately chaotic, it is irrational. Therefore natural morality and sin are illusory. Certainly Hunt viewed natural morality as a malignant doctrine. "Women taught not to sin are taught not to change," she insisted, and affirmed the insight of Boston College's Mary Daly:

"Elemental Being *is* sinning; it requires the courage to sin." The final note I made, the last bit of wisdom I carried away from the American Academy of Religion, was the dictum that served as the keystone of Mary Hunt's address. Our present task, she concluded, is to explore fully the implications of the first and the greatest commandment of the new dispensation: "Go, and sin some more!"

As I made my way to the airport I couldn't help but notice the familiar Midwest roadside piety of billboard and bumper-sticker: *God So Loved The World ... If You Love Me Keep My Commandments ... Jesus Loves You.* It struck me that "love" was a word I hadn't heard pronounced—at all—in the past three days. My thoughts were carried back to the (naive? prescient?) confidence of NABL's Dr. Peritz, who could write, in the year of Hitler's accession to power, that biblical religion provided the only solution of the problems of universal citizenship. Clearly the AAR had come a long way from its beginnings. As I boarded my plane I saw that, by an odd coincidence, the man in front of me was one of the stray Shriners I had bumped into at the Convention Center. He was still buoyed by the recreations of his own weekend, and was cheerfully yodeling in the jetway. "Everything's up t' date in Kansas City," he sang. "They've gone about as far as they kin go!"

"Yes," I said to myself. "Yes, I suppose they have."

Academic Religion: Playground of the Vandals

"When you say 'hill,'" the Queen interrupted, "I could show you hills, in comparison with which you'd call that a valley."

"No, I shouldn't," said Alice, surprised into contradicting her at last: "a hill can't be a valley, you know. That would be nonsense—"

The Red Queen shook her head. "You may call it nonsense if you like," she said, "but I've heard nonsense, compared with which that would be as sensible as a dictionary!"

—Lewis Carroll, *Through the Looking Glass*

Last year a national committee of Presbyterians composed a statement on sexuality called "Keeping Body and Soul Together." The document evidenced characteristics increasingly distinctive of the productions of American church bureaucracies: a cute journalistic title, a manifesto-like rhetorical swagger, the facile syntax of *Psychology Today*, and a predictable exhortation to Do What Thou Wouldst, caringly. It was rejected in the General Assembly by a vote of 534 to 31.

The resounding *No* given to "Keeping Body and Soul Together" is emblematic of a crisis affecting American religion as a whole: the profound and widening gap between ordinary churchgoers and the administrative *nomenklatura* which, largely through the oblique pressure of committee and caucus, has either gained control of the church executive or enfeebled those it doesn't control. This division is not (as yet) a rift between people and pastors; considering the number of highly publicized instances of grave scandal on the part of prominent clergy, the trust still extended by the laity to their ministers is astonishing. The suspicion and despair felt by those in the pew is directed, in the main, not toward those with a "cure of souls" but rather toward a new class of curial politician—or rather toward the ecclesiastical triumphs of this class, since the individuals responsible for them are often hidden from the faithful by many layers of bureaucratic anonymity.

Originally published in *First Things*, May 1992.

It has long been a commonplace of theological polemic to impugn the good will of a rival faction by attributing to it political motivations and cunning rather than genuinely religious zeal. All the more interesting, consequently, when a self-defined religious bloc claims political motives for itself. Some years ago theologian Hans Küng boasted of how many clandestine partisans he knew "at the switching points of the ecclesiastical apparatus," and more recently there has been talk in American Catholic circles of a "party of change" that "dominates the fields of liturgy, religious education, justice and peace offices, campus ministry, Catholic higher education, much popular theology, and the discipline of theology as a whole."

Now the fact remains indisputable that, in proportion as it has made a conquest of officialdom, the new clerisy, the "party of change" operating across the denominational map, has further repelled and alienated the overwhelming majority of churchgoers, *viz.*, simple people who pray, who worship God. Nor is the cause hard to find, for this new clerisy is by and large contemptuous both of the beliefs of the faithful and of the tradition in which these beliefs are nurtured. Indeed, the prime effort of this detachment of the knowledge class is precisely to insulate the common man from authentic religious tradition, so as to render him more easily manipulable by conventional political pressures.

The new clerisy (in which I include both lay and ordained functionaries) defies analysis in terms of standard ecclesial boundaries; a Catholic, Lutheran, and Methodist who belong to this set are likely to have more in common with one another than each has with his own bishops or with those of his co-religionists who are not of the "party of change." What is shared is not a set of doctrinal propositions but a culture: in this case, a culture institutionally cradled by the liberal seminaries, religion departments, and divinity schools of North America. As a consequence, what is common to all is seldom made explicit, for it is in its unreflective or unconscious operations that a culture is most profoundly unitive. Every culture protects its integrity by oblique means of discipline; every culture breeds its own skepticisms and its own credulities; every culture has peculiar bigotries and suffers certain fools gladly. To understand a society— including a society of churchmen—entails bringing to light what is hidden, making the implicit explicit, flagging those arguments which (for the insider) don't need to be made.

It is toward this end—elucidating the culture of the new clerisy and the crisis it has provoked—that the American Academy of Religion is useful, especially the AAR on display at its Annual Meeting. For it is when the filters are off, as it were, and it can speak to its own membership in its own voice that an institution is most revelatory of its purposes and convictions.

> "For instance, now," she went on, "there's the King's Messenger. He's in prison now, being punished: and the trial doesn't even begin until next Wednesday: and of course the crime comes last of all."

To the uninitiated, one of the most striking features of this learned society is the discrepancy between its professed policy and its actual conduct. We are told in its statement of purpose that the AAR exists to foster a "critical awareness about the study of religion"; further, that "there are no religious conditions of membership, and the organization itself is not advocative, save for the highest standards in the teaching and study of religion."

Now, the notion of critical scholarship is not univocal, but it seems to me that it requires, at a minimum, five procedural commitments. First, the belief that pedigree and accidents of upbringing are irrelevant to one's eligibility to enter a scholarly conversation and one's capacity to grasp the truths therein elicited. Second, a denial of a priori favoritism to truth claims of individual participants. Third, an understanding that the disputant is expected to test his own hypothesis more severely than those of his opponents; that is, in questionable matters, one always awards the benefit of the doubt to the adversary position. Fourth, the conviction that it is by superior argument and evidence that one defends a thesis, not in terms of intrinsic desirability. Finally, the concession that an opponent to one's thesis is not, simply in virtue of his opposition, a scoundrel.

The addresses I heard at the AAR, including those on which I reported earlier, were by and large so partisan, so blatantly advocative, that the pretense of a critical method of discourse was seldom even plausible. Most of the participants seemed to treat the Annual Meeting as a kind of party congress, with various scholarly colloquia as sideshows to the main events. Yet even here a curious asymmetry was perceptible. On the one hand, when more traditional believing

Jews and Christians spoke about their own religions, they were clearly expected to maintain the scholarly proprieties of the critical method, and for the most part they were compliant. (One speaker admitted, "I use the expressions B.C. and A.D. [in preference to B.C.E. and C.E.] and I'm proud of it!" and for his candor was hissed by the audience.) On the other hand, partisans of the new religions and opponents of the old were constrained by none of the critical commitments suggested above.

This asymmetry was clearly manifest in the discussion of "patriarchy"—one of the prime bogeys of the new clerks. The consensus—virtually unchallenged in liberal seminaries and divinity schools—has it that the special cultic authority reserved to males in Judaism and Christianity is not only a pernicious institution but one that was assumed by men, in bad faith, as a self-serving ploy to buttress political, economic, and sexual tyranny. Of course, it may be the case that there are good arguments for the truth of this claim; what is remarkable is that no speaker showed the faintest awareness that such arguments remain to be made. The "scandal of patriarchy" served not as a *demonstrandum* but as an axiom of discourse, with the result that the Christian hierarchy and Jewish rabbinate became simple embodiments of villainy, and contempt expressed for these institutions required no justification. I took some wry amusement from the fact that one of the controversies at the AAR concerned the propriety of using analytical reasoning in the abolition of patriarchy. The terms of debate were: "Is it right to use the Master's tools to demolish the Master's house?" At issue were the means to the end; the end itself was taken for granted. For these latter-day Catos, the major premise of every pertinent syllogism was *delenda est patriarchia*.

There is a telling historical irony in this particular indulgence of righteous indignation. The individuals currently reckoned by the new clerisy to be "patriarchs" include most of those whom traditionalist Jews, Roman Catholics, and the Christian orthodox regard as their rightful religious authorities, and it is impossible that the antipathy directed at such authorities should not spill over into antipathy for those believers who esteem their own leadership. Moreover, the successful overthrow of patriarchy would mean nothing less, in concrete terms, than the extinction of rabbinic Judaism and the apostolic

Christian churches. Thus, an institution that calls itself "an inclusive learned society" and takes pride in having "no religious conditions of membership" has proven supremely tolerant of the rhetoric of belligerence employed by those sectaries who, in earlier times, were most anxious to rid the world of popery and the Elders of Zion. Because the prophets of chastisement are no longer Roundheads or Klansmen but often well-spoken scholars at Ivy League divinity schools, and because the scandal of patriarchy enjoys the status of a self-evident truth, this bigotry goes largely unremarked by its defenders. As Chesterton observed, some men believe their dogmas so strongly that they can't recognize them as dogmas.

"Somebody *killed* something; that's clear, at any rate—"

Perhaps even more striking to the newcomer than its countermasculinism is the AAR's preoccupation with sexuality. If this aspect of human life was too often neglected by earlier students of religion, compensation for the lack has certainly been made—and with a vengeance. Indeed, some of the addresses at the Annual Meeting were devoted so narrowly to sexual detail that they might have been read with (at least) equal appropriateness at a conference on psychotherapy or anthropology. Many speakers made no attempt to relate the subject of their papers to anything recognizable as prayer or morality or worship of God. Now it is obvious that the notion of "Religion" with which the American Academy concerns itself is a rather commodious term—virtually any area of human enthusiasm seems to qualify—and it was likewise clear that, for many scholars present, sexuality constituted this most fundamental enthusiasm, this ultimate ground of meaning: there is no need to make explicit one's connection of sex with religion if, at bottom, they are one and the same thing. Once again it is crucial to notice the "dogma that doesn't bark" in this environment: what is significant here is not that someone should connect sex with religion, or even displace one by means of the other, but that such connection or displacement should be simply *assumed*, should be deemed unworthy of defense or explanation. In trying to understand the cultural gap between, say, the authors of "Keeping Body and Soul Together" and the churchgoing Presbyterian, it is the unspoken equations that are most illuminating.

Why should sexuality fascinate students of religion so disproportionately to the rest of the population, both the academic community and society at large? A partial explanation can be sought in the
sociology of education. Divinity schools tend to be one of the "soft
underbellies" of American universities, having lower academic standards than other professional schools, and they are obliged to accept
some students who (along with many highly qualified candidates) are
ill prepared, intellectually and emotionally, for the tasks of graduate-
level scholarship; thus, a borderline student obsessed with a particular
exotic topic might find Religious Studies the only department willing
to take him on. Further, since the perplexities of bedroom and bath-
room have never taken a firm or enduring purchase on the first-rate
minds of the Western university, there is much unexploited material
here for the less fastidious investigator. Finally, the "primary evidence" for sexually oriented research often proves of abiding interest
to those students discouraged in the attempt to master more formidable scholarly sources. To some extent, the AAR's emphasis on sex
stems from the fact that Toni Morrison is easier to read in the original
than Tertullian. (One speaker, in the course of a paper devoted to the
former author, enthusiastically assured us that "sensuality pervades
throughout her work.")

Yet I cannot rid myself of the conviction—admittedly subjective—
that there is another, less innocent, motive at work in this preoccupation with sex. For want of a better term, I would call it an impulse
to vandalism. The interest here displayed was overwhelmingly an
interest in aberrant sexuality—evidenced not only in repeated pro-
tests against so-called "compulsory heterosexuality" but in a macabre
litany of erotic pathology: mutilation, child abuse, incest, sadomas-
ochism, ritual castration, and so on *ad nauseam*. The most benevolent
spectator could hardly attribute more than a fraction of these "data"
to a disinterested study of religion. Surely the contempt for authoritative morality in general, and for sexual morality in particular, combined with the too-obvious relish in the details of deviant venery,
cannot be a coincidence.

The vandal's hatred is for the intact, the unstained, the integral; his
delight is to chip the nose off the perfect statue, to soil the white wall
with graffiti, to shatter the last unbroken window. His destruction is a
record not only of malice but of conquest; as a dog is said to foul trees

and lampposts as a way of marking territorial boundaries, so the vandal uglifies the yet-undefiled in order to chart the extent of his incursion into the world of order and decorum. By the same token, the ideals of sexual purity—consecrated virginity, the chaste yet fruitful marriage bed—have served as an emblem of the sacral function of Judaism and Christianity, as a redoubt of specifically *human* holiness: precisely the notion that the new clerisy wishes to expunge from religion. When scholars propose that the relation of nun to Church "might be re-imaged in terms of a lesbian butch-femme relationship," or that the story of "God sacrificing 'his' son legitimizes child abuse," we are not to imagine that their targets are chosen at random. There is an ill-concealed glee in this parading, as it were, the vivid sexual bells of Hieronymus Bosch through the ruined courtyards of Protestant academic propriety. The AAR, like the old-line divinity schools and seminaries which gave it birth, has become a playground of the Goth.

"Speak in French when you can't remember the English for a thing—and remember who you are!"

Markedly absent from that part of its world which the new clerisy put on display at the Annual Meeting was a sympathy for, or even awareness of, the struggles and achievements of Anglo-American analytic philosophy. Whereas the French connection (Lacan, Derrida, Foucault) was continually invoked, names like Fodor, Anscombe, Quine, Dummett, or Plantinga were never in play. Alasdair MacIntyre, it is true, was the subject of three addresses, all of which were critical; the English tradition was generally viewed as a hostile force. In part this is due to the fact that the linguistic precision and logical refinement common to analytic philosophy is unsuited to more subjective or intuitionist approaches to religious phenomena; it is unlikely, for example, that the author of "An Exploration of Quilt Design as a Reasoning Process" would find a congenial mentor in Elizabeth Anscombe. Yet it is also true that clarity, univocity, and universal intelligibility are neither valued in themselves nor productive of the ends to which language is put by many of the deconstructionist camp, regardless of subject matter. Ambiguity is the desideratum, and the effect, as in these excerpts from AAR abstracts, is striking:

Taylor's metaphorical "body," then, is an (ex)tension of the phallo-centric and phallocratic technology of modern theology, now con-fined to a two-dimensional wordplay indifferent to the cries and joys of a richly signed wor(l)d.

In Tibetan Buddhist systems there are hints of a compatible rela-tionship between reason and orgasmic bliss, in that developed prac-titioners seek to utilize the blissful and powerful mind of orgasm to realize the truth and the all-good ground of consciousness. The sug-gestion is that the sense of bifurcation between reason and orgasmic bliss is the result of not appreciating the basic nature of mind.

A feminist-informed, queerly placed interrogation is offered here of the representational matrices within which the stabilizing terms of gender may be opened up and overturned.

Thomas Kohler has brought to my attention the pertinent obser-vations of Eric Voegelin on the peculiar semantic "estrangement" he met in Heidegger and that is so often found in current postmodernist writing.

> We will all have the feeling [he says] as we read such texts that as far as linguistic expression is concerned, something is not in order, even if we can't immediately put our finger on what is wrong.... The text transposes factual relationships of our everyday world into a linguistic medium that begins to take on an alliterative life of its own, and thus loses contact with the thing itself. Language and fact have somehow separated from one another, and thought has correspondingly become estranged from reality.

Voegelin adds that after prolonged exposure to such texts we can "whip ourselves up into a reality-withdrawing state of linguistic delir-ium." It is important to stress that this linguistic delirium marks the success and not the failure of the rhetoricians who bring it to birth. As in Lewis Carroll's Looking Glass Land, sense and nonsense here become the sole property of the powerful, bestowed according to the royal will; certainly the AAR suffers no shortage of Red Queens.

> "When I use a word," Humpty Dumpty said, in rather a scornful tone, "it means just what I choose it to mean—neither more nor less."
> "The question is," said Alice, "whether you can make words mean so many different things."
> "The question is," said Humpty Dumpty, "which is to be master—that's all."

By traditional standards of liberal scholarship the culture of the new clerisy is in nearly complete intellectual disarray. But of course it is precisely these standards that the new clerisy has disavowed. The bigotry manifest in the campaign against patriarchy flies in the face of pluralism, but what should we expect? Scholarly honor is merely one more remnant of an alien ethics that can be debunked as easily as any other. The obsession with sexual deviance is distressing to the normal religious believer, but the normal/deviant distinction is rejected a priori, and sex and religion are simply different "moments" in a rhetoric of power. Language has become detached from shared meanings, but propositional truth itself has been dismissed as a myth of the male tyrant. In short, what those outside this culture lament as degeneration, those inside commend as deconstruction.

The ascendancy of deconstructionist thought at the divinity schools and liberal seminaries, though curious enough, is not entirely unprecedented. The fascination of American ministers with a number of European thinkers (Jung and Marx are prime examples) has far exceeded the concern for religion that the authors themselves took thought to express; and the zeal with which these men were institutionalized into certain aspects of church life often surpassed efforts for accurate theoretical assessment of their writings. The religious enthusiast (whether Lollard or Marxist) frequently has an innate contempt for halfway measures and a constitutional impatience at the hesitations of the theologian. So, too, it seemed to me that Derrida and Foucault were embraced at the AAR with an alacrity not paralleled by any proportionately serious attempt to come to grips with their thought. One speaker, it is true, qualified her otherwise ringing endorsement of Foucault with the admission that "he was, after all, a white male"; yet I didn't hear at the Annual Meeting a single citation from any *text* of Derrida or Foucault or Lacan—remarkable, considering how fervently the names were invoked. One can't help recalling Bernard Levin's quip that some people pass their entire lives under the mistaken impression that they have read *Das Kapital*.

For all that, the believers were true believers. To the extent that I could make it out the party line runs like this: Everything that purports to be "revelation"—that is, God's revelation of himself to men—is at bottom fiction. The authors of the fictions have constructed them so as to serve their own political purposes and have employed the myth of divine communication in order to impose the fictions, by terror and enticement, as normative for all: fears of sanction and hopes of reward are dangled as carrot-and-stick before the oppressed subject, who is forced into the state of false consciousness called "faith." Emancipation takes the form of exposing the frauds of the tyrants by pointing out the political motives latent in the structures of religion earlier supposed to be "divinely ordained." Further, members of oppressed populations are urged to invent (or rediscover) fictions of their own in which the notions of authority and obedience have been replaced by that of the lone individual as creator and bestower of value.

From a theological point of view, this enlightened religion has the awkward disadvantage of being atheist, but clearly the cavil carries little weight with adherents among the new clerks. The number of self-professed Catholics, Episcopalians, and other Christians who hold these or similar views without evident embarrassment illustrates the obvious corollary that, since all doctrines are instances of political artifice, the doctrine of God is as dispensable as any other. So too, whenever the word "heresy" was mentioned at the AAR, it was invariably preceded by the phrase "so-called"—and quite properly, given the belief that the categories of orthodoxy and heresy are equally and indifferently the malign inventions of an oppressor.

By the same token, most atheist Catholics and others of the new clerisy feel no pressure to leave the Church. In general, what they look for from a church community has so little to do with assent to propositional articles of faith that the deficiency doesn't register (any more than it would occur to a modern Roman to abandon his city once he became convinced that Romulus never existed). Moreover, when a man believes he has "seen through the bluff" on which some institution is run, he tends not to accept the judgments of those he regards as still deluded, especially the judgment that he doesn't belong in the institution.

Exposure of the fraud of revelation and the demotion of God from a fact to a fiction does not, in this culture, result in the anti-religious rancor typical of the propositional atheists of the eighteenth and nineteenth centuries, or in the tidy, well-lit materialism of Bertrand Russell and A.J. Ayer. Instead, "God" has become an infinitely plastic term, and the divine attributes can be tailored according to individual appetite and whim, with the sole proviso that God cannot be a jealous God, that is, he cannot require anyone's fealty nor pretend to the dignity of objective independent existence: such independence brings with it the inevitable structures of authority, emancipation from which is the very wellspring of the new religion.

Of course, in using the pronoun "he" of God, I have obscured the fact that divine fatherhood is one of the attributes most cheerfully dispensed with. Thus, Barbara Whitmer of the University of Toronto asked her audience at the AAR, "Is it too late to go back to the Goddess?" inviting us not so much to apostasy as to a heightened political awareness of our culture of violence. So also Anne Hunter of Drew University reminded us that "feminist theologies have thoroughly examined the all-powerful, judgmental, male God, but little has been said about the male God who is all-seeing and all-knowing." Hunter proposed to draw out "the implications of this all-seeing male God as a deterrent to the ability of religious women to free themselves from abusive relationships with men." Unspoken but clearly operative in these examples is the assumption that, like a body of law, one needs to drop, add, and amend one's deities according to the changing hardships one faces. And, just as he who writes the laws governs the nation, whoever controls its rhetoric controls religion. The question that absorbs the modern student of divinity is not what is true about God in himself but whose hands are on the levers of power, who controls the discourse.

Perhaps it is not so paradoxical after all that those who, in church-state debate, protest the incursion of religion into politics are often the same people who work most energetically to politicize the churches. Their objection, of course, is to religious *authority*, to the recognition of objective and durable realities and standards of conduct, to a magisterium (however realized) beyond the grasp of democratic manipulation. The game is to free both church and state from the illusion of unchanging obligations to divine commandments or to laws of reason. "There is no 'outside' of politics," announced one AAR speaker, thus formulating what I take to be the prime, crystalline *kerygma* of the new religion: "All relations are essentially relations of power." The struggle is to ensure that those who control the rhetoric by which power is exercised are fully enlightened individuals, those who can be relied upon to ensure that correct politics will triumph.

Implicit is the belief that power exists as a discrete, constant quantity and should be redistributed among those populations, such as homosexuals and women, who have traditionally received lesser shares. Here the penetrating remarks of Elizabeth Kristol on the rhetoric of power are worth repeating. Commenting on "the disturbing necrophiliac tendencies in much of feminist history, as authors rush to embrace the very concepts they have just killed off," Kristol observes:

> The same phenomenon occurs when feminists take on language and religion, and for the same reason women recognize that these ... realms *wield* the greatest political and social power, and they thereafter assume these realms *confer* the greatest power.
>
> But power isn't like a currency that can be passed from hand to hand—let alone be stolen. It is intimately linked with the creative forces that brought it into being. There is no question women's histories are capable of being imaginative; often too much for their own good. But crocheting pasts is a far cry from creativity. What would be truly creative, at this point, is if feminist historians permitted their gazes to drift away from the "power structures" they so covet and allow them to fall on historical topics that are genuinely in need of attention and illumination. As it happens, that is a real route to power.

Like such feminists, the new clerks are political reductivists *à outrance*, and like such feminists, they are more intrigued by the politics of power than by those of persuasion. In spite of their professing often radically democratic positions, they are rarely drawn to, or successful at, the consensus-building functions of political life, and this is true even within their respective churches. Just as in the civil domain the party of change has directed its energies more to victory in the courts than to constructing legislative majorities, so in the religious sphere it is in the growing bureaucracies that the party of change has found itself most welcome and most adept. As the North American churches have de-emphasized their pastoral and custodial responsibilities in favor of policy formation and management, the size and importance of the administrative apparatus has grown proportionally. The new clerisy has been quick to recognize and exploit the unique potentials of this intermediate level of influence—usually placed out of the reach of direct lay control, but at the same time resistant to pressures from the hierarchy. The earlier-noted list of functions "dominated" by the party of change bears repeating: "the fields of liturgy, religious education, justice and peace offices, campus ministry, [Catholic] higher education, much popular theology, and the discipline of theology as a whole." Few of us would disagree.

> "I know what you're thinking about," said Tweedledum; "but it isn't so, nohow."
> "Contrariwise," continued Tweedledee, "if it was so, it might be; and if it were so, it would be; but as it isn't, it ain't. That's logic."

After a sojourn among the new clerks in their native habitat (of which the AAR Annual Meeting is a prime example) the narrator finds himself in the unenviable position of Alice once she returned through the looking-glass to her family parlor. Not only are her traveling encounters exceptional, to put it mildly, but she has to admit that, for example, her implausibly Talking Egg exists on the more familiar level as a plausibly dumb cat. Objections were made to the mention in my earlier article of an address in which a speaker characterized race, class, and sexual orientation as "overarching structures of domination," reinforced by religion, from which asylum was found in African-American quilting. Was this, after all, a contribution to be taken seriously? Perhaps not. But the same scholar, it should be noted, served as an official consultant to the U.S. Catholic bishops for their project of writing a pastoral letter on women—that fact, I suggest, might prompt some reflection, and not just among Catholics.

The *Kulturkampf*, the battle of "cultures in collision" for the symbols of our common life, has migrated out of the universities into most institutions, including the churches and synagogues, concerns not *how* one should worship but *whom*, where it is entrenched with particular firmness. As long as we pretend that the new clerks don't really mean what they say, we will continue to fight the religious wars declared in the 1980s not between denominations but within them: to surrender the only essential clarity, forfeiting the father against son, daughter-in-law against mother-in-law, one named I AM to "he/she might be"—and functionaries against the faithful. For the dispute ain't logic. Nohow.

The Skimpole Syndrome:
Childhood Unlimited

Let me re-introduce you to Mr. Harold Skimpole. Skimpole lives in
the pages of Charles Dickens' *Bleak House*; he made his first appearance 140 years ago, yet those who are acquainted with the principal
hierophants of New Age spirituality may receive more than a slight
shock of recognition:

> He was a bright little creature with a rather large head; but a delicate
> face and a sweet voice, and there was a perfect charm in him. All he
> said was so free of effort and spontaneous and was said with such a
> captivating gaiety, that it was fascinating to hear him talk.... Indeed,
> he had more the appearance in all respects of a damaged young man,
> than a well-preserved elderly one. There was an easy negligence in
> his manner, and even in his dress (his hair carelessly disposed, and his
> neckerchief loose and flowing, as I have seen artists paint their own
> portraits), which I could not separate from the idea of a romantic
> youth who had undergone some unique process of depreciation.

Harold Skimpole took a bright disdain for the drudgery of adult
life—"I am a child, you know!" he frequently reminds us—and
delighted in the innocent pleasures around him. Speaking of himself
(far and away his favorite topic) he confessed to

> two of the oldest infirmities in the world: one was, that he had no idea
> of time; the other, that he had no idea of money. In consequence of
> which he never kept an appointment, never could transact any busi-
> ness, and never knew the value of anything! ... He was very fond of
> reading the papers, very fond of making fancy sketches with a pencil,
> very fond of nature, very fond of art. All he asked of society, was
> to let him live. That wasn't much. His wants were few. Give him
> the papers, conversation, music, mutton, coffee, landscape, fruit in

Originally published in *First Things*, May 1993.

the season, a few sheets of Bristol-board, and a little claret, and he asked no more. He was a mere child in the world, but he didn't cry for the moon. He said to the world, "Go your several ways in peace! Wear red coats, blue coats, lawn sleeves, put pens behind your ears, wear aprons; go after glory, holiness, commerce, trade, any object you prefer; only—let Harold Skimpole live!"

Thus, we are given a prototype of the consummate pluralist, the besotted lover of all creation, the friend of peace, the man who can tolerate anything but intolerance: with malice toward none, with kindness and caring toward all.

The best insight we have into Skimpole's character comes from his encounters with creditors and their agents—what would for another man be called "financial embarrassment"—but of course Skimpole has no capacity to blush for any reason. He lives in the house of a wealthy and indulgent friend; even so, he manages to accumulate spectacular bills. On one occasion the narrator, Esther Summerson, is summoned to Skimpole's room and finds him, to her shock, arrested for debt.

> "Are you arrested for much, sir?" I inquired of Mr. Skimpole. "My dear Miss Summerson," said he, shaking his head pleasantly, "I don't know. Some pounds, odd shillings and half-pence, I think, were mentioned."

The sum turns out to be more than twenty-four pounds—a staggering amount for the time, and it devolves on Esther and her friends to satisfy the officer and the debt.

> It was a most singular thing [Esther was afterward to reflect] that the arrest was our embarrassment, and not Mr. Skimpole's. He observed us with a genial interest; but there seemed, if I may venture on a contradiction, nothing selfish in it. He had entirely washed his hands of the difficulty, and it had become ours.

Drawing on their own savings, carefully accumulated through much ill-paid labor, Skimpole's acquaintances managed to placate the furious collecting agent, but Skimpole isn't through with him yet. "Did you know this morning, now, that you were coming out on this errand?" Skimpole asked him. "It didn't affect your appetite? Didn't make you at all uneasy?"

> "Then you didn't think, at all events," proceeded Mr. Skimpole, "to this effect. 'Harold Skimpole loves to see the sun shine; loves to hear the wind blow; loves to watch the changing lights and shadows; loves to hear the birds, those choristers in Nature's great cathedral. And does it seem to me that I am about to deprive Harold Skimpole of his share in such possessions, which are his only birthright!' You thought nothing to this effect?"

He is assured in emphatic terms that this was not the case.

> "Very odd and very curious, the mental process is, in you men of business!" said Mr. Skimpole thoughtfully. "Thank you, my friend. Good night."

Harold Skimpole never quite manages to lose his charm, and yet readers of *Bleak House* become increasingly appalled by him. He affects unselfishness, but is in reality fanatically, even maniacally, self-centered—existing in the soap bubble of an almost perfect solipsism. He insists in his sunny prattle that he is "a mere child," while he is in fact a grotesque parasite: a colossal tick, a leech, a tapeworm with a taste for Mozart, who, it turns out, is childlike in his pursuit of pleasure, but shrewd and willful in his studied neglect of responsibility. His sensibilities are exquisitely tender, and yet he has a talent for causing pain, for making his benefactors feel slightly soiled by their own honest labor. He professes universal tolerance and sweetness to all, though is willing to put his friends through shame, fear, and harm rather than see his own comfort threatened.

The burden of this essay is to demonstrate that the Skimpole Syndrome is alive and well today, particularly (though not exclusively) in the world of religion. I want to show that the churches have been victims of parasites, most often quite charming parasites, and that the exhaustion and despair we see in the faces of our pastors can, to some extent, be attributed to the energy sucked out of their veins by cheerful co-religionists who mock their host even as they grow fat on his livelihood, his patrimony. The difficulty before me—no small one—is to convince you that the good things that our modern-day

Skimpoles feast on are as precarious, are bought into being with as much pain and toil, as were the amenities of *Bleak House.*

The villainy of the Skimpole Syndrome does not consist in its choice of goods: papers, conversation, music, mutton, coffee, landscape, fruit, a little claret—few of us would argue that such things are inherently unwholesome. Nor is genial tolerance—"Go your several ways in peace! ... Go after any object you prefer!"—a bad thing in itself. The problem with Skimpolism is that it ignores, and refuses to acknowledge, the sources and causes of its own good fortune: the enormous human enterprise of toil, commerce, and distribution, the attendant fatigue, risk, worry, and vexation, the requisite virtues of foresight, prudence, honesty, and diligence—all of which are necessary for something as ordinary as a peach or a glove to end up in Skimpole's dining room. For the Skimpoles of this world, the ultimate source of bread is the baker's van, and there is no need to concern oneself with plowing, sowing, weeding, dunging, cutting, threshing, milling, and baking— not to mention the thousands of mercantile transactions, from mortgages to tire rotations—that must be in place, and continually attended to, so that Skimpole might have his honey on toast.

Skimpole believed himself set apart from other men by the fact that his needs were few. Of course, his needs were no fewer than anyone else's; rather, he was distinguished by his ignorance of his debt to prosaic necessities, by his confusing desires with needs, and by pretending that his wants were nobler than those of the multitude.

Consider, then, whether the following list of goods brings to mind a recognizable type: openness, sharing, compassion, diversity, dialogue, peace and justice, wholeness, growth. I am skating on thin ice here, and I know it. I should make it clear that I am not sneering at any of these objects, or the pursuit of these objects, as they are properly understood as components of Christian community. They are good things, and noble aspirations, and brave men and women have made heroic sacrifices so that they might be achieved and preserved. All this I insist on. By the same token, unless I am mistaken, this constellation of desiderata belongs in a special way to the Skimpole Syndrome of our own time, precisely comparable to the claret and newspapers and mutton that, to the mind of our perpetual child, simply came into being as gratuitously as sunshine and birdsong and warm breeze. The modern dream is just as illusory as the old, and decidedly more pestilent.

Take a fairly straightforward element in Christian life, the text of the Bible. Unlike the Book of Mormon, which is said to have been delivered on gold tablets by the Angel Moroni to the nineteenth-century copyist, the Word of God was not presented to Christians in final form. As Bible scholar Jon Levenson reminds us, there was in "biblical times" no such thing as a Bible, in New Testament times no such thing as a New Testament. Rather, the Bible was assembled over a number of years for the Church and by the Church—in particular, through liturgical usage and the ratification of bishops, who had already formed an inchoate hierarchy before the New Testament was itself complete.

Consequently, the Bible in the most physical sense—the written words on the page—comes down to us through two enormous efforts that overlap in practice though they are notionally distinct. On the one hand, the enterprise of copying, correcting, translating, and publishing texts—the business of scholarship; on the other, the enterprise of delivering to the Church an intact Old Testament and a New Testament that conforms to the mind of Christ: this involves setting the boundaries of the canon by choosing and rejecting among rival testimonies, selecting the best text of each canonical witness, suppressing additions and interpolations, suppressing mistranslations, and so forth. The human machinery—scholarly, administrative, legal, theological, editorial, custodial—that is engaged by the Church to put a Bible into our hands is beyond reckoning.

Not all of this machinery is especially gratifying to watch in operation. For example, it involves (and has always involved) censorship: the scrutiny of writings, the interrogation of authors of doubtful work, compulsory retraction of opinions found erroneous, and the suppression of those who refuse to recant their errors. Given the nature of their task, it is doubtful whether censors ever enjoyed great public esteem, but it is not doubtful that they cut poor figures today. Even in the civil sphere, the position of censor is not one that is likely to win invitations to fashionable parties or help to make an advantageous marriage. In an age with a warranted suspicion of bureaucracies and an unwarranted faith in the unconstrained intellect, censorship is seen as among the dirtiest of all dirty jobs, and for that reason alone is scorned by the Skimpoles.

The point is that the much-maligned structures of authority in the Church are as necessary to transmitting our faith as herdsmen are necessary to providing lamb chops. In the absence of censorship (and the sanctions that go with censorship) we would share no Bible, no prayer, no faith at all with the Christians of the Coliseum. Even the denominations that have minimal hierarchy and recognize no bishops have this reason to be grateful for those churches that do. Christians whose rule of faith is "by Scripture alone" are obliged to admit that the very Scripture they cherish not only produced the Church but was produced by it, and this production involved many of the very structures that they, several centuries later, were to find unscriptural.

And yet, the objection is frequently made, isn't it the case, once we have a firm and binding document—a genuine letter of St. Paul or a decree of an ecumenical council—that we can simply rely on the plain sense of the text to give us the teaching we need? This intuition is widely held, but the history of the Church shows us that there is no such thing as the plain sense of the text that is universally acknowledged—at least over time. It is simply impossible to lay the flooring of a document so tightly that someone, at some time, will not manage to fall through the cracks.

My favorite illustration of this point is the decree *Omnis utriusque sexus* of the Fourth Lateran Council, held in 1215. It holds that everyone, of both sexes, is required to go to confession at least once a year. It was, however, interpreted by a monk named William of Newcastle to mean that yearly penitential duty is incumbent only on hermaphrodites. Now Brother William, obviously, needed someone to point out the error of his ways. His Latin, incidentally, was flawless; the problem with his interpretation is that it was insane.

The upshot is that every article of faith we have, no matter how obvious or how arcane it may appear, has run a gamut of fatal threats throughout the centuries, and has been vouchsafed to us, *multa inter alia*, by bishops and censors and canonists and judges. As Chesterton points out, if you paint a fence post white and just leave it alone, it will eventually turn black. In the same way, the teachings of the Church have to be reappropriated in every generation—unglamorous work!—and protected from contamination, neglect, and the random predations of those Williams of Newcastle that stalk the pages of the history of doctrine in every age like a recurring nightmare.

In the Skimpole mentality, all the effort required to produce his wants is mere affectation, and as such requires no compensation, and no respect. So Skimpole gives us to understand, in narrating a conversation with his unpaid butcher:

> "Says he, 'Sir, why did you eat spring lamb at eighteen pence a pound?' 'Why did I eat spring lamb at eighteen pence a pound, my honest friend?' said I, naturally amazed by the question. 'I like spring lamb!' This was so far convincing. 'Well sir,' says he, 'I wish I had meant the lamb as you mean the money!' 'My good fellow,' said I, 'pray let us reason like intellectual human beings. How could that be? It was impossible. You had got the lamb, and I have not got the money. You couldn't really mean the lamb without sending it in, whereas I can, and do, mean the money without paying it!' He had not a word. There was an end to the subject.'"Did he take no legal proceedings?" inquired [Mr. Jarndyce]."Yes, he took legal proceedings," said Mr. Skimpole, "But, in that, he was influenced by passion, not by reason."

In the same way, present-day Skimpoles are fond of saying, "I don't believe in a hierarchical Church. I believe in a God of compassion," suggesting, of course, that the two notions are mutually exclusive. When we ask, "Now how do you *know* that God is a God of compassion?" they say, "Why, because it says so in the Prophet Amos and the Gospel of Luke!" When we ask further, "But how do you know that Amos and Luke are reliable witnesses to the truth about God, except in virtue of the decisions made by those same authoritative structures you reject?" they reply, astonished by the question, "Because these books speak about a God of compassion!" And so we will have come full circle, while they walk away, shaking their heads over the fact that the orthodox are still guided by emotion, not by logic.

Let me stress again that I do not for a moment sneer at compassion; it is right to rejoice in the knowledge that God is all-merciful. Skimpole's worldview is defective not in the things it includes but in the things it leaves out, and the same is true of his contemporary counterparts. They speak of peace and justice and compassion as if the notions themselves were obvious and spontaneous, springing up in the minds of men with no more trouble than the wine and strawberries that appeared on Skimpole's breakfast tray. What they ignore is the overwhelming struggle, the sheer human sacrifice necessary for the Church to articulate and transmit intact even the most rudimentary truths, as truths.

Has it, in fact, been universally obvious that our God is a God of compassion? Not to those whose religious experience regards forgiveness as weakness—to the Nazis, for example. Jon Levenson has pointed out that, for the Nazis, what they prized as the "Nordic type" was "not only a physical characteristic but a matter of fundamental spiritual posture." "According to them, the true Nordic practices an ethic that is the polar opposite of the ideal of humility, subservience, and non-violence that has so long been enforced by reference to the authority of Jesus." Their solution was to exalt the book of the Bible they found least offensive as communicating the "true faith" while pruning and cleansing the other parts of Scripture of false ideas. For Nazi theorist Alfred Rosenberg, the Gospel of Mark provided the true writ, other books having been contaminated by "womanish exaggerations" and "Syrian-African superstition."

More recently, Levenson suggests, feminists have begun to cleanse the Bible in precisely the same manner, based on the same appeal to religious intuitions—although these intuitions are, on the surface, at variance with those of the Nazis. Feminist thealogian Carol Christ sees the God of the Bible as a "God of war [who] stands for too much that I stand against." With regard to Drs. Christ and Rosenberg, Levenson has remarked, "It's hard to escape the conclusion that both are missing something."

Today's Skimpole is more likely to be a feminist than a Nazi, but both are indeed missing something—and not just a balanced picture of God. Both refuse to grow up; both insist on remaining "a mere child." Both have made the move "from the experience of religious authority to the authority of religious experience"; and to appeal to "the authority of religious experience" is a roundabout way of saying, "I like what I like because I like it."

Feminist Skimpoles are able to bring much of the heavy artillery of biblical scholarship to bear on their targets. In their lectures and articles and efforts to sift and winnow the Bible so as to expose the contaminations of patriarchy they may appear very sophisticated; yet once we blow away the smoke we will find that, at bottom, they are in the same intellectual position as a pouting child at the breakfast table picking the raisins out of the bran flakes. "I like what I like because I like it. I hate what I hate because I hate it."

Am I being too harsh? Bring to mind for a moment the people you have seen who conduct New Age weekends, or feminist workshops, or Peace Studies institutes, those who take glee in having "cut the knot" connecting them to patriarchal institutions, to structures of authority, to the unglamorous business of orthodoxy. Then recall the words in which Dickens first lets us glimpse the figure of Harold Skimpole: "He had more the appearance, in all respects, of a damaged young man, than a well-preserved elderly one.... There was an easy negligence in his manner ... which I could not separate from the idea of a romantic youth who had undergone some unique process of depreciation."

Skimpoles are, to my mind, a genuine threat to the integrity of the Church today. Their potential for harm comes in large part precisely from the good things in which they take delight. Let's face it: they're more attractive people than most of us, and certainly more attractive than the Vatican inquisitors—at least while the latter are at their tasks. They charm; they enliven; they amuse and provoke. They speak the sweet words of dialogue, tolerance, and innovation, while the authorities are obliged to talk of limits and penalties. They proclaim themselves on the side of freedom and portray the curiales as friends of ignorance, violence, and repression. They fire the popular imagination, while I would venture the claim that never, in the entire history of journalism, has there been a sympathetic "human interest" profile done on a man who suppresses books for a living. Because they engage so many of our wholesome affections, because they have a media monopoly on the consolations of Christianity, because they are chary of speaking the hard truths of our faith, Skimpoles continue to win support from inside and outside the Church. And just as their prototype had a knack for making his benefactors feel guilty about their earned wealth, so the moderns predictably work to turn their sympathizers against the Church.

Skimpoles are incapable of gratitude toward authority because they can conceive of no error they need to be protected from; like spoiled children—precisely, in fact, like damaged young men—they see all discipline as condemnatory and all condemnation as wicked. And, after all, who is more likely to despise and disparage his father's work: the teenager who bags groceries to supplement the money his father can spare him, or the coddled heir who draws all the cash he needs from a bottomless teller machine?

To stress the necessity of authority is not to say that it hasn't been abused in the past—it has, sometimes hideously—or that it will not be abused in the future. A man is not disqualified from objecting to another man's discharge of some office simply in virtue of the fact that he regards that office indispensable. That a father provides well for his son does not in itself sanctify the conduct of his business. The point of this essay is not to silence criticism but rather to reawaken the recognition that when we do criticize the ancient structures of authority, we are speaking with our mouths full, and our plates have been piled high by the labors of hands not our own. For a believer to remain "a mere child" may add to his charm, but it deprives him of a prime lesson of adulthood: orthodoxy is no servility; gratitude, no indignity.

Part Three

OF MANY THINGS:
REVIEWS, 1993–2019

Why Universities Went Secular

The Secularization of the Academy
Edited by George M. Marsden and Bradley J. Longfield

The Vice-Chancellor gives notice that presentation to the vacant benefice of Brantham, in the Diocese of St. Edmundsbury and Ipswich, devolves on the University. Candidature is restricted to graduates of Emmanuel College, Cambridge, who are either the kin of Sir Wolstan Dixie or who have been educated for one year at Market Bosworth School.

The source of the advertisement above is not P. G. Wodehouse, nor Anthony Trollope, nor even Mark Pattison. It appeared in the *Cambridge University Reporter*—in 1973. The eleven essays assembled by George Marsden and Bradley Longfield on the demise of university patronage of religion in the U.S., Canada, and Great Britain make it clear that the history of this development is not a straightforward one. Anachronisms abound: we find surprising vestiges of the old order, as with the benefice of Brantham, and surprising anticipations of the new, as in President Daniel Coit Gilman's success stimulating graduate research at Johns Hopkins. David Bebbington, Philip Gleason, D. G. Hart, Robert Wood Lynn, George Rawlyk, and James Turner add their own scholarship to that of Marsden and Longfield in attempting to track and illuminate the subtle, often paradoxical, forces that, in a century and a half, effected a nearly complete inversion of the religious culture of the academy.

The studies presented address the predicament of religion at state universities as well as that of church-supported colleges. Denominational schools of the nineteenth century characteristically placed great stress on cultivating a learned piety in their students; it is striking to what extent this concern was shared by the state institutions as well.

Originally published in *First Things*, January 1993.

Bradley Longfield tells us that "in the 1850s the first class on Monday morning for *all* students at the University of Michigan was Greek New Testament. This was intended not only to teach the Scriptures but also 'to keep the students from violating the Sabbath by pursuing secular studies.' In a similar manner, Minnesota did not hold classes on Monday for fear the students would violate the Sabbath." Prior to the Civil War, Michigan required attendance at chapel twice daily. A University of Wisconsin graduate in 1896 penned this recollection of her student days in Madison:

> I shall never forget my first evening in South Hall and the sweet, impressive voice of the Preceptress as she led the kneeling girls in prayer. Sunday afternoons we learned a Bible lesson which we recited in the evening.

Contemporary parents, baffled by the contents of the freshman orientation kits given their children, may find the contrast instructive.

The general problem addressed by this volume is set out by [American historian] George Marsden: "Why has Christianity, which played a leading role in Western education until a century ago, now become not only entirely peripheral to higher education but has also often come to be considered absolutely alien to whatever is import- ant to the enterprise?" The kinds of answers offered by these authors concern the process of "secularization" understood in a descriptive, rather than a normative, sense; the word is glossed by Marsden as "the removal of some activity of life from substantive influences of tradi- tional or organized religion," and thus bears no implicit judgment of progress or decline. The essayists, for the most part, are scrupulously attentive to the task of description and cautious in their imputation of motive.

While different kinds of pressures and populations are at work in British colleges and American, in church-supported institutions and those administered by the state, the overall picture of the change from 1850 to 1990 is one of growing intellectual confusion on the part of Christians—confusion about the nature of the university, the nature of the Church, and the social value of religion. When believ- ers can't explain to themselves or to sympathetic fellow citizens what precisely is to be gained by the academy's patronage of religion, it seems that secularization occurs by default. Several authors make the point that ideological hostility to religion, though present in some measure from an early date, played a very minor role in the transformation. Nor does it seem that the change which came over the believers corresponds to what is usually meant by a "loss of faith"; what was lost, rather, was the confidence and the ability to make a public argument for what was increasingly seen to be a private good.

While the authors are commendably stingy in bestowing praise and blame, a good measure of the blame they do bestow is accorded to university officials for their incapacity to give a coherent account of themselves and their institutions. George Rawlyk writes:

Despite the hollow moral platitudes offered by countless university administrators, the essential justification for the university is its technological usefulness, its crucial hegemonic role in the shaping of the consumer and the therapeutic culture.

Citing Edward Maloney's study of the place of religion at Catholic colleges, Philip Gleason says:

The catalogues of most of the institutions Maloney surveyed no longer stated their religious objectives in clear-cut terms, and in some cases remained entirely silent about them. The presidents he talked to confessed "an inability to articulate properly their religious objectives today, even though they want[ed] the college to have a religious orientation."

Robert Wood Lynn suggests that less creditable factors played a part in the transformation of some denominational schools into ecumenical seminaries:

Sometimes these institutions self-consciously embraced this transformation out of deep theological convictions. And then occasionally others simply drifted in this direction, prompted by "market imperatives" that lurked unacknowledged beneath the surface of talk about "service." In the latter instances, seminary representatives must be artful when supporters press them with questions about the school's tie to the sponsoring denomination. The answer given ... depends partly on who is asking.

Few of us who have watched at close hand these "artful" representatives in action will rejoice in the recollection.

The academicians, of course, do not deserve all of the responsibility
for secularization. Another common factor is that the churches themselves have gotten progressively murky about their self-understanding
during the period under consideration. A Methodist minister of 1850
could almost always explain to you on doctrinal grounds why he was
not a Catholic or a Presbyterian, without having to keep looking
over his shoulder as he did so; the arguments were public property.
But the vocabulary in which this kind of discussion must be conducted is simply not part of religious discourse in America today, and
hasn't been for some time—with the exception of those "cognitive
minorities" that define themselves consciously in opposition to the
dominant culture.

Evelyn Waugh once remarked that the West is dying of sloth, not
wrath. For the most part institutions are lost not because they are
stormed by hostile outsiders but because their custodians, overcome
by apathy, diffidence, and intellectual fecklessness, simply give them
away. A recent visit to the Braun Room of the Harvard Divinity
School found oil portraits of the nineteenth-century clerical worthies
in their doctoral gowns and preaching bands gazing down on "Sacred
Condoms," an exhibit of prophylactic devices filled with alphabet
soup, honey, etc., which was designed (according to the University) as part of "an important ministerial conversation." This tableau
might serve as an allegory of the history so skillfully detailed in *The
Secularization of the Academy*—a history ending not with a bang but
a whimper.

Assassins of a Lesser God

Jesus: A Life
By A. N. Wilson

Live from Golgotha
By Gore Vidal

Blasphemy is the derogation of God. To conceive of God apart from his holiness is intrinsically impossible. But to derogate God is precisely to deny his holiness. Therefore blasphemy is intrinsically impossible. While I'm not sure the syllogism above would withstand severe logical examination, it crystallizes my own more diffuse reflections on the failure of two well-established writers in two unusually inept and ugly books, *Live From Golgotha*, by Gore Vidal, and *Jesus: A Life*, by A. N. Wilson. The first presents itself as a novel and the second as biography, but neither author makes more than a half-hearted effort at instruction or diversion. Malice is the chief motive of both works; they are written to shock, grieve, and dismay Christian believers—goals easily enough achieved, one might think, and successfully attained by talents far more meager than those of Wilson or Vidal. The really intriguing question is, why should they flop? The answer to this question demands, paradoxically, closer scrutiny of these books than either deserves. There is a wholesome instinct that argues against granting certain works even the minimal dignity of a negative review: leave the dead to bury their dead.

Yet *Jesus* and *Golgotha* have received more than polite notice in the Christian press and have figured seriously in op-ed pieces in the *New York Times* and elsewhere. A fuller treatment is called for. The English writer A. N. Wilson was raised as an Anglican, became a Catholic briefly, reverted to Anglicanism, and has recently announced that he

Originally published in *First Things*, March 1993.

is an atheist. He is a successful novelist and has won respect as a biographer of Milton, Belloc, Tolstoy, and C. S. Lewis. Religion and the varieties of Christian churchmanship are principal concerns in all of his work. In 1985 he published a curious essay on his tottering faith called *How Can We Know?*, a work that irresistibly brings to mind Ronald Knox's Strato in *Absolute and Abitofhell*:

> For he, discerning with nice arguings,
> 'Twixt non-essential and essential things,
> Himself believing, could no reason see
> Why another other should believe, but he.

This was followed in 1990 by a tract titled *Against Religion*, in which the author declaimed, rather preciously, against religion. And now we have *Jesus*. Wilson seems unclear himself just what sort of book he intended to write. He claims that his focus is the Jesus of history, as opposed to "the mythological Christ of religion," yet he maintains that recovery of Jesus of Nazareth is "strictly speaking impossible."

> I do tell a narrative, based on the New Testament, which would not be satisfying to the most rigorous historian. For the sake of trying to convey what I think Jesus stood for, and what sort of man he was, I adopt the New Testament order of events. I hope that I have not written fiction, but I am aware that strictly speaking we cannot say as much about Jesus as I have in the final chapters of this book without an infinity of perhaps, perhaps, perhaps.

Taken by itself, such a disclaimer might suggest a reassuring skepticism on the author's part regarding his own reconstruction. But when it suits his purposes Wilson assumes a scholarly dogmatism few real historians would hazard:

> The Fourth Gospel tells us that the [Last Supper] took place well before the Passover. It was not a Passover meal, and in this account there is very conspicuously no institution of the Eucharist. This is perhaps the most glaring inconsistency in the Christian claim to be an historically based religion. The truth is that even if we were to believe the fantastic claim that Jesus wished to found a new religion, with a sacramental order of bishops and deacons, we could not believe that he instituted the Eucharist at Passover time as Paul and the Gospels aver.

But what happened to "perhaps"? The careful reader may be pardoned in finding Wilson methodologically capricious, when not entirely opaque, in his distribution of historical probability and doubt. The following sentence, unexplained in context, is a not-untypical specimen of his mind at work: "It is true, and indeed very likely, that Jesus caused some kind of disturbance in the Temple, overthrowing the money-changers' tables, though Christian interpreters of this event are likely to have mistaken its meaning." Except for the obvious moral—*chretiens ont tort; paiens ont raison*—I don't get it either. In broad terms, Wilson's Jesus of history will be familiar to anyone who has read a freshman World Religions textbook. Jesus was a Galilean *hasid* or holy man whose mission was to help Jews be better Jews. He made himself a nuisance to the Roman authorities, was executed, and was memorialized by his followers in a mythology colored by mystery religions of the East, a mythology that departed so greatly from Jesus' own Judaism that a new religion was born. For Wilson, Christianity is the invention of St. Paul, the product of personal neurosis and demagogic genius, and a good part of his work is devoted to a reconstruction of Paul's highly peculiar role in the whole business. Though admittedly provocative, Wilson's demonstrations are crippled beyond repair by his frequent use of the fallacy called "asserting the consequent," much loved of the *Chariots of the Gods* school of history, thus: "If there were an invisible cat on that chair, it would look empty; but it does look empty, therefore there is an invisible cat on the chair." To an inattentive reader the proof may seem convincing. Watch it at work in Wilson's argument that it was Paul, not Peter, who denied Jesus at the time of his arrest.

> The Acts of the Apostles tells us that Paul was responsible for the prosecution of Stephen, the first Christian martyr, for blasphemy; but this is very unlikely to have been historically correct. If Paul was actually concerned with the condemnation, not of Stephen, but of Jesus himself, this would have been a fact with which his conscious mind, in the Christian phase of his life, would have been unable to come to terms. The Synoptic Gospels and the Acts of the Apostles both draw on Christian traditions which are heavily influenced by Paul's interpretation and version of events. Their historical suppression or distortion of the truth would, if my theory is correct, correspond to the psychological suppression of the truth within Paul's own person.

[A-ha!] Further, if, as Galatians makes plain, Paul held strongly diver-
gent views from Peter, it would be natural that in the Pauline tradition, we should read accounts of Peter's denial of Jesus rather than
Paul's actual condemnation of the Lord to death.

Having once threaded our way through the snarls of conditional
syntax, we find that we are invited to reason thus: *If* Paul were dis-
guising his guilt for having sold out Jesus, we wouldn't find evidence
of his betrayal in the writings he influenced. But we *don't* find evidence of his betrayal in the writings he influenced, Ergo.... The
book is full of similar examples, but my favorite is Mary Magdalene's
post-Resurrection boner in the Gospel of John; it was *James*, the
brother of the Lord, whom she mistook for the gardener.

> As with Luke's Emmaus story, it is hard to see how someone who had
> known Jesus quite well should have been so slow to recognize him. If,
> however, the stranger were not the dear friend, but the dear friend's
> brother, who bore a strong resemblance, then this is just the sort of
> "double take" we should expect.

Several reviews of *Jesus* have remarked on the author's "scholarly approach." Rubbish. The book is emphatically, often laughably,
unscholarly. Footnotes are erratic and incomplete where they do occur.
The text is full of pointless pedantries (such as "The Fourth Gospel"
throughout for the Gospel of John) that seldom illuminate and often
obscure. Moreover, Wilson comes to the Bible innocent of Hebrew,
innocent of Aramaic, and with shaky sophomore Greek, yet these
handicaps don't deter him from making such claims as the following:

> One method of reconstructing the possible authenticity of Jesus' say-
> ings is to see how they are translated from the Greek in which they
> are written into the Aramaic in which they must have been spoken. In
> Luke 17:24, for example, we read of Jesus saying, "As the lightning,
> when it lighteneth out of the one part under heaven, shineth unto the
> other part under heaven, so shall the Son of Man be in his day." This
> is not a sentence which can be rendered into feasible Aramaic, and it
> can therefore be rejected quite certainly as something which Jesus did
> not say.

Again, the inference is ludicrous. It is as if we were to reason, "My
history book reports that Julius Caesar said, 'The die is cast,' once

he crossed the Rubicon. But Latin has no word for 'the.' Therefore it can be rejected quite certainly as something Caesar did not say." That Wilson is not a professional scholar of Scripture does not in itself disqualify him from the task of taking a fresh approach to the person of Jesus. It is sometimes the case that a perceptive amateur can spot connections that elude the micro-scholars, precisely because the latter are, in a sense, too close to the data. Housman maintained famously that if you want a really penetrating insight into Greek or Latin literature, the last person you come to is a classicist. Yet all this assumes that the one outside the guild be gifted with a logical acuity, literary perspicacity, and above all grasp of human nature great enough to outweigh any deficiency in technical knowledge. It is only fair to ask whether we have in Wilson this kind of inspired amateur. Can we trust him to recover the lost Jesus for us? The answer is given once-for-all in Wilson's argument that Jesus could not have been a carpenter, because he lacked the kind of knowledge true carpenters have.

> In one of his better-known carpentry analogies, Jesus again shows a fantastical imagination, and a sharp wit, but no practical knowledge of what it was like to work in a carpenter's shop. "Why beholdest thou the mote that is in thy brother's eye, but considerest not the beam that is in thine own eye?" It has become a proverb to express the archetypal human tendency to be observant of other people's faults and blind to one's own. Like much that Jesus said, it is hyperbolic to the point of farce. It is actually extremely funny. But no carpenter in real life came close to having a plank sticking out of his eye.... Jesus, then, does not appear to have been a practical man, or one well-versed in a trade.

Wilson is not much subtler when it comes to explaining how the Gospels came to be written:

> [Matthew] has been through the [Old Testament] Scriptures cheerfully lifting details, and then inventing "facts" to fulfill the "prophecies."

Or how the fix was in on the redaction process:

> We have to accept the fact that all the documentary evidence comes to us filtered via Christian witnesses, and that Christians, after their religion became the official creed of the Roman Empire ... busily set about destroying or altering any evidence which might conflict with the orthodox view of Jesus.

Or how the job was botched:

> Though the New Testament writers seem to have done their best to
> obscure Jesus altogether in an encrustation of fantasy, he won't quite
> be pinned down. He struggles free of the evangelists sometimes.

Those who, like Wilson, employ the stock hermeneutics of suspicion
baffle us as much by their credulity as by their skepticism. On the one
hand the Gospel-makers are portrayed as men of almost superhuman
cunning and malice, having succeeded by the end of the first century in convincing their contemporaries that their fraud, contrived
to foist an authoritarian hierarchy on the community of believers,
was an entirely authentic witness to Jesus. As editors, on the other
hand, they were preternaturally obtuse, failing to censor all kinds of
embarrassing counterevidence. Are we really meant to picture those
proto-patriarchs gathered in conclave, slapping their palms to their
foreheads like housewives who remember they left the iron plugged
in? "Good God, man! We forgot to take out the Beatitudes!" Read
Wilson on Mark 7:28:

> This saying, when taken with the other sayings of Jesus which the evan-
> gelists have forgotten to cut out ... makes us realize that the Gospels
> do, in spite of themselves, contain words which are almost certainly
> authentic memories of his teaching.

"In spite of themselves" is good. Flannery O'Connor once pointed
out that loss of Christian faith often coincides with an "awakening"
to the notion that Jesus is a *"beautiful! beautiful!"* human being: in
reference to one of her friends she called it the "eeeek eeeek eureka
stage." So too the newly enlightened Wilson presents himself as a
defender of the true Jesus (a good-hearted Jewish liberal, respectful
of women and the differently abled, with a "playful yet passionately
serious sense of the infinite worth of every individual") against the
arrant impostures of orthodox Catholics. Wilson's preoccupation
with the Church of Rome can fairly be called obsessive; I began a list
of the instances where he departs from his brief to make gratuitous
polemical jabs at specifically Catholic targets, and stopped counting
at twenty. Three examples from three different chapters will serve to
indicate the degree of his equanimity:

The world of Jesus has been more sharply focused for our generation than for any previous generation since 70 C.E., when his world was obliterated by the Romans, and the Catholic Faith, which had small interest in and less knowledge of Jesus' Semitic origins, pursued its own curious and in the end victorious course. Had [Jesus] attended the great Councils of Christendom—Nicaea, Chalcedon, Trent, or the First and Second Vatican Councils—his gratitude might have turned to dismay.... Even if it were even half possible that an historical personage existed who said the words attributed to him in the Gospels, there could be no greater insult to his memory than to recite the creeds.... Would [Jesus] have been tempted to found a church, or several churches, each accusing the other of heresy, and denouncing their fellow believers by the means of councils, papal bulls, inquisitions, and wars, until the capital of the empire stood thick with temples devoted to the worship of Jesus and altars where Gentile priests could, by pronouncing certain words, call down the very presence of Jesus into their midst?

Wilson's book, be it noted, was called by the Kirkus reviewer "a surprisingly dispassionate, respectfully skeptical study that makes the best biblical scholarship available to general readers." In *Jesus*, A. N. Wilson hoped he hadn't written a novel; in *Live from Golgotha*, Gore Vidal hoped he had. The hopes of both men are disappointed by their productions—in the former case, because an imaginative resentment could find no purchase on reality; in the latter, because a resentful imagination failed to attain the coherence of fiction. The conceit of Vidal's book (the word "plot" cannot be applied here without irony) is, as far as I can make out, this: Jesus is a repellent twentieth-century Jewish computer analyst named Marvin Wasserstein, a fanatical Zionist and Gentile-hater. The technology of time-travel is known, and Wasserstein has been able to discover Christianity's great dark secret: the man crucified on Golgotha was actually Judas, a grotesquely obese and epicene slob. St. Paul, working with his bisexual catamite St. Timothy, had concocted the story of a more presentable crucifixion victim because it would make for a more marketable new religion. The ruse worked, and Christianity was a smash hit. Wasserstein plots to take a film crew back through time to Golgotha to expose the fraud, destroy Christianity, and make the world retrospectively safe for Zionism. By a double-double-cross, Wasserstein is himself arrested at Gethsemane, is crucified *secundum scripturas*, and history proceeds unhappily ever after. Amused? A reviewer of *Live from Golgotha* labors under the obvious handicap that virtually none of his supporting evidence is printable. Imagine the movie version of *Ben Hur* or *Quo Vadis* produced by Robert Mapplethorpe: such is the tone of sexual squalor and Greco-Roman camp pitilessly trained on the reader by Vidal's narrator Timothy. In addition, there is a continuous descant of puerile Jew-baiting poking through the frequent gaps in the narrative. Why should such a novel, which we would hardly expect to find outside the restroom of the Camden Bus Station, warrant the attention of *First Things*? Because it is being discussed in deadpan earnest, by well-known intellectuals, in respected periodicals, as a legitimate contribution to the philosophy of religion. Irving Malin wrote the following lines in a review published in the Catholic weekly *Commonweal*:

> Although Vidal offers a *fiendish* gospel—a counter-gospel—he must be taken seriously. He is, after all, asking basic epistemological questions. He turns the tables on us. Why do we believe in miracles? Do we find truth by reason or faith? ... I suggest that Vidal's provocative, distasteful novel is perhaps one of his most sustained meditations on the nature of things. It will be read for many years.

One of Vidal's blander passages (still greatly edited) may help us understand the literary context of these basic epistemological questions, this sustained meditation on the nature of things. "Saint" is St. Paul.

> So Saint went sashaying around Asia Minor, setting up churches and generally putting on a great show, aided by the cousins Barnaby and John Mark. But although the Jerusalem Jews liked the money that Saint kept sending back to headquarters, they still couldn't, in their heart of hearts, stomach the Gentiles, and so they refused to eat at the same table with us, since our [obscenity deleted] were always on their minds. Finally, things came to a head when Saint took a shine to a young convert and stud named Titus and took him down to Jerusalem for a long weekend of fun.... The central office then leaned on James, an employee of the Temple, and James told Saint that in the future those goyim who became converted to Jesus must be circumcised. That tore it.

And that's the clever part. It is a disturbing fact about *Live from Golgotha* that all the elements of the Weimar aesthetic are here: the sexual violence, the thrill of sacrilege, the *haute couture* androgyny, the mock-jocular anti-Semitism with its underlying rage just peeking out from the high grass of countercultural chic: testing, testing. Most chilling of all to this reviewer is the straight-faced seriousness (for which Vidal is not responsible) with which literary aesthetes and academics calmly convert inarticulate rage into articulate social criticism, under the fashionable pretense that any and all anger is justified, provided it is subversive. And as long as subversion remains culturally chic, of course, any objections based on traditional morality, classical aesthetics, or scholarly propriety can be laughed out of court as mere naive prudery. The road from Weimar to Nuremberg used to be unclear to me; it is no longer.

Vidal's novel (his twenty-third, according to the publisher) does not exhibit the marks of a mature writer, nor even the disciplined intelligence of a literary journeyman. It is utterly devoid of wit. Vulgarisms abound, but none has been sharpened by the writer into a tool; we simply have squalor for the sake of squalor. In the place of wit are a number of gags, mainly obvious anachronisms—Shirley MacLaine "channeling in" to first-century Ephesus, St. Timothy watching televised ice hockey—that suggest Mel Brooks rather than Oscar Wilde. *Live from Golgotha* reads like an adolescent's work not only in the pointlessness of its obscenity but in its general self-indulgence: the author is too angry at his characters to crack a decent joke about them, too anxious that they be ridiculed to make them halfway credible first. He starts by making Saints Paul and Peter and Jesus himself into cardboard cartoons; then he riddles his own creations with bulletholes. As a consequence, the original targets of his malice remain curiously unscathed. Listen to St. Timothy's narration concerning St. James:

> As kid brother of Jesus, [James] insisted that the leadership of the church was his, and there had been times when he acted as if he and not his brother were the messiah. Fortunately, the Resurrection settled that bit of sibling rivalry. "The presence," said James, "of non-Jews is very distressing to many members of our congregation, particularly at table where we are entirely kosher, and often dairy." ...

James was staring with disgust at my hyacinthine golden curls and cornflower-blue eyes, the perfect Gentile youth so hated by every proper, self-loving Jew.... We were served quite a good kosher lunch by two wealthy Jewish widows, who are known in the community as yentas, a Jewish word meaning ladies-in-waiting for the return of the messiah. "I have already deposited the Jesus-tithing from Asia Minor at the bank in the temple, to your account." Saint smiled at James, who pretended indifference. Actually James was something of a financial wizard. Where Saint could raise money through salesmanship or creative bookkeeping, not to mention the all-important Follow-up strategies, James was a master of the Temple stock exchange, which so annoyed his brother, Jesus, or so we say.

There are 224 pages more of the same monotonously mindless tittering. A blurb citing a puff from *Vanity Fair* commends this book as "Hilarious! A full frontal assault on the New Testament!" Assailing the New Testament does not, perhaps, prompt hilarity outside the readership of *Vanity Fair* as reflexively as it does within; yet even allowing for this, the standard of humor seems curiously low. Is it possible that the amusement the book gives such a reviewer stems less from his own reading than from his delighted anticipation of the outrage it will provoke in the bourgeois believer?

While the genres in which A. N. Wilson and Gore Vidal have dealt with the early years of Christianity are quite distinct, there are many striking similarities in their treatment. For both men, the Christian religion is an enterprise entirely unconnected with the person of Jesus; for both, it is St. Paul who concocted Christianity to serve his own ends. For both men, Paul is endowed with great rhetorical and histrionic talent that is perverted by still greater psychological defects (in this respect they could hardly succeed in shocking, for at least one Episcopalian bishop has gone public with the same view). Both men see the establishment of the Church as a simple power ploy utterly contrary to the will of Jesus; and each brings James, the brother of the Lord, into prominence in the struggles for control. For Wilson as well as Vidal, God is a notion that is ridiculous for those who don't believe and malignant for those who do. Of course, this makes their efforts at debunking all the more strange. A man might find the claims of Sun Myung Moon preposterous; yet it would be odd if he spent most of his waking hours rebutting them. In fact, if his animus were sufficiently strong, we might begin to doubt that his disaffection was so total after all. In the same way, the slurs and sneers and adolescent forays into refutation directed by Vidal and Wilson at religion are wholly out of proportion to their professed contempt for it; religion is a kind of lantern that both scorches and fascinates the fluttering moth, a moth that curses the flame yet can't free itself from its orbit.

Nobler intellects than those that produced *Jesus* and *Live from Golgotha* have been trapped by the need to extinguish the source of *others'* credulity. One thinks in this connection of the master logician Georg Cantor, who, according to Bertrand Russell, spent his declining years obsessed with proving that Jesus was the natural son of Joseph of Arimathea. That is how a critic becomes a crank: first he provokes, then perplexes, and finally bores us.

It has become fashionable for intellectuals to paint, write, or compose music as a kind of psychotherapy. Since the reception given to *Jesus* and *Live from Golgotha* has so little relation to their scholarly or literary merit, it is worth asking whether we have in these works a kind of therapeutic auto-shamanism. Perhaps the authors believe that if demons can be exorcised by recitation of Holy Scripture, God, conversely, might be exorcised by blasphemy, by ritual incantation of what is calculated to infuriate pious men. Perhaps they are trying to rid themselves and similarly afflicted readers of a bad-faith *disbelief.*

They fail, of course; they couldn't do otherwise. Real holiness cannot be ridiculed; only sham holiness can. Caricatures of divinity make excellent, slow-moving targets for mockery, but they are, after all, the work of men's hands. Those who mistake an image for the reality might do irreparable damage to their own handiwork, might give lasting pain to the faithful, but sooner or later they will discover to their chagrin that the source of all holiness lives on, that they were assassins of a lesser god.

Mailer's False Messiah

The Gospel according to the Son
By Norman Mailer

The story is told of a prominent church historian, notorious both for his learning and his crustiness, who from time to time would find an over-excited grad student in his office, eager to win his master's applause for an original theological insight. Having waved his visitor into a chair, the historian would say, "I am very interested to hear your new theological idea, but before you explain it, let me tell you three things about it: One. It was already propounded by a fifth-century Syrian monk. Two. He expressed himself better than you will. Three. He was wrong."

It is a pity that Norman Mailer had no recourse to such a mentor, for it might have saved him, and us, the embarrassment of *The Gospel according to the Son*. The embarrassment in this instance is not primarily occasioned by the imputation of heresy. Mailer obviously wants to shock us with the book and has posed for interviewers as a kind of literary Dennis Rodman, delighting in his own naughtiness. Yet he is so far behind the Heterodoxy Curve as to be unaware that his shattering innovations are little more than the platitudes of New Age suburbia, and have long been superseded by those "weekend spirituality workshops" in which feminist nuns and retired orthodontists are taught how to deconstruct the New Testament and make pumpkin bread. Both heresy-hunters and bishop-baiters will feel somewhat let down by Mailer's Gospel. True, he does make an attempt to subvert the orthodox tradition by having Jesus "tell the real story" in his own voice. But, first, this ploy was already used by a Sister of Saint Jude in a summer creative writing seminar; second, she expressed herself better than he does; third, she got a B.

Originally published in the *Washington Examiner*, May 26, 1997.

The prime defect of *The Gospel according to the Son*, from which all others flow, is the author's own uncertainty about the kind of book he meant to write. Sometimes he sees himself as "re-telling the myth" (i.e., taking the Gospel story at face value), and sometimes he sets out to demythologize the traditional account (i.e., to chip away the encrustations of the Christ of Faith from the Jesus of History). These goals are mutually contradictory, and the resultant incoherence is fatal. Mailer's Jesus (Yeshua to his pals) turns out to be a Jewish seminary student who has converted to Methodism but isn't sure why. He shows no curiosity about the disciples who inexplicably collect around him and, in fact, seems unable to maintain interest in his own messiahship.

He tells his story in half-a-dozen different voices as his author struggles to get him into focus. As narrator, for example, he generally speaks in the kind of eco-aphorism that Hollywood scriptwriters put into the mouths of Comanche elders when they want them to sound like sages. "Such tales are to be leaned upon no more than a bush that tears free from its roots and blows about in the wind." "The Word had lived first in water even as the breath that carries our speech comes forth from our mouths in a cloud on a cold winter morning." "But a weight came upon my heart for cursing the roots of another." In fact, sometimes the clueless Yeshua forgets his Galilean Aramaic entirely and talks pure Tontoese: "Did I speak with a forked tongue?"

His pronouncements occasionally have the sonority and cadence of folk epigrams, but when cashed out add up to nothing at all. I doubt very much whether Mailer himself is aware of this, as some of his metaphors seem to have been accidentally welded together by his word-processor. Try parsing this one: "Yet his eyes were blue like the faded blue of the sky when the sky is white." As Wilde remarked, a simile committing suicide is always a depressing spectacle. (I picture the puzzled editor at Random House tapping his teeth with a pencil as he read the manuscript and ultimately acquiescing with a shrug of resignation: This must be how religious types talk.)

You can almost spot the yellow highlight stains in the books Mailer read to prepare for the writing of his Gospel, as when Yeshua speaks to us in the voice of a pedantic twentieth-century expert: "Joseph ... told us of a substance called pozzolana, an earth that came from the volcanoes south of Rome; this pozzolana, mixed with lime, became a cement." More often, however, particularly in recounting direct discourse, Yeshua resorts to Jacobean biblical English, spoken in the accents of Cecil B. DeMille: "And in the moment that Elizabeth saw my mother at the door, so did her babe leap in her womb. Overjoyed, she spoke out: 'Blessed art thou, Mary. All generations to come shall call you blessed.'" Again, notice the false pitch: not only the pointless and awkward shift from "thou" to "you" but the fruity "so did her babe leap," in which "so" exists merely to give the sentence a faux-antique veneer.

Elsewhere the eagerness to mimic the syntax of the Authorized Version turns the Gadarene swine into "the swine of Gadarene"— rather like rephrasing "Newtonian physics" as "physics of Newtonian." Sorry, Mr. Mailer, we just don't say it that way in our language.

In fact, except for the incidental archeology footnotes, the novel is unreadable. Perhaps its sentences aren't written to be read but to be listened to, to serve as a kind of Muzak that occupies the back third of our attention with a reassuring drone while the pictures pass before our eyes.

The book reads less like a novel than a B-movie screenplay. A cinematic rather than a literary sensibility governs the selection of material—both the incidents he has borrowed from the four true Gospels and the gaps in the life of Christ filled by Mailer's imagination. There is a distinct preference for DRAMA—here understood, as it is in westerns, to mean any scene that includes a weeping woman. My favorite is St. Joseph's discovery of his fiancee's pregnancy: "But then Joseph grew angry and said, 'Why did you bring this shame on yourself?' She began to cry. 'I am innocent,' she told him, 'and I have never known a man.'" Later, not surprisingly, the same imagination treats us to eight pages on Yeshua's encounter with the woman caught in adultery (that's Jn 8:1–11 in Gospels 1.0). Clearly we are meant to feel suspense here. Will our hero falter? "As I feared, she was beautiful. The bones of her face were delicate, and the hair flowed down her back." Mickey Spillane couldn't have put it better. Yeshua the celibate theology student is aghast to find his id in his cassock and, of course, is immediately in conflict with demons: "My abhorrence of fornication had filled my years with thoughts of lust. I had suffered from ravages of unspent fury. But now I heard the soft voice of a spirit." Relax; it all comes out all right. He remembers himself sufficiently to go beyond the merely physical and ask about her hobbies and interests ("Without the flesh," she says, "there is no life") and they part friends. Score that one a draw.

Mailer is not a theologian, not a biblicist, not a man who believes in the Gospel. None of that means he is disqualified from saying something interesting about Jesus. [French philosopher] Simone Weil shared all three characteristics with Mailer and yet was endowed with enough philosophical and literary intuition to come to original and valuable insights about the religion she rejected. But Mailer sets himself a tougher job than Weil. Not only does he want to get into the skin of God-become-Man—ambitious enough by itself—but the God with whom he tries to commune is, in his reckoning, neither omnipotent nor omniscient. Consider what this means. If God is defective, then his every attempt to reveal himself and his will to men is suspect, for the reason that no one, God included, can know with certainty what has been communicated or to whom. All Sacred Scripture, and all extra-scriptural tradition, is thus intrinsically unreliable. What then becomes of the project agnostics cheerfully call "man's search for God"? What can man possibly find at the end of his quest that he did not bring with him from the beginning?

Viewed in the terms of classical Christology, Mailer's Yeshua turns out to be a Messiah Lite. He had a supernatural conception, but his overbearing mother just wants him "to become a good Essene." The hand-wringing type, he is unsure when his divine Father is speaking to him and when not, and he repeatedly prays, "Help my unbelief." He performs miracles diffidently, and in fact they sometimes fail to come off. The miraculous feeding of the five thousand, Yeshua assures us, was really a feeding of five hundred—not a bad summation of the project of liberal exegetes, by the way: supernaturalism diluted to a 10 percent solution.

After the fast in the desert, Satan tempts the Messiah with "a leg of lamb, well cooked," apparently with some success. In the unintentionally hilarious scene in which he encounters John the Baptist at the river, Yeshua, for the nonce a fourteen-year-old Catholic, actually goes to confession: "I searched to find evil in myself and came back with no more than moments I could recall of disrespect toward my mother and contests in the night with lustful thoughts. Perhaps there had been a few acts of unkindness when judging others." Three Hail Marys is what I'd give him.

At the core Yeshua is no sacramentalist. He's bummed out by churches and by repetition of the same prayers. He's sensitive to the environment. He doesn't get bent out of shape by "men who did not know women but other men." He uses gender-inclusive language. Most wonderfully of all, at the supreme moment of eschatological revelation in which the Messiah makes known to his disciples that the world is to come to an end, he admits, "As I said this I could *feel their pain.*" Bingo. When the last veil is torn away, God is a New Democrat. Our Apocalypse is going to be a *caring* Apocalypse.

Pontifex Minimus

*Building a Bridge: How the Catholic Church and
the LGBT Community Can Enter into a Relationship
of Respect, Compassion, and Sensitivity*

By James Martin, S.J.

Is sodomy a sin? Perplexed readers of Father James Martin, S.J.'s [2017] book will want to put the question to him, if only to understand why he felt it important to write at all.

Father Martin describes his project as that of reflecting "on both the church's outreach to the LGBT community and the LGBT community's outreach to the church." From the outset the encounter is framed in political rather than pastoral terms. The term "community" in the phrase "LGBT community" is borrowed from the civil rights movement of the 1960s, and in its present employment the word corresponds to no discernible social reality. One does not find among lesbian, gay, bisexual, and transgender people—taken as a collectivity—distinctive commonalities of religion, nativity, culture, recreation, or fellowship. Their shared interests are political; they are aggregated not as a true community but as something like a caucus. It is noteworthy that Father Martin voices his wish that his readers understand the LGBT acronym expansively as LGBTQA—that is, to include "questioning or queer, and allies." The word "ally," designating not sexual appetite but political allegiance, gives the game away.

The truth is that the Church, as Church, has no pastoral interest in the LGBT bloc apart from her concern that those who compose it be protected from sin contemplated and rescued from sin committed—precisely the same concern she shows for everybody else. That is to say, the Church is concerned with the prospect of salvation and damnation, and persons with a propensity for a particular sin engage

Originally published in *First Things*, August–September 2017.

her pastoral solicitude in the degree that the sin is grave and the propensity stubborn. She wants us to get to heaven.

With this duty in view, the Catholic Church teaches that sexual relations are the exclusive privilege of married love—and that between a man and a woman. The sexual revolution not only rejects this doctrine but is violently disdainful of it, and the cultural and political triumphs of that revolution have made defense of the teaching increasingly costly. It has also made fidelity increasingly difficult for all, but especially for those whose sexual libido is not ordered to heterosexual love. Same-sex attraction has received exceptional attention inside and outside the Church. This is not because the sin to which it tends is somehow more mortal than other mortal sins but because both partisans and adversaries of the sexual revolution understand how much is riding on the preservation or elimination of the injunction against sodomy.

Father Martin is, of course, under no obligation, even in a book dealing with the Church and the LGBT caucus, to expound Catholic teaching on homosexual acts. Disconcerting, however, is his failure to acknowledge the existence of those afflicted with same-sex attraction who believe that the Church has it right today and has had it right all along. Priests who frequently counsel and hear confessions can attest that there are many such Catholics, who fully accept the difficult doctrines as the teaching of Christ and who struggle heroically to keep them. Such Catholics already live in the heart of the Church, as much as do any of the faithful, and no bridge needs to be built to them. Moreover, they do not need to be "accompanied," as the jargon has it, because they have already arrived at, or never left, the home they share with their would-be accompanists. Very few of these men and women identify themselves as "gay" or wish to be so designated. They are simply Catholics, neither more nor less, struggling (as do the rest of us) with the spiritual and moral hardships that come their way. It is astonishing that Martin seems never to have met such a person.

To his credit, Father Martin concedes that there exists a "chasm" between the Church and the LGBT bloc, whence his call for a bridge to span the divide. His plea is to reduce the distrust that makes each side wary of the other by encouraging mutual "respect, compassion, and sensitivity"—using the language of the *Catechism* (2358). But why do we not find comparable chasms of distrust between the Church and other populations afflicted by a sinfully inclined disorder—say, kleptomaniacs? Most of us see the reason plainly: If the man next to me in the pew is struggling with kleptomania, I have no reason to believe he denies Church teaching on property rights. But a person who announces himself as "gay" for that very reason (so it would appear) regards his same-sex attraction not merely as a libido experienced but as an identity embraced, and this embrace seems all but impossible to reconcile with Catholic doctrine. What percentage of those who claim membership in "the LGBT community" also endorse the teachings of the *Catechism* (2357) that "Sacred Scripture ... presents homosexual acts as acts of grave depravity" or that "homosexual acts are intrinsically disordered"? There are a stalwart few, no doubt, but their number is tiny. In consequence, the mistrust that Martin deplores is not misplaced. The chasm is real, and reasons for its existence reveal themselves as more sound the more closely they are studied.

However well-intentioned, Father Martin's book does not advance the Church's response to the crisis of disordered sexuality; it waves a white flag. For all that, Martin is right to lament the antagonism that persists and correct in pointing to the need of spiritual assistance for same-sex-attracted persons. Here, too, I believe that recourse to the Church's broader pastoral experience would go far to remedy the problem. Those with extensive experience in the confessional will have encountered penitents with many different disordered and objectively immoral desires, some associated with behaviors that even today are universally regarded as felonies. The Church is right to teach that all such people are deserving of respect, compassion, and sensitivity, which are their due simply as human persons, not as those who have achieved a given standard of probity or of psychological health. But her own task, carried out by means of her sacraments and the pastoral exertions of her ministers, is to reconcile the sinner and to strengthen the weak, so as to be a conduit of supernatural aid—that is to say, of graces that have their effect in spite of the human limitations of those who transmit them.

By an entirely understandable paradox, the seal of the confessional means that the Church's pastoral successes in this regard almost never meet the light of day. The pastors are forbidden to speak and their penitents disinclined. Yet the parable of the Pharisee and the publican

(Lk 18:10–14) is an admonition to remember that authentic spiritual renewal may not take place in the well-lit areas at center stage—where everyone is watching and public congratulations are fulsomely exchanged—but often occurs out of sight, in the darker and more private precincts of the temple, where humility and remorse seek the truth and are rewarded with new life.

Waugh on the Merits

Evelyn Waugh: A Life Revisited
By Philip Eade

Arthur Evelyn St. John Waugh was born in 1903 to upper-middle-class Anglicans who lived in a suburb of London. He attended a boarding secondary school (Lancing College), read history at Oxford, published his first book (a biography of the painter Dante Gabriel Rossetti) at age twenty-four, then his first novel a year later. Waugh married that same year (1928), divorced after two years, and converted to Catholicism. After the first marriage was declared null, he married a Catholic by whom he had seven children. He served honorably but ineffectively as an infantry officer in World War II and was to publish thirteen novels, as well as seven travel books, three biographies, a volume of autobiography, and numerous essays and book reviews. Lionized in the 1920s as a trendy man of fashion, he became increasingly conservative in politics and churchmanship and notorious for his truculent contempt for the sham enthusiasms of modernity. He died on Easter Sunday 1966 at his house in Somerset.

In addition to works published in his lifetime, Waugh left behind several hundred pages of diaries and thousands of letters. And in reading these we become aware that sometime between the ages of fifteen and seventeen, he acquired an almost freakishly mature mastery of English prose. For the remainder of his life, he was all but incapable of writing a boring sentence. Even in his commonplace and perfunctory communications—business correspondence, military reports, letters to agents and headmasters—Waugh wrote a clean, elegant, beautifully precise English that is appetizing in the most unpromising circumstances. Just as it's unsettling to be reminded that Bach's *Well-Tempered Clavier* was a set of keyboard exercises composed "for the

Originally published in *First Things*, October 2017.

profit and use of musical youth desirous of learning," it's remarkable how much eerily flawless craftsmanship Waugh displays even when the occasion of his writing is casual or mundane.

The most outstanding characteristic of Waugh's prose is its lucidity. Every sentence is clear. Even where his subject matter is thorny, I don't believe I've ever had to read a sentence twice over to get its meaning. His friend and fellow novelist Graham Greene remarked that what struck him about Waugh's writing was its transparency, that you could see all the way to the bottom, as with the Mediterranean in days gone by. This transparency is partly attributable to perfect syntax—grammatical solecisms are almost non-existent—and partly to Waugh's care in choosing the right word, the word that not only conveys but illuminates. Sometimes Waugh employs a recondite word from his compendious vocabulary, but never an obscure word for the sake of its obscurity. As a boy I learned the meaning of many words I had never before encountered from the perfect fit they were given by Waugh in a single memorable phrase. Reading Waugh, you don't need a dictionary at your elbow; the sentence provides sufficient light on its own.

Waugh also had a genius for conveying spoken English matched only, perhaps, by James Joyce. Like Joyce, he lets us *hear* the speakers through their dialogue—their accents; their treble or contralto, their coughs, stammers, and lisps; their whining or their barking— and he does this with almost no departure from standard spelling. We recognize cockneys without resort to dropped aitches and Scotsmen without resort to tripled *r*'s; we recognize them because the speeches Waugh gives them convince us that only *this* cockney or only *this* Scotsman could utter them. Their language informs us about his characters' class, age, education, and provenance with a certainty that makes further description superfluous. So too their brief speeches give us a glimpse into his characters' souls that clumsier authors would require many pages of narrative to communicate.

Almost miraculous in this respect is Waugh's first novel, titled *Decline and Fall*, whose minor characters, though mere props in a farce, have a kind of inevitability and immortality: Once having read the lines Waugh gives them, you can't imagine their ever saying anything else. Something imperishable has been created out of nothing. You feel you'd know Dr. Fagan and Lady Beste-Chetwynde were you to overhear them in a bus. The quality persists in Waugh's later works, but only sporadically and only in the minor characters.

A third characteristic of Waugh the prose stylist is the concord between the rhythm of the paragraph and its meaning—a concord that is easier to perceive than it is to analyze. By the operation of some deep poetic instinct, the rise and fall of the narrative augment and reinforce the sense of the words that underlie it. Here is one example, from the travel book *When the Going Was Good*, describing an encounter with a young American on a lake steamer on the way to the Congo:

> I offered him a drink and he said "Oh no, thank you," in a tone which in four monosyllables contrived to express first surprise, then pain, then reproof, and finally forgiveness. Later I found that he was a member of the Seventh Day Adventist Mission, on his way to audit accounts at Bulawayo.

As with Edward Gibbon, every sentence in Waugh has a kind of architectural perfection; as did Gibbon, Waugh knew how to maximize the blunt impact of the monosyllabic word by its well-timed departure from a stream of elegant polysyllables. Waugh strove for economy of expression, such that the structural elements of this prose would each carry as much weight as possible. He frequently compared the writer's craft to that of a cabinetmaker or carpenter and saw the joinery of words as an indispensable task of artisanship. In a 1949 letter to Thomas Merton—who had sent him a draft of his book *The Waters of Siloe*—Waugh criticizes the monk for shirking this chore:

> In the non-narrative passages, do you not think you tend to be diffuse, saying the same thing more than once. I noticed this in *The Seven Storey Mountain* and the fault persists. It is pattern-bombing instead of precision bombing. You scatter a lot of missiles all round the target instead of concentrating on a single direct hit. It is not art. Your monastery tailor and boot-maker would not waste material. Words are our materials.

Waugh loathed the pretense of artists as members of a secular priesthood and insisted that exalted art did not exist apart from the humble craftsmanship that was a necessary, but not a sufficient, condition of its existence.

Yet the differences between Waugh and Thomas Merton were not limited to prose style, and this brings me to my second subject: Evelyn Waugh the Catholic. Both Merton and Waugh were converts to Catholicism, yet it would be difficult to find coeval co-religionists with more sharply contrasting approaches to their faith. Merton, the monk with the irrepressible ego, put the self on center stage to an extent that stood classical monasticism on its head; Waugh prized his religion precisely because it was objective, was doctrinally immutable, and by its inflexible demands aimed at mortifying the querulous self and its appetites. The English Jesuit Martin D'Arcy, who instructed Waugh prior to his conversion, remarked that he'd never known a convert for whom the *truth* of Catholic teaching was more closely scrutinized and, once accepted, more central to his faith.

It's important to stress that Waugh, himself an artist, was not attracted to the Catholic Church by any aesthetic appeal. As he remarked, the hymns, the great cathedrals, the ancient titles, the liturgy written in the heyday of English prose—all were the property of the Church of England. Had he been guided by his own taste, he would have remained an Anglican. The appeal of the Catholic Church was simply her universal claim to authority, which, once found valid, required submission of mind and will, without regard to whether and to what extent it was gratifying or irksome. The faith Waugh embraced could be called "impersonal," if by that term we mean not hostile to the person but sternly indifferent to the cravings and pleas of the ego. C. S. Lewis wrote that the Real is that which says to us, "Your preferences have not been considered." So too for Waugh, it was the fact that the Church had not consulted him, or any other creature, in the formulation of her doctrines that made her claim plausible. It's telling that when changes were proposed in the celebration of the Mass during the 1960s, Waugh rejected the accusation that defenders of the Latin Mass were either conservatives or aesthetic thrill-seekers, citing his own conversion as evidence:

> I was not at all attracted by the splendour of great ceremonies—which the Protestants could well counterfeit. Of the extraneous attractions of the Church which most drew me was the spectacle of the priest and

his server at low Mass, stumping up to the altar without a glance to discover how many or how few he had in his congregation; a craftsman and his apprentice; a man with a job which he alone was qualified to do. That is the Mass I have grown to know and love.

Waugh does not deny that the Catholic Church has aesthetic splendors to offer; what he denies is that such splendors provide a reliable basis for accepting the Church's claims as true. The feelings such splendors produce are sporadic and transitory, and those who wallow most deeply in them will feel cheated and distraught on the day their magic fails. Rather it is the ordinary daily Mass, the *opus operatum*, performed and assisted at out of duty rather than desire, that points to the objective reality of a universal immutable faith: your preferences have not been considered.

One of Waugh's lesser-known short stories is instructive in this respect. Its title, "Out of Depth," makes reference to the hero's being out of his depth in his collision with black magic, and simultaneously to the *De profundis clamavi*—the incipit of Psalm 130: "Out of the depths I cry to thee, O Lord." In the tale, the hero Rip, a languidly sybaritic bachelor, is thrust forward five hundred years into the future, to find London nothing but a marshland marked by hummocks and wattle huts inhabited by grunting white savages—a mirror image, in fact, of the Thames valley as it was twenty-five hundred years prior to his adventure. Dazed and disoriented by the vanishing of everything familiar to his senses, he sees imperial conquerors from Africa making their way up the Thames in a launch ("a large mechanically propelled boat, with an awning and a flag; a crew of smart Negroes, all wearing uniforms of leather and fur though it was high summer; a commander among the Negroes issuing orders in a quiet supercilious voice"). Rip is taken downstream with some other natives to a mission compound. The story concludes as Rip regains awareness of his surroundings. Waugh writes:

And then later—how much later he could not tell—something that was new and yet ageless. The word "Mission" painted on a board; a black man dressed as a Dominican friar ... and a growing clearness. Rip knew that out of strangeness, there had come into being something familiar; a shape in chaos. Something was being done. Something was being done that Rip knew; something that twenty-five centuries had not altered;

of his own childhood which survived the age of the world. In a log-built church at the coast town he was squatting among a native congregation; some of them in cast-off uniforms; the women had shapeless, convent-sewn frocks; all round him dishevelled white men were staring ahead with vague, uncomprehending eyes, to the end of the room where two candles burned. The priest turned towards them his bland, black face.

"*Ite, missa est.*"

In part, "Out of Depth" is a dig at Hilaire Belloc's view that "the Faith is Europe and Europe is the Faith." In part, it is a sly reference to Macaulay's famous tribute to the perpetuity of the Catholic Church given in his 1840 review of Leopold von Ranke's *History of the Popes*:

> She may still exist in undiminished vigour when some traveller from New Zealand shall, in the midst of a vast solitude, take his stand on a broken arch of London Bridge to sketch the ruins of St. Paul's.

Yet there's more to Waugh's story than a poke at Belloc or a nod to Macaulay. In Rip's projection into the future, all the political, cultural, and social solidities of twentieth-century Europe have disappeared; every complacency has been demolished. The contingencies of history have made conquering races out of the conquered, and new empires carry their civilizing schemes to the barbarian wilds that were once Piccadilly and Grosvenor Square. Only the spiritual realities remain unchanged, realities that are symbolized by the Mass but that include the moral and evangelical efforts of the missionaries, which are as deathless as the Church herself. We're not to imagine Rip as a pious, churchgoing Catholic—quite the contrary—yet the unsensational gestures and rhythms of the Low Mass provide, across the centuries, a touchstone of intelligibility: as Waugh puts it, "a shape in chaos."

A shape in chaos. This is the key phrase in "Out of Depth." The story is not a lament that Western civilization will decay into savagery. The point, rather, is that the sophisticated man-about-town and the grunting, scurrying savage are equally engaged in endeavors that are vain, transient, and, from the viewpoint of eternity, meaningless. External circumstances may flatter the one and humiliate the other, but in Waugh's perspective, the bushman and theatergoer are both immersed in a maelstrom of futility against which the Catholic faith is an unchanging, if dimly understood, still point and touchstone of the good, the true, and the beautiful. It's not that London's glitterati might become the great-great-grandsires of savages; to the extent they are disconnected from the true Church, the worldlings are already savages themselves.

Throughout his professional life, Waugh was both admired and feared for the lethality of his tongue and pen. Some have suggested that his practice of satire was incompatible with the Christian vocation. When Waugh was asked, "Are your books meant to be satirical?" he answered:

> No. Satire is a matter of period. It flourishes in a stable society and presupposes homogeneous moral standards—the early Roman Empire and eighteenth-century Europe. It is aimed at inconsistency and hypocrisy. It exposes polite cruelty and folly by exaggerating them. It seeks to produce shame. All this has no place in the Century of the Common Man where vice no longer pays lip service to virtue. The artist's only service to the disintegrated society of today is to create independent little systems of order of his own. I foresee in the dark age to come that the scribes may play the part of monks after the first barbarian victories. They were not satirists.

Like any author, Waugh bridled at having his works pigeonholed so as to be approved or rejected with reference to a single category; on these grounds, he is justified in rejecting the label of satirist. From our vantage point, however, we can smile at Waugh's claim that in his time (he wrote those words in 1946) vice no longer paid lip service to virtue. More to the point, Waugh the writer indisputably engages in the exaggeration of polite cruelty and folly, which on his own terms must be reckoned satire, however subsidiary he would rank satire among his artistic intentions. The attempt to illustrate Waugh's satiric art is beset by a disadvantage. His satire was not, like Dorothy Parker's, expressed in epigrams or pithy one-liners. It cannot be separated from the context from which it emerged so as to be repeated at a dinner party. His literary wit finds its poise in the balance of character, circumstance, and sudden felicity of language.

I want to argue that Waugh could not have been a great satirist were he not a Catholic, and, more controversially, that his satire had its source in appropriation of the truths of Catholicism rather than in extenuation of its precepts. Most fundamentally, it was Catholicism that made "Waugh the insular and class-conscious bully" into an internationalist taking the side of the underdog. His satire was subversive, and deliberately so. It is essential to grasp that his satire subverts the social and political tyrannies of our time.

There is, I admit, a good deal of subjectivity here. Both parties to a dispute may view themselves as David up against Goliath, and one man's needle may be another man's cudgel. We find in literary satire the same spectrum of moral and artistic value displayed in political cartoons. The best caricaturists help us see a new truth in an arresting and witty way. The worst—think of Julius Streicher of *Der Stürmer* and Boris Efimov of *Pravda*—strive to make their target not so much an object of ridicule as an object of hatred. Their exaggerations are indifferent to truth or falsehood and make a clandestine appeal to complacency—that is, they help us take pride in our bigotries and thus reinforce our vices. By the same token, satire may be used to fortify our contempt for some disfavored class, but it may have—and with the best authors does have—an emancipating element.

Consider the following passage in Waugh's 1942 novel, *Put Out More Flags*. It takes place in a Bloomsbury garret in which communist artists and atheist graduate students are gathered at the outbreak of World War II. They are unsure whether, as good Marxists, they should join the fight against Nazi Germany (and thus become unwilling defenders of bourgeois Britain) or else ignore the conflict entirely (and to that extent assist Hitler by weakening the war effort and spreading despondency). Waugh writes:

> There was a young man of military age in the studio; he was due to be called up in the near future. "I don't know what to do about it," he said, "Of course, I could plead conscientious objections, but I haven't got a conscience. It would be a denial of everything we've stood for if I said I had a conscience."
>
> "No, Tom," they said to comfort him. "We know you haven't got a conscience."
>
> "But then," said the perplexed young man, "if I haven't got a conscience, why in God's name should I mind so much saying that I have?"

Note that Waugh does more than get off a jest at the expense of Marxist intellectuals. He exposes and illuminates a radical flaw in Marxist orthodoxy, and that so concisely that it would take many pages of philosophical exposition to make the same point. We aren't moved to hate or despise leftists by this spoofing, yet we are inoculated against a great deal of nonsense by the wit displayed in the deftly revealed incongruity. Perhaps it's also worth mentioning that in the 1940s, Marxism enjoyed a great deal of prestige—certainly more than did Catholicism—among educated elites. Yet it's the Catholic David, whose faith has taught him what the word "conscience" means, who pulls the whiskers of the Stalinist Goliath.

As Dr. [Samuel] Johnson said, "A man had rather have a hundred lies told of him than one truth which he does not wish should be told." Anarchists hate to be exposed as autocrats. I think in this connection of Waugh's "Open Letter" to Nancy Mitford, in which he affected to find fault with her proposed model of an upper-class English family. Waugh objected that her portrait was inaccurate in that it included too few children. "Impotence and sodomy are socially OK," he wrote, "but birth control is flagrantly middle class."

Of course, Waugh was only feigning sympathy with Mitford's project and feigning a social rather than a moral objection to contraception. His inflexible Catholic convictions, as everyone understood, were provocatively masqueraded as class consciousness. The outrage that greeted this remark—or better, the humorlessness of the outrage—proved that Waugh's shaft had found its mark. He had hit on a truth—namely, the ill-hidden bad conscience of heathen England—it did not wish should be spoken.

One of the distinguishing characteristics of the Christian satirist—so I would argue—is that he places himself under the same moral judgment as his targets. That is, he acknowledges a single system of morality governing the satirist and the satirized and holds himself responsible to the same precepts. I believe few critics of Waugh have adequately emphasized the extent to which his satire cuts most deeply at his own pretensions and illusions. This is most evident in the semi-autobiographical novels, such as *The Ordeal of Gilbert Pinfold* and the *Sword of Honour* trilogy, but detectable in nearly all his fiction. Consider the following excerpt from *Helena*, Waugh's historical novel about the mother of the emperor Constantine. She was the wife of the Roman general Constantius Chlorus, and Waugh fancifully makes her the daughter of King Coel of Colchester. On a military mission to Britain, Constantius takes notice of Helena and asks her father for her hand. Coel is transformed from a mossy minor prince to become the upper-class Edwardian father, alarmed at the prospect of a southern European for a son-in-law. As did all fathers in similar situations, he tries to dissuade the suitor by pleading ignorance of his antecedents. "I daresay we seem old-fashioned in Britain, but we still care a great deal for such things."

> At last Constantius spoke. "You have a right to the information you seek, but I must beg you to respect my confidence. When I tell you, you will understand my hesitation. I would have preferred you to accept my word, but since you insist"—he paused to give full weight to his declaration—"I am of the Imperial Family."
>
> It fell flat. "You are, are you?" said Coel. "It's the first time I've ever heard of there being such a thing."
>
> "I am the great-nephew of the Divine Claudius.... Also," he added, "of the Divine Quintilius, whose reign, though brief, was entirely constitutional."
>
> "Yes," said Coel, "and apart from their divinity, who were they? Some of the emperors we've had lately, you know, have been"—very literally—"nothing to make a song about. It's one thing burning incense to them and quite another having them in the family. You must see that."

"Apart from their divinity, who *were* they?" An unsurpassably devastating verdict on the insularity, snobbery, and narcissistic delusions of the British upper class—and it comes from the pen of a Waugh. The capacity to make oneself the target of one's own mockery is, though not exactly humility, a kind of second cousin to humility, and points to the universalizing moral scope of a satire that instructs and does not merely deride. In his writing, Waugh made use of both Christian and un-Christian satire; I would argue that a blanket condemnation and blanket exoneration are equally misguided and that each specimen should be judged on its merits.

Judging on the basis of merit is a distinctive virtue of Philip Eade's new biography, titled *Evelyn Waugh: A Life Revisited*. Building on the achievements of Waugh's earlier biographers, Eade retells the story of Waugh's life primarily from the standpoint of relationships: father, mother, brother, schoolmasters, schoolfellows, wives, lovers, military superiors, children, and the many, many individuals of all ranks whom Waugh outraged or enchanted vividly enough to leave behind a report of the collision. Eade worked with the advantage of several documentary sources that the passage of time and changes in notions of literary propriety have made newly available to investigators, most notably the account of their marriage by Waugh's first wife, and the diaries of his commanding officer during the Battle of Crete. It is to our advantage that Eade presents his material with a scholar's eye: respectful of conflicting testimony, balanced in judgment, alert to bias in his sources, with a measured sympathy for Waugh and for the claims of those he failed or wounded. His biography restores, to some extent, many damaged reputations, and damages, to a lesser degree, a few others.

With commendable moderation and, I think, insight, Eade permits the severest judgments on the character of Waugh—and they were severe—to be those attested by Waugh himself, whereas the evidence for virtues contrary to his self-constructed image of truculent misanthropy comes from the first-person testimony of recipients of his silent but exceptional and exceptionally frequent acts of generosity. One gets the sense throughout his work that Eade has set his hounds to sniff out the documents and interviews that give the truth, even if unsensational, rather than the racy or amusing anecdote; yet in the end his evenhandedness serves to sharpen rather than blur the likeness he has crafted. In sum, Eade succeeds in giving a convincing picture of a complex man—one more interesting, in human terms, than the portrait the artist gave us of himself.

I conclude with a passage that touches on Waugh's early manhood and continues in various ways to resonate throughout his life. It occurs in the novel *Decline and Fall*, when Paul Pennyfeather, expelled from his Oxford college, seeks employment as a schoolmaster and is granted an interview by Dr. Augustus Fagan, headmaster of Llanabba School in Wales:

> "I understand, too, that you left your university rather suddenly. Now—why was that?"
>
> This was the question that Paul had been dreading, and, true to his training, he had resolved upon honesty.

"I was sent down, sir, for indecent behaviour."

"Indeed, indeed? Well, I shall not ask for details. I have been in the scholastic profession long enough to know that nobody enters it unless he has some very good reason which he is anxious to conceal."

Dr. Fagan's sublime cynicism is never more than half a degree below room temperature and is expressed by unhurried, syntactically flawless disgust; his squalid criminal enterprises seem impelled more by boredom than venality. In moral terms, he is the point-by-point antithesis of Gervase, the saintly aristocrat and father of Guy Crouchback in the *Sword of Honour* trilogy. As creations, these equally urbane and imperturbable English gentlemen stand at the beginning and toward the end of Waugh's authorial life, yet the virtuous elder Crouchback is one of the very few minor characters in Waugh's repertory who fail to amuse. Endowed from boyhood with the ability to give pain and give delight, Waugh found it a lifelong task to learn how to edify; neither by his pen nor in his personal life did he wholly succeed. It is a testament to his character, and his faith, that he tried at all.

The Gospel according to David Bentley

The New Testament: A Translation
By David Bentley Hart

David Bentley Hart's new single-handed translation of the New Testament will strike the fair-minded reader by turns as startling, incisive, audacious, smug, shrewd, and quirky to the point of exasperation: everything, in short, the author intended it to be. The book sets out to be provocative and succeeds. A philosopher, theologian, scholar of patristics and mythology, and frequent contributor to *First Things*, Hart maintains that his dissatisfaction with the standard renderings of the Bible—each the product of committees and therefore of numberless harmful compromises—convinced him of the value of starting from scratch and making a one-man job of it.

The work consists of the twenty-seven books of the New Testament, transmitted in what Hart calls his "almost pitilessly literal" translation. Framing the translation itself are a lengthy introduction and a "Concluding Scientific Postscript," written with the lucidity and cheery truculence characteristic of Hart's essays. In these sections he sets out the purposes of his project, explains his strategy of translation, declares independence from a priori doctrinal and theological constraints, and provides a discussion of his more controversial renderings of key words that, somewhat paradoxically, amounts to an original theology of the New Testament in miniature.

It is a truism that those who know the Bible only through translations are cut off from a good deal of what is communicated in the original texts. It is also widely recognized that translations made over-familiar by liturgical or personal repetition tend to steer the mind of the reader down habitual paths and for that reason insulate him from what is terrible or perplexing in the text. Hart acknowledges this, but he also makes a point more rarely considered: that scholars

Originally published in *First Things*, November 2017.

accustomed to reading biblical documents in the original languages—
especially those who believe they have "gotten a feel" for the voice
of the ancient author—likewise glide over much that is ambiguous
and problematic, and that it isn't until one is forced to *translate*, that
is, to reformulate the familiar phrases using the equipment of another
language, that the difficulties announce themselves with full impact.
Says Hart:

> To translate a text is to be conducted into its mysteries in a way that
> no mere act of reading—however conscientious or frequent—makes
> possible. At the very least, the translator is obliged to confront the
> words on the page not merely as meanings to be received, but as prob-
> lems to be solved; and this demands an attention to detail for which
> most of us never quite have the time.

The problems Hart refers to are of two sorts: places where we
know what the Greek says but find English (or whatever the receptor
language may be) inadequate in conveying the meanings, and places
where the meaning (or text) of the Greek is itself in doubt. In addition, many readers have doctrinal or theological commitments that in
effect cut them off from readings that the original texts permit, and
sometimes compel.

Hart is well aware that few scholars will applaud all his decisions,
and admits his preference for choosing the "unfamiliar or more baf-
fling interpretation" because it is unsettling—and because it is sometimes more accurate. Even those of us convinced that the Holy Spirit
is the author of Sacred Scripture are rarely attentive to how many
purely human anticipatory choices, based on purely human prudence,
are involved in deciding for each particular verse which text, which
grammatical and syntactical analysis, and which translational rendering best reflect the sacred author—and thus end up on the printed
page of our English Bibles. Inasmuch as one goal of Hart's eccentric
formulations is to make us rethink the validity of the accepted ones,
he provides a useful service, even where we judge him wrong, in
pushing us back to the original texts to assess the plausibility of the
rival claims. If, after considering the evidence, we decide the conventional expression remains superior to Hart's alternative, our preference is no longer a sentimental loyalty but a choice more alive to the
ambiguities of the original.

This New Testament is not intended for liturgical use. The awkward bits are not smoothed over. "Where an author has written bad
Greek," says Hart, "I have written bad English." If he is to wake
us from our dogmatic slumber, his prose must not purr. But it is
in his choice of diction that Hart anticipates (and perhaps deserves)
the greatest resistance. *Gehenna*, *Ioudaios*, and *kosmos*, for example,
are programmatically rendered "Vale of Hinnom," "Judaean," and
"cosmos" in place of the familiar "hell," "Jew," and "world." In his
"Concluding Scientific Postscript," the author provides justification
for his treatment of these and another dozen key terms. Hart translates
Greek *makarios* not "blessed" but "blissful," explaining that it was
a word "whose original connotations meant something like 'divine
blessedness' or 'the bliss of the gods.'" The result is that we get "How
blissful those who mourn ... how blissful the peacemakers" as well
as (at Caesarea Philippi) "Blissful are you, Simon bar-Jonah, for flesh
and blood did not reveal this to you."

After the initial shock, and after consulting the explanation in the
appendix, most of us will concede that by foregrounding the nuance
of *divine* beatitude, Hart has extended our appreciation of the term
makarios in a valuable way. Yet Jesus was not speaking Greek but
Aramaic, which raises a deeper question of methodology: In making a translation of a translation of a lost original, is it legitimate to
make use of a term which pivots on a nuance that obtains in the
transmitting but not in the transmitted language? That is, in turning
into English first-century Greek that was itself recording spoken discourse (to which we have no independent access) in Aramaic, are we
justified in trading on refinements of Greek for which there was no
Aramaic counterpart?

It seems to me it can be argued both ways—which are equally cir-
cular. Scholar A asserts that by finding distinctions in the Greek that
didn't exist in Aramaic, the English translator risks making "ghost
claims" impossible or irrelevant to the original speaker. Scholar B
replies that, in default of the speaker's actual words, we simply trust
that the author (here, the evangelist), in applying refinements of Greek,
accurately conveyed meanings presumably expressed by paraphrastic
locutions in the Aramaic original. Given the rival contentions—"We
have to know what a man *could* say before we know what he *did* say"
and "We have to know what a man *did* say before we know what he

could say"—I see no way of deciding the matter that doesn't beg the question at issue.

The difficulty is more vexing in the consideration of what is perhaps Hart's most earnest and ambitious novelty: the translation of the Greek adjective *aiōnios*—where it has been conventionally rendered "eternal"—by the formula "of the Age" (with variants). This innovation will be particularly controversial because it has consequences for our understanding of the biblical basis for the theological concepts of eternal life, eternal punishment, and the eternity of God. Hart makes a convincing case for a meaning of *aiōnios* in Jewish Hellenistic Greek of the first century that supports his rendering, but I remain unpersuaded by his argument as a whole, for the reason that *aiōnios* almost certainly continues the corresponding terms in biblical Hebrew (*ōlām*) and Aramaic (*'ālam*), whose lexical history only partially overlaps that of *aiōnios*. Now Hart is fully aware of this, yet he contends (implausibly, in my opinion) that the Old Testament *ōlām* also means "age" in a sense congruent with Greek *aiōn*. Of course Hart might with perfect consistency concede that biblical Hebrew *ōlām* sometimes means "eternity" and yet deny that this meaning is shining through the adjective *aiōnios* as used in the New Testament. Once again, it boils down to conflicting intuitions about biblical semantics and the uses to which the sacred author put his semi-Semitized Greek.

These pedantries should not obscure the measure of Hart's achievement and the principal virtue of his translation: he conveys exceptionally well the *urgency* of the New Testament. The message itself is of supreme and burning importance, and the authors were in a hurry to get it out, and Hart lets us feel this "from the inside"—most successfully in his version of the Gospels. His translational prose is emphatically non-professorial. He conscientiously preserves the rough-and-ready grammar of the original and its "wartime-footing," functional vocabulary that combines homely household words with sublime theological concepts, with the result that the peculiar tang of New Testament Greek comes through with vividness and immediacy. Here is his rendering of Luke 23:50–52:

> And look: A man named Joseph, who was a member of the Council, a man good and just—This man had not agreed with the Council and their actions—from Arimathea, a city of the Judaeans, who was

awaiting the kingdom of God. Approaching Pilate, this man requested the body of Jesus.

Hart lets us hear a man who, though not precisely breathless, does not have a complete sentence in view before he begins it but is nevertheless concerned to communicate all the essential information and whose second thoughts and explanations interrupt and crowd their way into his exposition. The prose itself—we don't need a footnote—reminds us that St. Luke was not an essayist or a biographer but an evangelist, a man with a message of life-or-death importance to deliver.

Hart's version of the Pauline and Catholic epistles likewise gives voice to the insistent earnestness of the authors, and evidence of the blood, sweat, and tears of the translator himself in grappling with the manifold thorny difficulties (textual, syntactical, theological) of these documents. He does a particularly thorough job of disentangling the diction of Romans from the theology of Reformation controversy but displays throughout an alertness to covert theological claims hiding in the ambiguity of the Greek. One need not agree with Hart's judgment as to whether the claims were or were not made by the sacred author to be grateful for his flagging the problems. Or again, the great anthems at the beginning of Colossians and Ephesians, so melodious in the Latin of the Liturgy of the Hours, are dismayingly clunky at first reading; however, having chewed through the difficulties while reading Hart synoptically with the originals, one returns to the familiar beauties inoculated against several misunderstandings.

For whom is the book intended? Hart avers that a new translation is likely to cause consternation "in countless breasts," but this surmise is predicated on the assumption that the alarm will be caused by encountering the unfamiliar in place of the expected. Yet how many are there today for whom *any* translation of the Bible could be called familiar? Apart from a pious remnant, most readers would find the Authorized Version no less exotic than Hart's. My hunch is that those who will best profit from this work are serious students of the Bible: theologians, seminarians, clergy with a sermon to prepare, and, most of all, New Testament exegetes (for whom the cant phrase "target audience" is, in this instance, only partly metaphorical). My own review copy has been on my desk for less than a month, and I

have already consulted it a couple dozen times on questions of interpretation, sometimes concurring, always learning something new. I
can picture a similarly shabby clergyman or academic crouched in his
study a hundred years from now, flummoxed by the syntax of Galatians or 1 Peter, giving up and stretching an arm to his bookcase with
a sigh: "I wonder what sense that wild man Hart managed to make
of this shambles."

Historical-Critical Qur'an

The Qur'ān and the Bible: Text and Commentary
By Gabriel Said Reynolds

This book is misleadingly named. The blame, if blame there be, rests with the stingy conventions of contemporary publishing. The work deserves one of those splendidly prolix seventeenth-century titles, of the kind that required three progressively diminished fonts in order to fit on the title page: *A New English Rendering of The Qur'an, being a Revision by the Author of the celebrated Translation of Ali Quli Qarai, together with a seriatim Commentary shewing the manifold narrative Tributaries ultimately derived from the Old and New Testaments of the Bible, with particular Attention to various Syriac Christian Vehicles of Transmission, enriched by the Annotations and Explanations of sundry eminent Scholars: Muslim, Jewish, and Christian alike, together with a compendious Bibliography, &c.*

A professor of Islamic studies and theology at Notre Dame, Reynolds has given us a complete Qur'an—highly useful in itself—annotated so as to illustrate and expound those pre-Qur'anic sources indirectly descended from the Bible. Of a typical page, two-thirds might be devoted to verses (*'ayāt*) of the Qur'an, and the remainder to interspersed commentary citing and explaining parallels that can plausibly be regarded as tributary. Reynolds has consciously limited his focus, centering on what he calls the "conversation" by which "the Qur'ān alludes to, and develops, earlier traditions." Says Reynolds:

> The absence of direct quotations of Jewish and Christian texts in the Qur'ān reflects the path these texts took to reach the Qur'ān's author. As Sidney Griffith has argued, neither the Bible nor other Jewish and Christian texts were available in Arabic at the time of the Qur'ān's origins. The author of the Qur'ān would have heard only descriptions or

Originally published in *First Things*, November 2018.

paraphrases of such texts rendered into Arabic orally, most likely from some form of the Semitic language known as Aramaic.... My argument that the Qur'ān is so closely, or organically, related to the Bible represents a departure from traditional ideas that the background of the Qur'ān is largely pagan (and partially Jewish).

Reynolds' mention of the Aramaic language points to a key element in his "conversation." From the eighth century B.C., Aramaic had been the lingua franca of the Near East, and with the rise and spread of Christianity, the dialect of Aramaic known as Syriac became a major literary language in Eastern Christendom, operating as the vector not only of liturgy and theology but of a plebeian Christian folk culture as well. Following the path laid out in the 2011 Princeton dissertation of Joseph Witztum, *The Syriac Milieu of the Quran*, Reynolds is particularly attentive to the ways in which Syriac literature had fastened upon certain biblical accounts and reshaped them in characteristic fashion, traces of which are discernible in their Qur'anic adaptations. Syriac literature included creations of high intellectual culture but was not limited to them. We also have documents produced by folk religion and the often giddy imagination of popular piety. Some of the apocryphal infancy narratives of the life of Jesus belong to this latter category. The literature displays a recognizably Syriac fable-forming mechanism with a folkloristic proclivity, otherwise familiar to us in the way Christmas carols make use of the Bible, re-fashioning the narrative in the service of apologetic or didactic or sentimental purposes, yet always so as to foreground the gestural and picturesque.

An instructive example of Reynolds' bringing biblical and Qur'anic episodes into conversation is found in the story of Joseph and the wife of Potiphar. The story the Bible tells in fourteen verses (Gen 39:7–20) is expanded into thirty-one by the Qur'an (12:23–53), and from the outset it is evident that the reticence of the earlier author is to be remedied:

> The woman in whose house he was, solicited him. She closed the doors and said "Come!!" He said, "God forbid! He is indeed my Lord; he has given me a good abode. Indeed, the wrongdoers do not prosper." She surely made for him; and he would have made for her [too] had he not beheld the proof of his Lord. So it was, that We might turn away from him all evil and indecency. He was indeed one of Our

dedicated servants. They raced to the door, and she tore his shirt from behind, and they ran into her husband at the door. She said, "What is to be the requital of him who has evil intentions for your wife except imprisonment or a painful punishment?" He said, "It was she who solicited me." A witness of her own household testified [saying]: "If his shirt is torn from the front, she tells the truth and he lies. But if his shirt is torn from behind, then she lies and he tells the truth." So when he saw that his shirt was torn from behind, he said, "This is [a case] of you women's guile! Your guile is great indeed! Joseph, let this matter alone, and you, woman, plead for forgiveness for your sin, for you have indeed been erring" (12:23–29).

In his commentary on the passage, Reynolds gives us, by way of contrast, the spare text from Genesis, then points to an exegetical fable in the Babylonian Talmud in which Joseph had decided to relent to the woman's importuning but corrected himself after receiving a miraculous vision in which his father, Jacob, upbraids him; it is suggested this may account for the "proof of his Lord" mentioned but not explained in the Qur'an. The test for determining Joseph's guilt or innocence, that is, the location of the rip in his shirt, has no basis in Genesis and is missing from other Jewish sources but is to be found, Reynolds notes, in the Syriac Christian homilies of Narsai and Pseudo-Narsai (fifth century A.D.).

What the Qur'anic author (or his yet undiscovered sources) has himself contributed are the words of the husband's address to his wife and, in admonishment, to womankind; the sententious truism of Joseph ("wrongdoers do not prosper"); and, most characteristically, the kind of narrator's apostrophe—editorially indicated by the capitalized "We" and "Our"—by which the reader is addressed in the first person plural (we Muslims) in order that the proper moral lessons are made explicit. That is to say, the Qur'an distances itself from its own narrative just far enough to pass judgment on its truth and godliness. Equally interesting is what is not made explicit in the Qur'an. The author's many oblique references and allusory technique depend upon a common knowledge of stories told elsewhere. Almost certainly we have to postulate an extensive oral culture that provided the background information needed to make the stories cogent and complete. Where we lack the "story behind the story," the Qur'anic discourse often seems gauzy and perplexing. (Compare the Qur'an's account with the unity, lucidity, and economy of the account of the serpent and the woman in Genesis 3.)

Figures from the Old and New Testaments are often given a second life and novel history by the Qur'an, in accordance with the particular interests and sentiments of the author. The Qur'an has the newborn Jesus speak to Mary, telling her to shake the trunk of the palm under which he was born so as to feed herself on the dates that drop (19:25). Jesus announces to the Israelites that, as a sign to them, he will shape birds out of clay and vivify them by his breath (3:49); he is raised alive to heaven by God (3:55), though it is not altogether clear that he died first. Mary is herself the sister of Aaron (19:28), taken as an infant by Zechariah to live in the sanctuary of the Temple, where he tended to her and God miraculously fed her (3:37). Reynolds indicates the pertinent parallels with apocryphal Scriptures of the early Christian centuries. The Qur'an displays a strong affinity for the anecdotal among these episodes: those which present themselves vividly to the pictorial imagination or which conclude with a striking and memorable utterance, usually aphoristic in nature.

The Qur'anic treatment of Abraham illustrates a more evident moralizing. In the Bible, Abraham becomes the father of true worship of the one true God by virtue of his divine election and obedient response. Whatever cult he paid to native deities before his call is not mentioned, and we are not told that Abraham destroyed paganism and graven images so as to clear the ground in anticipation of his election. In later Jewish midrashic texts, however, Abraham's father, Terah, is depicted as a maker and seller of idols. In the account given in the *Genesis Rabbah*, Abraham demolishes these idols on the day he is left in charge of his father's shop. In the Qur'an (21:51–66), Abraham finds himself in a location with many idols and smashes all but the largest one among them. When arraigned for the sacrilege, he answers that it was the large idol itself who had shattered the smaller ones, taunting the idolaters, "Ask them, if they can speak," thereby confounding his accusers and winning his acquittal. Here again it would appear that the biblical account—if indeed it was known at all—was regarded as insufficiently explicit and insufficiently memorable to serve the author's didactic purposes, among which communicating a detestation of idolatry was paramount. Thus, the tidily dramatized moralism of the midrash was brought into service.

Unlike the rabbis or the Syrian monks of the time, the author of the Qur'an was not part of a literary culture working within a tradition of manuscript recension and transmission. Reynolds makes an important point: "The Qur'ān is the first book in the history of Arabic literature. There was no preexisting canon of Arabic works to which the Qur'ān's author could turn. Accordingly he benefited from a variety of different linguistic and literary traditions which were transmitted orally in the Late Antique Near East." If there was no tradition of monoglot writing at this place and time, it stands to reason that, by the same token, there was no tradition of reading, that is, of reading silently by and for oneself. We are obliged to consider that the first Arabic book was not offered to its first audience as a folio placed in the hands and consumed in private but was itself read and expounded aloud and to that extent partaking of the same cultural energies that produced it. In tracing the development of the sources of the Qur'anic text, Reynolds may have provided some clues toward its exegesis as well, just as the historical-critical methods have illuminated the Old and New Testaments in interesting and useful ways.

This is a well-produced book, and a book laid out with working scholars in mind. The commentary is not placed in footnotes but on the main pages, in a legible font, immediately following the verses discussed. Reynolds is generously redundant in his annotations, reiterating arguments and bibliography that apply to more than one passage instead of obliging the reader to chase down cross-references, endnotes, appendices, etc., so as to patch it all together by himself. This considerateness has fattened the tome beyond a thousand pages but makes it that much easier to use. Reynolds' own writing is pleasingly plain, clear, undoctrinaire. He is out to inform rather than dispute, and succeeds.

His Excellency

American Priest: The Ambitious Life and Conflicted Legacy of Notre Dame's Father Ted Hesburgh
By Wilson D. Miscamble, C.S.C.

In 2008, Father Theodore Hesburgh (1917–2015) gave an interview to the *Wall Street Journal* in which he said, "I have no problem with females or married people as priests, but I realize that the majority of the leadership in the Church would." True, he was ninety-one at the time, and had long been retired as the president of Notre Dame, but the debonair self-confidence with which he conflated doctrine and discipline was entirely characteristic of the man, as was his subordination of both to the imperatives of liberal sentimentalism. He was an American priest.

Father Wilson Miscamble, like Hesburgh a priest of the Congregation of Holy Cross, joined the history faculty at Notre Dame in 1988 and knew Hesburgh personally. When he approached Hesburgh in 1994 with the proposal of writing his biography, Hesburgh was initially hesitant: "He ... explained that it would be hard for a single historian to capture in a full and meaningful way the extent of his actions over the years." Hesburgh was not one to underestimate the magnitude of his accomplishments, and throughout his career was actively, even punctiliously, concerned with the curatorship of his reputation and legacy. Miscamble prevailed, happily, and brings to the task the extraordinary advantages of firsthand acquaintance with the man himself, intimate knowledge of Notre Dame and many of the key players in the pertinent period, and approximately thirty hours of interviews recorded in the summer of 1998, conducted expressly for the purposes of the biography.

Originally published in *First Things*, April 2019.

For all that, Miscamble starts with a singular disadvantage, namely, that his protagonist had none. Most biographers have a level of interest built into their narrative simply by recounting the struggles of their subject in overcoming adversity: the usual ups and downs, setbacks and triumphs, that attend the early lives of the famous. Never was Hesburgh an underdog. His career, from the time he left high school, was an unbroken series of advances, successes followed by more successes, rescued from monotony only by one's curiosity as to how long the string might remain intact. Hesburgh was a man of exceptional energy, ambition, charisma, and self-control, endowed with a precise knowledge of his own abilities. He focused on using those abilities to advance himself and the institutions in which his allegiances were enshrined. In this he succeeded brilliantly.

In Miscamble's telling, Hesburgh's loyalties as a young man were typical of an upper-middle-class American Catholic of his era. He was conventionally patriotic in his churchmanship and citizenship, and studies in Rome and France in the late 1930s resulted in few strong attachments in either place. They did, however, give him a familiarity with the mechanisms of ecclesiastical influence, which he used to his benefit throughout his career. Assigned in 1945 to the Holy Cross community at Notre Dame, he immediately caught the attention of administrators, acquitted himself masterfully in a series of progressively demanding positions, and was named (by his religious superior) president of the university in 1952. On Hesburgh's retirement in 1987, Notre Dame's annual budget had grown from less than $10 million to $176 million, its endowment from $9 million to $350 million, student enrollment from five thousand to ten—and his own stature in the public eye increased proportionately. The evolution of Hesburgh's allegiances is a more complicated story.

Hesburgh seems to have been almost preternaturally astute at choosing subordinates: men of exceptional competence and energy willing to put both at the service of their leader's direction. Hesburgh didn't surround himself with yes-men, but he was nervous in the company of assistants as ambitious as himself, and displeased whenever football coaches received more media attention than he. More than once in this biography one is reminded of Herodotus' account of Thrasybulus of Miletus, who, when asked for instruction in the art of autocracy, strode silently through a field of wheat, snicking off with his switch the head of every conspicuously higher stalk. By the same token, Hesburgh became resentful of direction—which he viewed as interference—on the part of agencies claiming superior authority, most notably the Holy See and his own religious congregation. Much of his career as a churchman and educator was spent in declaring, and effecting, independence from the Church, even as he emphasized the atmospherics of pious, picturesque Catholicism: choirs, clerical garb, the Marian grotto.

An instructive example is found in the history of Hesburgh's ideas on the nature of Catholic higher education. Already in his first term as president he was lecturing on the subject. In a 1953 address to the faculty titled "A Theology of History and Education," he said, "We do not rest in human reason, or human values, or human sciences—but we certainly do begin our progress in time with all that is human in its excellence. Then, after the pattern of the Incarnation, we consecrate all our human excellence to the transforming influence of Christ in our times." In a 1954 talk, called "The Mission of a Catholic University" (note, by the way, the last-word-on-the-subject swagger of his titles), Hesburgh said that the task of a Catholic university was one "that no secular university today can undertake—for they are largely cut off from the tradition of adequate knowledge which comes only through faith in the mind and faith in God, the highest wisdom of Christian philosophy and Catholic theology." Deprived of context, one might be forgiven for thinking that these passages came from *Ex Corde Ecclesiae*, Pope John Paul II's 1990 apostolic constitution on the Catholic university. Yet by 1990, Hesburgh was vigorously opposed to *Ex Corde* and its ecclesiology. Says Miscamble, "He and Dick McBrien [then chair of the Notre Dame theology department] let no opportunity pass to express their opposition to what they saw as a dangerous challenge to the institutional autonomy of Notre Dame and a wrongheaded assault on the American approach to higher education."

Much had happened in the intervening years; most important—at their midpoint, in July of 1967—Hesburgh summoned a group of carefully chosen Catholic educators to an informal caucus at the Land O' Lakes villa in Wisconsin, including sympathetic college presidents from the U.S. and Canada and Father Theodore McCarrick, president of the University of Puerto Rico. The discussion resulted in a manifesto insisting on the independence of the academy:

The Catholic university today must be a university in the full modern sense of the word, with a strong commitment to and concern for academic excellence. To perform its teaching and research functions effectively, the Catholic university must have a true autonomy and academic freedom in the face of authority of whatever kind, lay or clerical, external to the academic community itself.

The term "excellence" has become so debased today as an empty buzz-word that it is hard to believe it was once taken seriously. It was in fact a key concept, a non-negotiable, for Hesburgh, who Miscamble shows was caught up in the "near-mania for excellence" (Philip Gleason's phrase) that intoxicated Catholic educators after the issuance in 1958 of a Rockefeller Brothers Fund report called, without embarrassment, *The Pursuit of Excellence*. Hesburgh believed excellence in higher education to be objective and measurable, metered by the volumes in the university library, faculty salary levels, value of government research grants, percentage of faculty with doctorates in hand, and so forth. Nor was he in doubt about the way forward; Miscamble quotes Hesburgh more than once as saying that the ten greatest universities in the United States are those with the ten richest endowments, and he made it his goal to do the fundraising necessary for Notre Dame to buy its way into the premier league. It was an era of confidence in "the best and the brightest," of Management by Objectives. The Land O' Lakes statement's insistence on a secular notion of excellence, and Hesburgh's enthusiasm for it, should be viewed against this background of managerial optimism. Yet his fellow priests and religious spotted the flaw in Hesburgh's project of severing the mooring lines between Church and university; Miscamble's verdict on Hesburgh is as devastating as it is understated: "Without making a major and formal decision he began to allow what might be called the pursuit of excellence approach to supplant the pursuit of the truth."

Among the good things on offer in the book is Miscamble's perspective from inside the religious community that founded, and remains connected to, the University of Notre Dame. We learn, for example, that in 1969 priests of the Holy Cross accounted for fifteen full professors, twenty associates, and twenty-two assistants at Notre Dame—numbers unimaginable today for any order at any university. He describes how Hesburgh, resentful of his order's prerogative of naming its members to university posts, negotiated a two-tier trustee system on the Harvard-Berkeley model with a lay majority; how he outmaneuvered his superiors in their plans that Notre Dame fund a seminary on its campus; how he arranged that presidents succeeding him, though restricted to priests of the Holy Cross Congregation, would no longer be assigned to the job by the superior but proposed to the board for confirmation. We see too how the balance of power shifted, as a man in charge of an enterprise with a couple thousand employees and a budget of over a hundred million dollars not only gained ascendancy over his nominal religious superior but was able to advance, stall, or redirect the careers of many of his brother priests. Hesburgh was seldom bashful in wielding his influence.

Hesburgh's climacteric year was 1968. The political turmoil of the time affected the student body, no longer docile under traditional measures of campus discipline, even when conveyed by Father Ted. Sentiment for and against the Vietnam War alienated Hesburgh from friends and political contacts on both sides of the issue. His steadfast and courageous stance on civil rights was inadequate, in some circles, to the new urgency in racial grievances. But for Hesburgh the Catholic, Hesburgh the priest, it was *Humanae Vitae* that starred the mirror once and forever.

The policy wonks of *The Pursuit of Excellence* generation were perfectly capable of devising countermeasures against political threats; what they failed to grasp was the depth of the lifestyle revolution, and its promise of sexual freedom, communicated to the younger generation through its headphones. Like the three hundred foxes Samson used to terrorize the Philistines, the issues that convulsed the universities in 1968 were joined by the tail.

Well before 1968, Hesburgh himself had large areas of sympathy for the sexual revolution. Since 1961, he had been on the board of directors of the Rockefeller Foundation, which advocated "population control" measures—including abortion, sterilization, and contraception—in underdeveloped nations. While he consistently dissented from the Foundation's promotion of abortion, he concurred with the other proposals, and his priesthood as well as his personal prestige helped—as the Foundation and he knew it would—to defuse some of the Catholic resistance. Further, Miscamble documents that

Hesburgh lent support to a series of meetings held at Notre Dame annually from 1963 to 1967, sponsored by the Rockefeller and Ford Foundations in collaboration with the Planned Parenthood Federation, ostensibly aimed at the "population problem" but intended to provide, in the words of historian Donald Critchlow, "a liberal forum to create an oppositional voice within the Catholic Church on the issue of family planning." Having done what was in his power in the matter, Hesburgh was confident that Pope Paul VI would accede to a change in Church teaching and was shocked when, in July of 1968, he was proven wrong.

[Protestant moral theologian] Stanley Hauerwas remarked, "It has been the project of liberal political and ethical theory to create just societies without just people, primarily by attempting to set in place social institutions and/or discover moral principles that ensure cooperation among people who share no common goods or virtues." To some extent, Hesburgh's support of population control measures was of a piece with the "management control systems" approach to problem-solving associated with Robert McNamara and the Whiz Kids of the early 1960s, predicated on the conviction that, if the right policies were implemented by the right personnel, personal moral choice became irrelevant to social change. On the other hand, Hesburgh, together with many liberal Catholics, had been infected by the sentimentalisms that the "human face" of the sexual revolution transmitted through its summer-of-love mawkishness.

For Hesburgh's fellow academics in the main, the permissibility of contraception had long been accepted, and they had moved on to push for easing constraints on homosexual activity and abortion. Miscamble relates a telling moment during an address at Yale in 1973 when Hesburgh included a few sentences in strong opposition to abortion, and female members of the audience hissed him into silence. Miscamble claims this was a turning point, in the wrong direction, for Hesburgh:

> Whatever his response to the hissing Yale feminists, he thereafter failed to make abortion and the right to life one of the great issues that he chose to address forcefully. To have pursued it vigorously would have put him at odds with the liberal establishment figures with whom he wanted to associate in tackling global poverty and world peace.

Hesburgh, painful as it is to acknowledge, was not the same man who in 1953 had urged his faculty to consecrate themselves to "the transforming influence of Christ in our times." Though he occasionally growled at the disappearance of traditional Catholic decorum in matters of courtship and sexuality, fear of being lumped with the defenders of *Humanae Vitae*—the thick-necked "red meat and rosary" folks who typified working-class Catholicism—robbed him of his voice. We're told that when Notre Dame's Student Life Council voted to allow women's visitation in the male dorms, he "yielded without a murmur." The prestige he had won for himself was, quite simply, too precious to lose. In all matters, Hesburgh was as idealistic as expedience allowed.

Miscamble provides another glimpse into the character of his subject that merits reflection. He tells us that while Hesburgh had great affection for Pope John XXIII and deep sympathy for Paul VI, he never warmed to John Paul II, put off by his hardline anticommunism, his dismantling of Vatican *Ostpolitik* (which Hesburgh strongly favored), and his robust defense of Catholic teaching on abortion and sexual morality. Still, Hesburgh accepted an invitation by President Jimmy Carter to a reception for the pope on the South Lawn of the White House, at the conclusion of his pastoral visit to the U.S. in October of 1979:

> Father Ted, who was seated close to the front of the animated crowd, remembered being struck that everyone was straining and reaching out for the pope when he and the president walked by. He made a point of reaching out to Carter and assuring him: "We love you too, Mr. President."

Hesburgh may have felt that Carter was in need of reassurance, but it's hard not to see a twinge of regret at the admiration shown John Paul II. No one could call Hesburgh a mere spectator in regard to the problems of the world; he worked assiduously, and at the highest levels, to confront the crises of his time. But his work took place in committee rooms. John Paul II was a man who had experienced danger firsthand, a man who had helped make history by heroic fidelity to his Catholic faith, a man of exceptional and genuine intellectual attainments, a man—most of all—who patently believed in the truths that Hesburgh had himself professed in 1953 but abandoned at the hissing of a New Haven lecture hall. Small wonder if the moment was awkward for him.

Walking around the Notre Dame campus in his retirement, Hesburgh saw his legacy enshrined in two substantial buildings that already bore his name: one is the Hesburgh Center for International Studies, the other is the university library, bearing the famous *Word of Life* exterior mural depicting Jesus surrounded by apostles, saints, and scholars. Hesburgh told Miscamble he came to regret the absence of any women in the mural, a remark that dates the change in his sensibilities and those of our own time (according to which exogenous gender assignment is itself iniquitous). What is dismaying is Hesburgh's inability to unwind, his ceaseless need to fine-tune his reputation, here—as in the *Wall Street Journal* interview—by his genuflection in the direction of feminism. He passed his life in the gaze of the Lidless Eye of his obituarist. Perhaps for this reason he fails to humanize himself convincingly, even in the indiscretions confided to his biographer. Like Evelyn Waugh's Apthorpe, he "tended to become faceless and tapering the closer he approached." Were his private correspondence to be published, it would almost certainly reveal nothing he didn't already make sure that we knew about himself.

There is one delightful exception, an occasion in which Hesburgh cashed in his chips and gratified an impulse for its own sake. Having done some favors for Jimmy Carter, he browbeat the president into muscling him onto a Lockheed SR-71 for a wholly gratuitous supersonic flight. Able for once to be a boy as well as a man, the author of *The Humane Imperative* got himself a ride on the fire truck to end all fire trucks. He had bought much shabbier wares at a much dearer price; one hopes he enjoyed it.

APPENDIX

THE DRINAN FILES—A MEMORANDUM

Memorandum on the Drinan Candidacy and the NE Prov Archives

Paul Mankowski, S.J.
April 2007*

I—Background

In 1991 I was living at Faber House (42 Kirkland Street) in Cambridge, Massachusetts, while doing doctoral studies at Harvard. On February 5 of that year, Father William Guindon, S.J.,[1] the Provincial of the New England Province from 1968 to 1974, was a dinner guest at Faber House and reminisced for the assembled company about the recently dead Father Arrupe. One of his anecdotes went like this:

> Well, I was over in Beirut at the time and Arrupe summoned me to Rome. That's when I was still Provincial. He said, "I want you to tell Fr. Drinan to withdraw from the election"—this was his first run for office—"it is in violation of canon law!" I told him, "No no no, you don't want to do that; you don't understand American politics; you'll cause more trouble than it's worth. That's not the way to do it; just pray that he loses." Then Arrupe said, "All right. But this is the last time! Never again for him or anyone else!" So Bob had the permission of all three ordinaries. Then when I got back to province I found John McLaughlin in my office asking for permission to run for the Senate in Rhode Island. I said, "Can't give you permission, John." He said, "Why not?" I said, "For one thing Fr. Arrupe has forbidden it. For another I think you've got a wheel loose."

Guindon's language recorded here is very close to verbatim. Immediately after the dinner I made notes transcribing his account

---

*The background to and rationale for the publication of this memorandum is found in the Introduction. Ed.

[1] To aid narrative clarity and avoid the appearance of unequal respect, Jesuits will be identified fully the first time their names occur and thereafter only referred to by surname.

and sent a copy to Father Joseph Becker, S.J., then director of the Jesuit Center for Religious Studies at Xavier University. He wrote back saying that he placed my transcript in his archives; if they still exist, it may well be on file.

By his own account, Guindon deceived Arrupe about his motives and interest in Drinan's candidacy, not only concealing his own efforts to launch Drinan but, in his urging Arrupe to pray that Drinan would lose, falsely pretending to be opposed to his election. By presenting himself as an exasperated but cautious administrator who was unsympathetic to Drinan, instead of the partisan that he was in fact, Guindon led Arrupe to think that they had a common interest in the outcome of the affair. By this ruse, Guindon won from Arrupe, if not a green light for Drinan, at least an agreement not to oppose publicly his (first) candidacy. In his account of using Arrupe's general prohibition to refuse permission to then-Father John McLaughlin, S.J.—on canonical and religious grounds the obviously correct decision—Guindon shows both that he understood Arrupe's mind perfectly well and that he exploited the General's leniency for his own ends: using Arrupe's grudging one-time concession in order to advance the career of a like-minded Jesuit, and his ban in order to undercut an uncongenial one.

I should declare up-front that—while I never met the man—my attitude toward Drinan was not neutral. Pro-lifers (of whom I am one) regarded Drinan as one of their most formidable and injurious opponents in the U.S., despite his insistence that he accepted Church teaching on abortion. I've yet to meet a politically aware pro-life Catholic who wasn't baffled and exasperated by the damage Drinan was permitted to do as a priest-congressman and a priest-lawyer. Therefore, presented with firsthand testimony that Drinan was complicit in a ruse from which he launched his career as a pro-abortion legislator, I was fully disposed to challenge his moral authority by making the knowledge public.

I wrote Father Richard Neuhaus, editor of a journal of religion and public life called *First Things*, proposing an article to be titled "*Arrupe ab omni naevo vindicatus.*" The essay was to exonerate Arrupe of the charge that he had acquiesced in Drinan's pro-abortion work. I intended to emphasize the very point volunteered by Guindon, *viz.*, that the Drinan candidacy was stage-managed from the U.S. in such a way that Arrupe was deprived of the information he needed to make a prudent and just decision. A hoped-for collateral effect of the article would be to discredit Drinan by laying out the details of his road to office. Neuhaus was mildly interested and suggested I work on a rough draft, after which he would decide whether or not it was suitable for *First Things*. The project ran up against the obvious difficulty that, apart from Guindon's indiscreet account of the affair, there was no publicly available evidence to suggest that Arrupe was not content to make Father Drinan an exception to his own stated policy against Jesuit political activity.

In the summer of 1992 I got a call from Father Paul Shaughnessy, S.J., at the time a doctoral student in moral theology at the Gregorian University. His dissertation concerned the moralist Father John Ford, S.J., and he was working in the New England Province archives—then at the Campion Center in Weston, Massachusetts— going through those of Ford's papers that were stored there. Shaughnessy told me about the existence of a box of archives dealing with the Drinan candidacy and asked if I wanted to have a look at them. At the same time, he suggested, I might be able to help him with the material in the Ford file (much of which was in Latin) and to help in combing the documents for matter pertinent to his dissertation. The Province archivist, Father John Walsh, S.J., was perfectly aware of who I was and of my activities in the archives; in fact I had to get the key to the archive room from him on two or three different occasions. In working through the Ford papers Shaughnessy and I found numerous cross-references to files in the Drinan Candidacy Archive. In fact, it was Ford who first informed Arrupe that Drinan was planning to run for Congress. This was my entrée into the Drinan candidacy correspondence.

A word on the disposition of the archival material: the boxes containing the Drinan Candidacy Archive were in no sense specially confidential—that is, they were treated as any other material in the archive. The boxes were simply side-by-side with the other materials in the room, unsealed, containing no notice of embargo or need for extraordinary permission for consultation. The files contained no originals of Jesuit correspondence, and the photocopied documents were obviously prepared for normal archival use—confidential or irrelevant paragraphs were blocked out by the persons who assembled the file, so that no internal forum or otherwise morally confidential matter was before the eyes of the researcher. The intended use of the material is obvious from a memo (April 6, 1976) the then-socius Father Joseph Devlin, S.J., sent to the then-provincial Father Richard Cleary, S.J., in which Devlin complains of the size of the Drinan-abortion correspondence and says:

> I'd simply give [the recently arrived letters] to Jimmy Powers to store downstairs (if there is any more room!). Someone, years from now, should have plenty of material for a good book/thesis *re* our two Washington beauts, 1970–75. Both of us could certainly add a few animate versions!

It should be stressed that the Jesuits who assembled the Drinan Candidacy Archive took pains to remove material they felt to be private, and indisputably understood that what remained was intended for normal archival consultation—in fact, that everything in the archive was (in theory) destined to become public sooner or later.

After a first glance at the material, I sought out Walsh and explained to him that I was working on an article on Drinan for *First Things* (he had no reason to know this earlier) and that I had come across relevant material in the province archives. I asked him if I could make photocopies of material from these Drinan candidacy files, and he gave me his permission to do so. Both my request and his consent were entirely routine. I did not ask Walsh's permission to show the material to another Jesuit, or to show it to a non-Jesuit, or to publish the material itself, or to publish an account summarizing the material. I simply asked, and received, permission to make photocopies.

II—What the Files Show

The material in the Drinan files corroborates Guindon's *viva voce* account mentioned above in all its essential points and shows further that had Drinan, Guindon, and Cleary dealt truthfully with Arrupe, the bishops, and the public, Drinan's candidacy would have been impossible. Here follows a summary of the principal facts of the case.

The correspondence shows that Guindon was aware of Drinan's intention to run at least five weeks before his nomination acceptance was announced (February 21, 1970). Arrupe, informed of Drinan's intent by Ford, wrote Guindon on February 9 explicitly excluding the possibility of Drinan's candidacy:

> I am taking the opportunity of this communication to refer to another matter. As you know, many reports come to me from the Provinces, some of them valid and others not so in their specifications. Recently a letter arrived which indicated *Father Drinan* plans to run for the Congress of the States. If my interview with Spanish reporters regarding Jesuit political activity has been incompletely publicized in the American press, I did mention that Ours cannot espouse the action of any political party. Jesuits should explain the doctrine of the Church which in some instances has strong political implications, but we can never be identified with a government or a political party.

The files indicate that Guindon left Boston for the Middle East on February 20, the day before Drinan's candidacy became public knowledge. On February 25, Arrupe sent a telex for Guindon to be relayed via the Jesuit Conference:

> FOR WILLIAM GUINDON. NEWSWIRE REPORTS ROBERT DRINAN ANNOUNCED HIS CANDIDACY FOR PUBLIC OFFICE CONTRARY TO POLICY STATED IN MY LETTER TO YOU. FATHER DRINAN MAY NOT RUN FOR OFFICE AND IF ELECTED MAY NOT SERVE. ARRUPE

Guindon's socius, Father Paul Lucey, S.J., clearly acting on pre-arranged instructions, telexed Arrupe immediately.

> TO FATHER GENERAL. MEMORANDUM EXPLAINING DRINAN CANDIDACY BEING MAILED TO YOU. REQUEST NO STATEMENTS TO PRESS PENDING GUINDON'S VISIT. LUCEY (N.E. PROV.)

Drinan, simultaneously contacted by phone, dictated to Br. Ed Babinski, S.J., a reply to Arrupe's telex that was to be signed and sent by Lucey. A draft version, with Lucey's edits penned in by hand, began with the patently false statement, "Your telex message, received today, with regard to Father Drinan was very surprising and unexpected." Some instructive paragraphs:

After your letter of February 9th to Father Provincial, he did not disclose its contents to Father Drinan. I brought up this matter with Father Guindon prior to his departure for the Middle East on February 20th. At that time, Father Guindon indicated to me that he felt no necessity of acting on what he felt was a mere suggestion in your letter of February 9. . . .

Father Drinan, if he were in effect elected to the Congress, would not be affiliated with any particular political party in any pejorative sense. Clearly, he is not being nominated or endorsed by a political party, but rather by a group of citizens.

I have not disclosed the contents of your telex message of today, February 25, 1970, to anyone. I think that disclosure of its contents would have the most severe consequences on the Society and upon the Church in America.

I feel that the carrying out of the suggestion in your telex message would be a violation of due process for Father Drinan, who has complied in every way with his obligations of obedience and has, in effect, received affirmation from both Father Provincial and from myself to be nominated by this group for the Congress of the United States.

In the final version of the letter, mailed the following day (February 26, 1970), Lucey does not include the statement that he'd explicitly asked Guindon if he planned to disclose Arrupe's prohibition to Drinan. Instead, Lucey makes it understood that he surmised that Guindon did not read Arrupe's remarks as a veto:

Father Drinan informed me that he had not been informed of the contents of your letter of February 9 (70/10) to Father Provincial. I take it that Father Provincial, who is sensitive to the directives of Society legislation, did not interpret your remarks as expressing a legal prohibition.

At the same time that Lucey sent his modified version of Drinan's text to Arrupe, Drinan dispatched a copy to Guindon to await his arrival in Rome, enclosing for Guindon's eyes only handwritten "talking points" for selling his campaign to the General:

I am sure that you are aware of the disastrous consequences which would follow if the General reversed your permission and that of Father Paul Lucey. May I mention a few:

(1) The Catholic and general press has generally praised my candidacy and has not pointed out a single reason against it.

(2) The American Civil Liberties Union is prepared to make a statement that *no* Church-State issue is involved in my candidacy.

(3) At least 3000 persons are now involved in the campaign that has been launched.

In view of the foregoing, an edict from "Rome" forbidding a candidacy would be nationally and internationally practically a "scandal"!

The method by which Father General has intervened is open to the most serious criticism. Without consulting at all he had issued a directive in a way contrary to the mandates of Vatican II and the last General Congregation of the Society.

I feel certain that any attempt by Father General to enforce his incredible directive would impeach his own authority, could bring about a crisis of authority in the American provinces of the Society and would have other seriously adverse consequences.

These four themes

- the *ipso facto* impropriety of Arrupe's intervention,
- the crisis of religious authority resulting therefrom,
- the injustice to Drinan's supporters and contributors,
- and the catastrophic consequences for the status of the U.S. Church,

were to be employed as weapons against Arrupe's reluctance as long as he held office in the Society. Assuming—correctly as it turned out—that Arrupe would honor their request not to make public his prohibition of the candidacy, Guindon and Lucey, often coached by Drinan, systematically proceeded to misinform Father Arrupe, most of all, but also bishops, perplexed laity, and fellow Jesuits about their intentions and the attendant circumstances.

Their project was not without obstacles. A March 12, 1970, letter from Arrupe to Guindon makes clear that they spoke in Rome after Guindon left Beirut ("for the record let me place in writing the conclusions from our conversations"), but that Arrupe was not persuaded to change his mind about Jesuits' running for office:

I feel it is your responsibility, Father, to work out a plan with Father Drinan to withdraw as a candidate for Congress, because it is contrary to the policy of the Society enunciated in the Collection of the Decrees of the General Congregations, N. 239 (Epit. 700 §2), which was supported by my letter of February 9, 1970 (New England 70/10), but never communicated to Father Drinan, and by my telegram of February 25th. Such a candidacy is likewise contrary to Canon 139 §4. Be assured, Father, that I appreciate the delicacy of the situation but the reasons for this candidacy do not outweigh the wisdom and grave need at this time for the policy in the Society.

Guindon was not to reply to this directive from Arrupe until April 10. On April 1, however, he wrote John McLaughlin denying him permission to run for Senate, in a startlingly cynical letter:

> Since your visit here on 17 March 1970, I have taken counsel with the Province Consultors, during the recent Provincial Congregation, regarding your proposal to run for elective office. The great majority of Consultors feel that you should not enter this campaign. Father General has been embarrassed by another Jesuit running for elective office. For me to approve another candidacy would be not only inconsiderate of Father General's position, but disloyal to him as well. In these days of turbulent change, we ought to respond to his views on the appropriateness of campaigning for political positions.

Guindon did not respond to Arrupe's March 12 directive until the following month. In a six-page letter to Arrupe of April 10, 1970, he gave an extensive explanation of his inability to comply, conceding in fact that there was a clash of wills.

> I found myself in a quandary of obedience for the first time in my Jesuit life, having to choose between the Superior's expressed wish and my own conscientious judgment. I felt strongly the obligation to carry out the wishes of Father General and to prevent or relieve his embarrassment over the situation in which Father Drinan's candidacy has placed him. Yet, on the other hand, there was a morally unanimous opinion of all persons whom I contacted that I should not take any action to cause Father Drinan's withdrawal from the race. I must say that, to me, these latter opinions seem the much more convincing to me and much more conducive to the good of the Church and the Society of Jesus, especially in America, at this time. I have concluded that I simply cannot order Father Drinan to abandon pursuit of the office he seeks in the elections next fall.

Guindon further attempted to finesse the delicate problem of the requisite permission of the relevant diocesan bishops:

> Unaware that Canon 139, 4, requires also the approval of the Ordinary of the place until after my return from Rome, I concluded then that implicit approval had, in fact, been achieved since no objections had come from either of the two chanceries (Boston or Worcester) within whose diocesan boundaries Father Drinan's Congressional District lies. In fact, Father Drinan had contacted, unofficially, officials of the Worcester chancery, who told him not to ask for approval explicitly, but commended his entry into the election campaign. Later on, the Boston chancellor came to talk to me, in confidence, about Father Drinan's candidacy; the only question he asked was, "is it true that Father Drinan has run for office, having been forbidden to do so by Father General?" My reply was that I had given approval for his candidacy; this satisfied the chancellor completely.

Later correspondence from the hand of this chancellor gives reason to doubt Guindon's estimate here. More to the point is the suspension of truthfulness Guindon permitted himself, as he goes on to explain:

> To be honest and complete, I added that the fact of my approval did not at all mean that Father General was happy about Father Drinan's candidacy; I felt, however, that no good, and possibly much harm, could come from my explicit statement to the chancellor that you had asked me to ask Father Drinan to withdraw. In any event, you had requested action only by me directly and only indirectly by Father Drinan, to whom I had not given any orders in the matter. Furthermore, his entry into the race was certainly not after he had been forbidden by anyone.

Obviously, the last statement is true only on the understanding that Arrupe's February 9 letter was not a prohibition. More telling is Guindon's admission that "I felt ... that no good, and possibly much harm, could come from my explicit statement to the chancellor that you had asked me to ask Father Drinan to withdraw." Guindon goes on to argue the catastrophic effects of ecclesiastical tampering in terms that, to put it mildly, are surprising in a man that, ten days earlier, squelched another Jesuit's campaign on the grounds that it would be "inconsiderate" to Father General to permit it to continue:

The major argument which motivated me and the consultors against requiring Father Drinan to withdraw from his candidacy on the grounds of religious obedience is the very real danger of scandal. We would do incalculable damage to the Church and to its image as supporter of individual freedom, particularly as a respecter of the proper autonomy of civil and ecclesiastical spheres. An order to withdraw would necessarily be interpreted in this country, at this time, as an international and ecclesiastical interference with local politics. The Church is only beginning to recover from the petty interferences of over-zealous pastors in ward politics in the cities of America, where there is still some of this activity going on; it is also only beginning to recover from the major blunders of Vatican blundering in Italian politics, as seen in the early history of Christian Democracy, which had a direct effect on the growth of Fascism in Italy, and more recently in the pressure tactics affecting the formation of governments in Italy in the time of crisis over the divorce issue. The Church in America, at least, simply cannot afford to interfere in these ancient ways any more.

The fact, or even the allegation, of ecclesiastical interference in American politics would be disastrous, even apart from the consideration of the policies on which Father Drinan bases his campaign; in these policies and issues, one finds another strong argument for the Church's interest in not seeming to oppose his campaign. Father Drinan is campaigning for the elimination of racism from American life, he is against war, and specifically the war in Vietnam, he is for increasing the miniscule contribution America makes from its vast resources, through non-military aid to developing countries. No matter what fine statements might be made concerning alleged reasons for asking Father Drinan to withdraw, the conclusion would inevitably be drawn, and exploited throughout the campaign, that Father Drinan's voice in the campaign was silenced by Church authorities, unwilling to displease persons or groups of racists, militarists, and selfish nationalistic practices and policies. Above all, the Church and the Society must not allow the Church's name to be associated with such opinions, as it would be if Father Drinan were forced to withdraw from his advocacy of their opposites.

Guindon next gives Arrupe the "human background" to the candidacy controversy in terms that suggested misgivings on the part of responsible persons were virtually non-existent:

Literally, no one here whose opinion I value has even hesitated about this issue: not one of the consultors nor one of my staff members could see how I possibly could order Father Drinan to withdraw from the campaign. I have received only a very few letters on this topic, one from an embittered older Jesuit, to whom everything modern seems wrong; the rest, two or three from otherwise unknown lay folk, apparently upset by change.

Both internal and external evidence supports the likelihood that the "embittered older Jesuit" to whom Guindon refers was John Ford. Guindon had earlier sent a letter to Arrupe (March 18, 1970) making Ford out to be an irresponsible obstructionist:

> I find it increasingly annoying and frustrating to have to occupy time and energy in replying to obstructive and reactionary tactics such as Father Ford feels compelled to use. Not merely does this sort of thing distract me from attention to those who need help, and from the real problems of the Province, but these tactics are the very ones which are making some of our most creative members feel that the Society is sick, beyond hope of recovery.

The tactic of undermining Jesuit-initiated criticism by traducing the men who gave voice to it was to be employed by Guindon throughout his official involvement in the controversy. Returning to the April 10 letter: Guindon, having assured Arrupe that "Father Drinan's candidacy has received almost universal approval in Catholic publications, with no opposing reasons being offered or commended," concluded by repeating his resolution to disregard the directive:

> I did not intend to write such a long letter, or even such a bold one, even though I am seriously disturbed at not finding myself able to carry out your explicit wishes in this matter. Neither did I intend to delay so long, leaving you wondering what action—if any—I had taken about Father Drinan's candidacy. For my original approval, made in good faith, for my being unable to carry out your wish, and for being so slow in responding, I ask your pardon. I think it will be seriously wrong for me to press Father Drinan to withdraw from the race; perhaps the voters will, but I cannot.

Whatever the causes of the tardiness of Guindon's response to Arrupe, that delay doubtless worked to his (and Drinan's) advantage, since Drinan's political momentum increased week by week, thereby giving more force to the claim that his supporters and donors would be defrauded if he were compelled to withdraw.

At this point Arrupe made a fateful step from which there was no turning back. On April 18, 1970, with Guindon's April 10 letter to hand, he wrote all the U.S. provincials: "This is a strictly confidential letter to seek your advice on whether Father Robert F. Drinan, S.J., should be permitted to continue to be a candidate for the office of Representative to the U.S. Congress from the State of Massachusetts." Having given Guindon three explicit commands in writing (and at least one face to face) forbidding Drinan's candidacy, his solicitation of advice regarding that command provided Guindon with the opening he needed. As a superior, Arrupe was pinned—and remained so, in spite of his many second thoughts.

Drinan wrote Arrupe on June 26, 1970, assuring him the local ordinaries were enthusiastic in their approval of his candidacy:

Sometime ago I visited personally with the Most Reverend Bernard Flanagan, the Bishop of the Worcester Diocese.... Bishop Flanagan was very receptive and cordial. He volunteered to write a letter to all of the priests of the Diocese indicating his approval of my candidacy. By mutual agreement it was decided between Bishop Flanagan and myself that such a letter be postponed until or unless it seemed to be necessary.

My Provincial, Father William Guindon, S.J., saw the Chancellor of the Archdiocese of Boston several weeks ago just around the time that a private citizens caucus of some 2,000 individuals invited me along with others to be the candidate of this citizens caucus for a seat in the U.S. Congress. I have heard directly from an individual who talked with Richard Cardinal Cushing that the Cardinal declared with enthusiasm that my candidacy was "a great idea."

On July 9, 1970, Arrupe sent Drinan a cautiously written letter which, while short of a grant of permission, accepts Drinan's assurances of episcopal approval and implicitly concedes that he will no longer actively oppose the candidacy:

Your personal conversation with Bishop Flanagan of Worcester and your reported enthusiasm of Cardinal Cushing for the "great idea" of your candidacy, communicated through his Chancellor to the Provincial, happily seem to fulfill the requirement of Canon Law, that the Ordinary of the place, where the election is held, should approve the candidacy of a cleric.

In your knowledge of the international field I am sure that you will understand that in the future the Society through the general will have to weigh relative benefits and clearly evaluate the issues involved and forces operative in a political situation before sanctioning the candidacy of a Jesuit. Modern means of communication can transform a simple, local question into a grave and complex problem for Jesuit life and work in the far distance provinces of the Society.

My prayers shall be joined to yours, Father, that your candidacy may advance the objectives of the Society in promoting the public morality of your country and to some extent of the entire world.

Drinan was elected to his first term in Congress in November of 1970. The rest of the story, until a new pope put an end to it in 1980, involves a series of feeble thrusts and forceful parries in which Drinan invariably emerged the victor. It is a story that, as told by the archives, becomes more complicated after Drinan's first election. Partly this was due to the *Roe v. Wade* decision of January 1973 and the controversy attendant on Drinan's fervid pro-abortion partisanship. Partly it was due to the dispute about whether or not Drinan had the permission of the ordinaries of Boston and Worcester to run for re-election.[2] Reading the archived material, one understands the extreme, almost frantic, desire of interested parties that it not become public. The excerpts from the correspondence that follow provide a highly schematic synopsis of key moves:

Arrupe to Drinan, January 19, 1972:

The Boston area possesses outstanding and qualified Catholic laymen who are well-suited for the position of Congressman in the House of Representatives. Therefore, I do not approve of your becoming a candidate for re-election.

[2] U.S. Congressional Representatives serve two-year terms. After election in November 1970, Drinan was a successful candidate again in 1972, 1974, 1976, and 1978. His candidature in 1980 was terminated by order of Pope John Paul II.

Guindon memo of conversation with Drinan, January 25, 1972:

Father Drinan asked me to keep this information, and the letter of Father General, as private as possible; I told him that I had told only Fathers Lucey and Nolan on the Provincial Staff that I would strive to keep it as private as possible. Furthermore, if I were asked in public I would simply reply "no comment." (N.B. Father Lucey pointed out to me that Father General did not "forbid" Father Drinan from running for reelection, he simply "did not approve" such an action.)

Guindon to Arrupe, January 25, 1972:

I was more than a little unhappy that you sent your letter of 19 January 1972 to Father Drinan, giving me a copy the next day, without having had any consultation with me, or giving me an opportunity to discuss the matter, although I was in the Curia.... There is no, I repeat no, layman, Catholic or otherwise, who has these qualities and, therefore, no one to take his place at this time. There are many prophetic voices in the Church today. You yourself are one. Father Drinan is another.... Therefore, I beg of you—do not become involved at this point. You can do such harm to the Society in the United States, to the American Church, to the New England Province in particular, and to Father Drinan's constituents that it will take a generation for us to recover.

Arrupe to Drinan, February 10, 1972:

I am unable to reconsider my decision denying you permission to run for reelection, until you or Father Provincial send me the approval in writing of both Archbishop Medeiros of Boston and Bishop Flanagan of Worcester, in whose dioceses the election will be held.[3]

Arrupe to Drinan, March 13, 1972:

I am in receipt of a letter, written on March 3, 1972, by Bishop Bernard J. Flanagan of Worcester, concerning your being a candidate

---

[3] Bishop Bernard Flanagan was the Ordinary of the Diocese of Worcester, Massachusetts (which included part of the congressional district in question) until March 1983. Humberto Medeiros succeeded Cardinal Richard Cushing as Archbishop of Boston in September 1970 and served until September 1983.

for re-election to Congress. The Bishop states that he discussed your proposed candidacy with Archbishop Medeiros, and it was the conclusion of both himself and the Archbishop that they were unable in conscience to approve of your being a candidate for Congress.... In the light of this statement, Father, I am unable to reconsider my decision communicated to you on January 19, 1972, not approving of your becoming a candidate for re-election.

Guindon memo of conversation with Drinan, April 3, 1972:

Drinan is firmly convinced that he had all the permissions required for approaching the election campaign, having approval of myself, Cardinal Cushing (implicitly), and Bishop Flanagan (implicitly). There is no provision in canon law for reelection.... At this time apparently Father Drinan feels that we should play it very cool, making no public statements or responses.

Drinan to Arrupe, April 11, 1972:

In view of all of the foregoing circumstances—and particularly after my conversation with your Reverence—it was my understanding that I, like every other Member of Congress, would be automatically a candidate for re-election. There was no reason to think otherwise.... In the recent past, pursuant to your suggestion, I visited with Bishop Flanagan.... Bishop Flanagan stated that, since permission was given for the original election, "re-election is incidental." He stated firmly that the original permission is valid and that it continues "as long as the office continues."

Arrupe to Drinan, May 29, 1972:

In recognition of the statement of Bishop Flanagan, that you may rightfully run for reelection because his original approval endures, and of the uncertainty communicated to me by Archbishop Medeiros on whether Cardinal Cushing's permission remains in force, I shall not require you to submit in writing their explicit approval. I too shall not give a positive approval for your candidacy, but at the same time I shall not prevent your placing your name as a candidate for reelection.

Cleary press release,[4] September 29, 1974:

I further state that in 1970 Father Drinan did receive the permission of his Major Superior, Rev. William G. Guindon, S.J., to run for election. He also received the permission of Father Guindon to seek reelection in 1972, and this permission was ratified in writing by Rev. Pedro Arrupe, S.J., Superior General of the Society of Jesus.

Joseph O'Connor, S.J.,[5] memo to Cleary, February 25, 1975:

Perhaps, if you can get him antecedently to pledge absolute confidentiality on the matter, it might be time to give the Cardinal the present story on Bob Drinan; if he realizes that Bob will leave the Congress at the first moment that he can do so without bringing odium on the hierarchy, I should think it might change his attitude on a lot of things. It is, in short, in my judgment, time to bring this pious sonofabitch into the real world. Who'd have thought your vocation was to midwife the birth of a baby that fat?

Bishop Thomas Daily to Mrs. James Connell, June 17, 1975:

Although Father Drinan claims that His Eminence, Cardinal Cushing gave him permission to campaign, we have no record of that permission in the Chancery office, nor in the records of the Archdiocese. His Eminence, Cardinal Medeiros, has never given permission to Father Drinan, either orally or in writing, to campaign for public office.

Arrupe to Cleary, July 1975:

I must in all honesty say that I still do not see adequate reason for reversing the decision I have made and conveyed to Father Drinan, telling him not to run again for office.

Drinan to Arrupe, September 23, 1975:

I have found nothing in political life which causes me to "compromise" any moral principles. I vote according to my convictions and

---

[4] Cleary succeeded Guindon as New England Provincial in 1974 and served until 1979.
[5] New England Provincial Office staff member.

my conscience,—independently of and indeed not even thinking of any political consequences which might result from a particular vote.... In view of the foregoing, it is my judgment that any involuntary withdrawal on my part at this time cannot be supported by reason, by contemporary Catholic attitudes in America or elsewhere or by anything in recent Jesuit or Church teaching.

Arrupe to Cleary, April 24, 1976:

The best that I can do is to repeat my desire that [Drinan] find a convenient way to withdraw from Congress, but leave the time and manner of that withdrawal up to him, in consultation with yourself. However, I recognize that it is too late now for him to withdraw in 1976.

Gerald Sheahan, S.J.,[6] to Cleary, May 24, 1977:

As I predicted when you and I talked, Fr. Gen's first question was about Drinan. He definitely wants Drinan to terminate with Congress at the end of this term. Please keep me informed on this one.

Arrupe to Edward O'Flaherty, S.J.,[7] February 5, 1980:

I am content to accept your judgment on the basic question of giving Father Drinan more time to extricate himself from Congress, but it is difficult to understand his stance on the question of federal funding of abortions. I am acquainted with the careful distinction he makes between a moral position and public policy. This may resolve his conscience on the issue itself, but how does he resolve his conscience on the deep scandal that his stance causes for large numbers of people and disturbance of the whole American Hierarchy?

III—Stalemate

Having made a copy of most of the relevant material, roughly 350 pages, I resumed work on the interrupted article. In the late summer

---

[6] U.S. Regional Assistant.

[7] O'Flaherty succeeded Cleary as New England Provincial in 1979 and served until 1985.

and early autumn of 1992, I gathered material from contemporary newspaper and magazine accounts of Father Drinan's congressional career, attempted to contact Congressman Robert Dornan (unsuccessfully), and spoke with Congressman Henry Hyde about Father Drinan's presence and influence on the abortion issue. By this time I had a fairly full picture of the story, the central points being that Father Drinan's work to expand abortion rights was anything but reluctant, and that the files prove Father Arrupe demanded Father Drinan's withdrawal at least twelve times over the pertinent period but was successfully outmaneuvered on every occasion.

My own predicament had changed from a deficiency of hard documentary proof to an over-abundance. The new problem was how to tell the truth about the Drinan candidacy without being preempted by those Jesuits complicit in or sympathetic to the subterfuge made plain by the archival material.

For advice on this predicament I consulted several friends, including Chicago Province Jesuits Becker and Paul Quay, as well as Edward Hanify, an attorney and Holy Cross trustee, Prof. Mary Ann Glendon of Harvard Law School, and Prof. James Hitchcock of St. Louis University, to whom I gave a set of the photocopied material. Hitchcock had done considerable research in U.S. chancery archives and knew the protocol that attaches to quotation and so forth. It should be stressed that the contemplated publication was to be my effort and not that of Professor Hitchcock. By this time, however, the original purpose of the article began to seem doubtful. Drinan's effectiveness as a pro-abortion partisan appeared to be on the wane, and although he wrote articles in both the *Boston Globe* and the *National Jesuit News* reiterating his false claim to have had ecclesiastical permission to run for office, my sense was Drinan had done all the damage he could do and that making public his imposture would not materially benefit the situation.

At no stage in this process did I consult my Jesuit superiors. Some of those superiors had pro-abortion sympathies; others, while not pro-abortion, were plainly disinclined to admit the existence of pro-abortion Jesuits wherever the reputation of the Society was thereby imperiled. Added to these factors, and still more problematic, the nature of the case excluded a neutral deliberative ground: the very fact of informing a superior of the existence of material showing the perfidy of Jesuit provincials would shift the moral responsibility onto that superior's shoulders, whatever course was ultimately taken. I believed that, for these superiors, the prospect of confronting their fellows for unseemly malfeasance would be distressing enough to overwhelm the considerations of justice (i.e., justice toward potential victims of abortion, and justice toward those who had been misled by Guindon, Cleary, and Drinan) and that the only foreseeable reaction would be a defensive blackout on the damning evidence combined with a counterattack on my own loyalty as a Jesuit. This surmise was to be shown correct.

IV—The Article Revived

I was wrong, however, in thinking that Drinan was a spent force in terms of harm on the abortion front. On May 31, 1996, Drinan published an article in the *National Catholic Reporter* applauding President Clinton's veto of legislation outlawing partial-birth abortions.[8] On June 4, Drinan published an op-ed in the *New York Times* restating his support for the veto.[9] Drinan put the full prestige of the Society of Jesus behind his opinions ("I write this as a Jesuit priest who agrees with Vatican II," he stated in the *NYT* op-ed, "which said abortion is virtually infanticide") and stressed heavily his former role

[8] Partial-Birth Abortion, also called "intact dilation and evacuation" (IDE) or "dilation and extraction" (D&X) is a procedure whereby a late-term fetus is partially delivered by the abortionist such that the limbs and trunk of the fetus are pulled outside the birth canal and only the head remains inside. The base of the skull is broached by a forceps and the cranial contents removed by suction, causing the death of the child. The legislative debate surrounding the attempt to ban the procedure forced many Americans to confront the moral reality that earlier forms of abortion succeeded in keeping obscure. This explains the overwhelming public opposition to the procedure and the willingness of some moderate Democrats in Congress to vote in favor of the ban.

[9] On November 1 and December 7, 1995, respectively, the U.S. House and Senate approved HR 1833, the "Partial Birth Abortion Ban Act." On April 10, 1996, President William Clinton vetoed the bill. For a presidential veto to be overridden a two-thirds majority of both houses of Congress is necessary. During the period in question (the summer of 1996) in anticipation of the vote to override the veto, interested parties on both sides of the issue conducted campaigns to rally public support, as well as lobbying efforts directed at Congress, concentrating less on the House of Representatives, where the needed majority was secure, than on the Senate, for which it was in doubt.

as a congressman, no doubt having shrewdly gauged the impact this would have on wavering Catholic legislators. Pro-lifers were appalled by Drinan's statements and told one another that here, at long last, Drinan's superiors would issue a counterstatement repudiating his position. Until August 30, 1996,[10] there was no response whatsoever on the part of Jesuit superiors. Clinton's veto was upheld.[11]

I did not—and still today do not—understand why no counter-statement was made, but I realized that whatever rationale Jesuit superiors used to justify a laissez-faire approach to Drinan applied *a fortiori* to my project of making public the real circumstances of Drinan's candidacy. If Drinan was at liberty to justify infanticide, no Jesuit could feel himself constrained in opposing him.

I was, however, prohibited from setting out the projected article under my own name. The previous autumn (October 1995), I had published in *Catholic World Report* an article on the sexual abuse of minors by Catholic clergy that included the controversial proposal that gay priests be dismissed from the clerical state. This essay occasioned a swift response from the then-Chicago Provincial, Father Bradley Schaeffer, S.J., who forbade me unequivocally from publishing any material before the completion of my doctorate: "I do not wish to see your name on any article, essay, book or written text until your doctoral dissertation has been accepted and defended" (October 25, 1995).

In the summer of 1996 this prohibition was still in force (I defended in the Spring of 1997), and publishing the account of the Drinan candidacy would be a direct violation of Schaeffer's order. In order to honor the ban while addressing what I understood to be an urgent obligation in justice, I asked Prof. Hitchcock to summarize the material and publish the article himself, which he did. It appeared in the July 1996

---

[10] On this date Fr. William A. Barry, S.J., issued a press release affirming Drinan's support for Church teaching on abortion and stating that "the legal nuances are often lost in the public arena, and [Drinan's] stance in this case has sincerely offended many good people." He went on to distance himself from Drinan's position: "Since it might appear, by my silence on the issue, that the Society of Jesus supports Fr. Drinan's position, I want to say publicly, as his religious superior, that I disagree with Father Drinan and have told him so. In fact, I wrote to President Clinton in May to protest his veto."

[11] The veto override succeeded (as expected) in the House of Representatives (285–137) on September 16, 1996, but failed in the Senate on September 27 by a vote of 58–40 in favor of the override—i.e., nine votes short of the requisite two-thirds majority.

issue of *Catholic World Report* under the title "The Strange Political Career of Father Drinan." It was almost completely narrative in content, with a bare minimum of analysis and editorial evaluation. I read the proofs of the article prior to publication and made half-a-dozen minor corrections; the text was from Hitchcock's pen entirely. Had I authored the piece myself, there would have been very few differences of emphasis and on the truly controversial points no differences at all. Prefaced to the article, at my insistence, was a note making clear the circumstances of publication: that it was I who made photocopies of materials from the Drinan Candidacy archive and it was I who gave them to James Hitchcock.

V—Initial Reactions

On July 12, 1997, New England Provincial Father William A. Barry, S.J., faxed the following memo (Province Memorandum 96/14) to the houses of his province:

> The July issue of *The Catholic World Report* has an article by James Hitchcock on Bob Drinan's political career which is, apparently, based on material taken from the province archives. Prior to the article, in what seems to be the editor's explanation, it is stated that Father Paul Mankowski of the Chicago province, while a graduate student at Harvard, was given permission by the New England Province archivist to make photocopies of the correspondence and office memos pertinent to the issue of Bob's term in Congress. Fr. Mankowski, it is said, decided not to write the article he was planning with his research. "However, he then sought the opinion of a professional historian, James Hitchcock, in determining how the various documents could be of use for the historical record; he provided Hitchcock with a copy of the correspondence for that purpose." Because of Bob's recent articles defending President Clinton's veto of the "partial-birth abortion bill," it was decided that "the documentation now has a new timeliness." The article itself quotes letters to and from Father Arrupe and three provincials and letters and memos between the provincials and Bob Drinan himself. Interoffice memos are quoted as well.
>
> I am writing to let you know this has happened and to let you know that I am appalled that somehow the correspondence of Fr. General and three living provincials and of a living Jesuit and his major

superiors has been allowed to escape from our offices and to be used in a publication. One thing that we have counted on in our Jesuit life is that we could be honest and open with our Jesuit superiors without the fear that our letters and conversations would become public. I do not know how this outrage was perpetrated. In the article the date 1992 is given as the time when Fr. Mankowski finished his "research." I became provincial in June of 1991. I knew nothing of such a permission and can assure you that I would not have allowed it. John Walsh, our archivist, not only never gave him permission for such research, but has never seen the file(s) supposedly photocopied. He, too, is outraged that such documents could become public. Let it be said that Fr. Mankowski has done the Society a great disservice if he was, indeed, the source of the photocopies used by Professor Hitchcock. I want to assure you that we keep our correspondence secured and do not give permission to Jesuits or anyone else to examine correspondence.

I am writing to you, my brother Jesuits, because I believe that our life is founded on trust in one another and, especially, on trust in our superiors. I am sure that you join me in outrage and sadness that another Jesuit is said to have been the source of this breach of trust.

In this memo Barry omits any mention of the gravamen of Hitchcock's article, focusing exclusively on my own violations of ecclesiastical protocol and confidentiality. Yet Barry's presentation of the protocol issues is inaccurate in several important respects. Contrary to what he claims, Jesuit letters or inter-office memos were not—and deliberately were not—quoted in the article; the sole quotation from archival material is from a document to which we had independent access outside the archive, *viz.*, a 1975 letter from the chancellor of the Archdiocese of Boston to a pro-life laywoman, Mrs. James Connell, with whom both Hitchcock and I were acquainted. Further, Barry implies that I was using the province archives without the consent of the province archivist. The implication is false. The archivist knew perfectly well what I was doing in the archives, to which he more than once gave me the key—as well as explicit permission to make photocopies from the Drinan candidacy file—and this after I told him I was writing an article on Drinan. Most importantly, Barry gives the impression that the material in question was morally confidential, referring to "our correspondence" and "our letters and conversations." He does not distinguish between the closed archive used to store internal forum material and the open archive containing material pertinent to conduct of province business. Nor would readers of his memo have reason to understand that the materials consulted had already been censored by province officials and placed in the non-secret part of the archives precisely in order to be consulted by future researchers. Barry's reference to material "allowed to escape from our offices" and his indignant suggestion that moral secrecy was breached ("one thing that we have counted on in our Jesuit life is that we could be honest and open with our Jesuit superiors without the fear that our letters and conversations would become public") were clearly intended to convey to his fellow Jesuits that I had committed a violation of the internal forum and was deserving of the odium attending such a violation. In this Barry was successful.

It goes without saying that the purpose of internal forum confidentiality is to make it possible, not to lie with impunity, but to tell the truth with impunity. Thus, if a Jesuit had admitted a sin or a shameful weakness to his superior, it would indeed be an abomination to make that fact known. But the misdeed manifested by the archives is not a misdeed *confessed* but a misdeed *perpetrated*—a misdeed in which institutional secrecy was cynically used to maintain false beliefs about Drinan and his candidacy. Guindon lied to Arrupe; he didn't confess a sin to him. By his suggestion that I was in the secret archives rather than the non-secret ones, and by his implying that I had revealed painful truths communicated in secret rather than a lie protected by bureaucratic protocols (a lie whose effects continued to perpetrate a fraud and an injustice), Barry focused the moral indignation of Jesuits onto Mankowski. The awkward and potentially explosive reckoning with the mischief committed by Guindon, Cleary, and Drinan never took place.

Shortly after the transmission of Barry's memo, I was contacted by my own province and asked to explain my actions. I replied in a July 29, 1996, letter to Schaeffer, which gave a summary of the events leading up to publication (in effect, a briefer version of this document), and concluded as follows:

My decision to go public with the imposture is, I believe, vindicated by Fr. Barry's memo issued in response to it, since it indicates the degree of objectivity I could expect to encounter had I channeled my request through his offices. Although I have been resident in the New England Province since June 10th, Fr. Barry has never attempted to make contact with me to clarify the facts of the case or to ask for an account of my motivation. The memo omits any indication of concern for the thrust of Hitchcock's article, focusing entirely on my own breach of trust. As should be obvious, such an approach necessarily negates itself:

> The article (and I) maintain that Fr. Drinan and Fr. Guindon are guilty of perfidy, and that Fr. Cleary was complicit in their perfidy. This is, or ought to be, an extremely serious charge. It is so serious, in fact, that the stance taken by the Society of Jesus toward me and toward Frs. Drinan, Guindon, and Cleary ought to hinge entirely on the truth of the allegations. If my allegations are false, then I am guilty of a grievous libel and have grave responsibility to make amends for the damage done to their reputations. If my allegations are true, then I deserve not censure but congratulation, and the Society owes an apology to all those people, Jesuit and lay, who made objections in good faith to Fr. Drinan's conduct and whose trust was abused. What is not coherent, on any possible understanding of the situation, is to fail to rebut the concrete allegations of perfidy and then accuse the whistle-blower of damaging our foundational "trust in our superiors."

To this letter, Schaeffer replied on August 5, 1996, with a very measured and sympathetic communication in which he acknowledged the earnestness of my motivations but expressed his own "serious concerns" about my decision not to consult any Jesuit superior before letting the article be published, my circumvention of his October 1995 order by triangulating the material through Hitchcock, and the extent to which I might regard, not just the New England provincials, but all government in the Society as "malign and dishonest." After at least one *viva-voce* conversation about the fall-out from the *Catholic World Report* article, Schaeffer sent me another letter dated October 30, 1996, reviewing the situation and concluding with the following directives:

> In order for the Society to judge whether or not you are apt for tertianship and final incorporation, you must take this matter to prayer, rebuild the trust with your superiors and brothers which has been significantly damaged, demonstrate the quality of obedience expected

of Jesuits, and attend fully to the mission assigned you by the Society. Specifically, this is what I want you to do:

(1) Find a spiritual director with whom you will work closely in considering these matters in prayer;

(2) Destroy immediately any materials from the New England archives which are in your possession;

(3) Direct anyone to whom such materials have been transmitted that these are not to be used in any way;

(4) Complete and defend your dissertation in the timely fashion you outlined;

(5) Dedicate yourself fully to the mission assigned you at the Biblicum and to your "professional development" as a Scripture scholar through research, writing, and participation in professional organizations and conferences;

(6) Get the specific approval of your local superior for any ministry beyond your work at the Biblicum;

(7) Get the permission of your rector to publish anything, make any public statement, or take any public action. If he judges any of these to be "controversial," then the Delegate and the Chicago Provincial are to be consulted for their respective permissions in such matters. You are to abide by their judgment.

On the day I received Schaeffer's letter, I made a copy for my local superior, Father Robert O'Toole, S.J., and with it turned over to him all the required materials, with the suggestion that he read them before seeing to their destruction. I have no reason to think he did so.[12]

VI—Aftermath

The disposition set down by Schaeffer has essentially remained the *status quo*. Barry has made no attempt to rectify the impression that I had access to internal forum material and was guilty of betraying it. Since July 1996 I've received no communication, written or otherwise, from the New England Provincial Office, nor had any contact

[12] Although those most embarrassed by the documentation may affect not to see the conflict of interest in the directive given me to "destroy immediately any materials from the New England archives which are in your possession," others can spot the problem—including the non-Jesuits who furnished the correspondence quoted in this memo.

with Guindon, Cleary, or Barry. Roughly three years after the *Catholic World Report* article I had a friendly dinner in Rome with the former archivist Walsh, in the course of which he told me that had he known that I would make the Drinan material public, he would have refused me permission to make photocopies. I have remained under the prohibition from publishing non-academic material (corroborated by the then-Provincial Father Richard Baumann, S.J., in a letter of May 29, 1998, to which a prohibition from giving interviews to reporters was later added by the same provincial).

For his own part, Drinan continued the original bluff, as late as November 2004 making the false claim that he'd had Cardinal Cushing's permission to run for Congress, in addition to the claim that his 1980 resignation was the consequence of restrictions introduced by Pope John Paul II in the revised Code of Canon law—issued in 1983.

Guindon died in October 2006, Drinan in January 2007.

My use of the Drinan archives has surfaced in nearly every conversation I've had with a superior regarding final vows in the Society. Though it has not been stated in so many words, the clear implication is that a statement of remorse on my part is a necessary though not sufficient condition of advancement. I, in turn, made the explicit request of my provincial superiors in June 2001, December 2001, January 2003, and December 2003 that they obtain copies of the Drinan candidacy files from the New England Province in order to acquaint themselves with their contents. In each case this request was ignored or refused. The reason given was that, by awarding myself permission to make sensitive material public, I had violated the bond of trust and co-responsibility between a Jesuit and his superior, whence the content of the files was itself irrelevant.

As a consequence I have been unable to offer a complete explanation of the genesis of the *Catholic World Report* article to my fellow Jesuits and unable to vindicate myself of the discredit attached to me by Barry's July 1996 memo. Every Jesuit understands the reasons, and most, including myself, concede the need for the confidentiality in which the Society's business *ad intra* is conducted— even business that does not involve internal forum material. Truly exceptional circumstances must obtain to justify an exception to the norm. My claim is that truly exceptional circumstances were present in the case at hand and that any fair-minded person who takes the following circumstances into account would agree that they are indeed exceptional:

(a) superiors manipulated and lied to the General of the Society of Jesus in order to help place and keep a Jesuit in political office;

(b) that same General understood the stance of that Jesuit as causing a "deep scandal ... for large numbers of people and disturbance of the whole American Hierarchy";

(c) the stance at issue was the Jesuit officer-holder's repeatedly voting to use tax dollars to pay for elective abortion and his opposition to a constitutional amendment outlawing abortion;

(d) the same Jesuit was again endangering the lives of children by his public support for Clinton's veto of the partial birth abortion ban. At the time I acted it was still possible that innocent human lives could be saved by an override of that veto.

I cannot vindicate my claim that exceptional circumstances justified my action if these facts are excluded from consideration and the content of the candidacy correspondence is deemed irrelevant. The official information loop is a closed one and operates, in this case at least, as a vicious circle.

The whistle-blower chooses to occupy a vulnerable position. His gamble is that, while his actions make him a target of retaliation, persons with a broader concern for rectitude than those impeached by his unwelcome revelations will be perturbed more by the abuses than by their disclosure, more keen to remedy the former than eliminate the latter. He is hopeful that justice will be done in the long run; he is willing to submit to vexations in the interim.

Chronology of the Drinan Candidacy as Reconstructed from Key Archival Documents

Key:

ACV   Andrew C. Varga, S.J., General Assistant (Roman Curia of the Society)

ASC   Anne Stewart Connell, pro-life laywoman

EO'F   Edward O'Flaherty, S.J., Provincial of the New England Province

JJM   John J. McLaughlin, S.J.

JVO'C   James V. O'Connor, S.J., Executive Secretary of the Jesuit Conference

OL   *ordinarius loci* (local bishop)

PA   Pedro Arrupe, S.J., General of the Society of Jesus

PTL   Paul T. Lucey, S.J., Socius of the New England Province

RAM   Robert A. Mitchell, S.J., President of the Jesuit Conference

RFD   Robert F. Drinan, S.J.

RTC   Richard T. Cleary, S.J., Provincial of the New England Province

TVD   Bishop Thomas V. Daily, Chancellor of the Archdiocese of Boston

WG   William G. Guindon, S.J., Provincial of the New England Province

DATE	EVENT	REFERENCE
± Jan 15 1970	Drinan phones Guindon, receives "permission to enter negotiations"	PTL to PA, Feb 26 1970
Feb 9 1970	Arrupe reports rumor of candidacy to Guindon, reminds WG of prohibition of involvement	PA to WG, Feb 9 1970, p. 1 WG to PA, Apr 10 1970, p. 2
Feb 18 1970	Drinan writes Guindon that he will accept nomination on Feb 21 1970	RFD to WG, Feb 18 1970 PTL to PA, Feb 26 1970
Feb 20 1970	Guindon leaves for Middle East	PTL to PA, Feb 26 1970, p. 1
Feb 20–21 1970	Candidacy announced in NYT, Boston papers	PTL to PA, Feb 26 1970, p. 2
Feb 21 1970	Nomination by citizens' caucus announced	PTL to PA, Feb 26 1970, p. 2
Feb 25 1970	Arrupe cables Guindon, forbids candidacy	PA to WG, Feb 25 1970 (telex)
Feb 25 1970	Lucey cables Arrupe, asks no public statement	PTL to PA, Feb 25 1970 (telex)
Feb 25 1970	Drinan dictates Lucey response to Arrupe	note on draft of PTL to PA
Feb 26 1970	Lucey writes Arrupe reasons for ignoring cable	PTL to PA, Feb 26 1970
Mar 9 1970	Guindon returns to Boston	WG to PA, Apr 10 1970, p. 1
Mar 12 1970	Arrupe writes to Guindon repeating prohibition	PA to WG Mar 12 1970
± Mar 24 1970	Guindon discusses PA's mind w/RFD, "did not order him to withdraw"	RFD to WG, Mar 31 1970 WG to PA, Apr 10 1970
Apr 1 1970	Guindon forbids McLaughlin candidacy	WG to JJM, Apr 1 1970

DATE	EVENT	REFERENCE
Apr 10 1970	Guindon writes Arrupe refusing to comply	WG to PA, Apr 10 1970
Apr 18 1970	Arrupe writes Guindon and Ordinaries of Boston and Worcester (content unknown)	WG to PA, April 24 1970
Apr 24 1970	Guindon replies to Arrupe reiterating refusal to comply	WG to PA, Apr 24, 1970
Apr 27 1970	J.V. O'Connor writes Guindon relaying message from PA to Small (US ass't) that no SJ may run for office without explicit approval of PA	JVO'C to WG, Apr 27 1970
May 6 1970	Varga (Gen. Ass't) writes Guindon saying neither OL has given Drinan permission, asks that Canon Law be observed	ACV to WG, May 6 1970
Jun 26 1970	Drinan writes Arrupe that conversations with Flanagan and the Boston Chancellor approve his campaign	RD to PA, June 26 1970
Jul 9 1970	Arrupe writes Drinan that Drinan's assurances of conversations with Flanagan and Boston Chancellor count as approval of OL	PA to RFD, Jul 9 1970
Nov 5 1970	Drinan informs Arrupe of election	RFD to PA, Nov 5 1970
Feb 22 1971	Guindon and Drinan speak *re* PA's conditions: not oppose bishops, not run for re-election	memo of WG, Feb 22 1971
Feb 26 1971	Guindon invites PA to pray in Congress, opposes PA's conditions	WG to PA, Feb 26 1971
May 1 1971	Arrupe and Drinan meet in Cambridge, MA	memo of WG, Jan 25 1972
Jan 9 1972	Cardinal Krol (archbishop of Philadelphia) says on TV that Drinan is acting contrary to the bishops	memo from George Nolan to WG, Jan 8 1972
Jan 19 1972	Arrupe refuses Drinan approval for re-election	PA to RFD, Jan 19 1972

DATE	EVENT	REFERENCE
Jan 25 1972	Guindon phones Drinan, promises to keep Arrupe's decision "as private as possible"	memo of WG, Jan 25 1972
Jan 29 1972	Guindon writes Arrupe, claiming no layman exists qualified to replace Drinan	WG to PA, Jan 29 1972
Feb 10 1972	Arrupe writes Drinan and Guindon denying RFD run without written permission of OLs	PA to RFD, Feb 10 1972 PA to WG, Feb 10 1972
Mar 3 1972	Bishop Flanagan of Worcester writes Arrupe claiming neither he nor Archbishop Medeiros (of Boston) approve candidacy of RFD	PA to RFD, Mar 13 1972
Mar 13 1972	Arrupe writes Drinan citing Flanagan's letter, reiterating his own non-approval	PA to RFD, Mar 13 1972
Apr 1 1972	Arrupe asks Drinan whether he has withdrawn, citing lack of OLs' and his own approval	PA to RFD, Apr 1 1972
Apr 3 1972	Drinan phones Guindon, says "we should play it very cool," making no responses; says Canon Law states nothing about re-election	memo of WG, Apr 3 1972
Apr 11 1972	Drinan writes Arrupe, claiming support for his candidacy from conversations with both OLs	RFD to PA, Apr 11 1972
May 29 1972	Arrupe accepts Drinan's assurances of approval	PA to RFD, May 29 1972
Sep 24 1974	Cleary issues press release saying Arrupe has "ratified" Guindon's permission	NE Prov SJ Release, Sep 24 1974
Nov 9 1974	Arrupe writes Drinan, forbidding him to run again	PA to R. Mitchell, Aug 29 1975 PA to RTC, Apr 24 1976
Jun 17 1975	Bishop Daily (auxiliary of Boston) writes Anne Connell affirming that Archbishop Medeiros never gave permission	TVD to ASC, Jun 17 1975
Jul 24 1975	Arrupe informed Cleary that he has forbidden Drinan to run again	PA to RTC, Jul 24 1975

DATE	EVENT	REFERENCE
Aug 29 1975	Arrupe writes R. Mitchell: "more confirmed than ever" not to let Drinan run	PA to R. Mitchell, Aug 29 1975
Dec 75–Jan 76	Arrupe decides Drinan must "get out or else"	memo of Joe Devlin to RTC, Jan 27 1976
Apr 24 1976	Arrupe admits it is "too late" for Drinan to withdraw from 76 campaign, expresses "desire" that he quit Congress	PA to RTC, Apr 24 1976
Feb 5 1980	Arrupe writes EO'F acceding to giving RFD "more time to extricate himself from Congress"	PA to EO'F, Feb 5 1980
Mar 12 1980	Archbishop Medeiros complains to EO'F that PA "promised him" RFD would not run again	memo of EO'F, Mar 12 1980

October 1976 Letter from the Congressional Liaison
Staffer of the National Committee for a Human Life
Amendment to Bishop Driscoll of Fargo, ND, concerning
Drinan's Congressional Impact on the Abortion Issue

National Committee for a Human Life Amendment, Inc.

October 8, 1976

The Most Reverend Justin A. Driscoll
Bishop of Fargo
Box 1750
Fargo, North Dakota 58102

Dear Bishop:

My apologies for the delay in responding to your request respecting
Congressman Robert Drinan, S.J. and the abortion issue. During July,
August and September, I worked entirely on attempting to help stop
the federal funding of abortions, and consequently am just beginning
to catch up on informational requests. You specifically were interested in Congressman Drinan's position, his votes on key measures,
and his impact on efforts to achieve a Human Life Amendment to the
Constitution and to stop the federal funding of abortions.

Congressman Drinan's position on abortion has changed. In 1967,
he wrote "However convenient, convincing or compelling the arguments in favor of abortion may be, the fact remains that the taking of
life, even though it is unborn, cuts out the very heart of the principle that *no one*'s life, however unwanted and useless, may be terminated in order to promote the health or happiness of another human
being." ("The Inviolability of the Right to be Born," *Abortion and
the Law* 123 (Smith, ed. 1967). In March, 1970, he opposed state laws
to protect unborn children in an article entitled, "The Jurispruden-
tial Options on Abortion," published in *Theological Studies*, 149–696.
His position here is best described and critiqued by Professor David
Granfield in his book, "The Abortion Decision":

"A more drastic attempt to accommodate all points of view is proposed
by Robert Drinan, S.J. He is opposed to abortion. He believes that to
compromise on an American Law Institute type of statute, is to lose the

ideological battle for the right-to-life. He insists, as fundamental, that the state should not be put in the position of determining who shall be born and who shall die before birth. He recommends, however, the removal of all local restrictions on abortion and answers the accusation of inconsistency by appealing to the lack of agreement in this pluralistic society about the morality of abortion. The net result of this rationale is to justify the community, if not the state, in lethal discrimination against one class of underdeveloped people, the unborn. This position is not a compromise, but rather an abdication of local concern for a clearly identifiable group of the unwanted. Despite protestations to the contrary, this accommodation does establish a precedent for state determination of who shall live and who shall die—the simple expedient of removing legal protection for any class that enough of the community feel is expendable. The state itself does not kill; it leaves the decision, however, to the liberal conscience of the citizens of a pluralistic society." (Doubleday & Co., Inc. 1971, p. 191).

Since the January 22, 1973 Supreme Court decisions on abortion, Congressman Drinan has been adamant in his opposition to any constitutional amendment, arguing that the issue should be relitigated through the courts based on the experience of the Black minority. This argument has been effectively criticized by Bill Cox, Director of the NCHLA. The fallacy here is apparent when one considers how far the Black community would have gotten without the Thirteenth and Fourteenth Amendments to the Constitution. The success of the Black community in the courts is directly attributable to the fact that they had strong constitutional support for their position. Also, all efforts to date to relitigate the issue have been fruitless. We have seen the U.S. Supreme Court decisions on abortion broadened and expanded by the federal courts, rather than tightened and restricted. It is true that in two or three generations, a different court might reverse the 1973 decisions; but it may in fact never happen and, if it did, 25 to 50 million lives would have been lost in the interim. The price in life is too high to wait.

Respecting the Congressman's voting record and his impact on efforts to achieve a Human Life Amendment and stop federal funding of abortions, I believe a chronology of events would be the most effective and objective way to respond.

June 21, 1973—Voted in favor of the involvement of Legal Services lawyers as advocates in pro-abortion litigation.

June 22, 1973—Voted against fetal experimentation.

April 25, 1974—Voted for fetal experimentation.

May 29, 1974—Voted in favor of anti-poverty funds being used for medical assistance and supplies in cases of abortion.

June 28, 1974—Voted in favor of federal funding of abortions.

October 8, 1974—Voted against Congress creating a select committee to conduct a full and complete study of the abortion question.

May 9, 1975—Congressman Drinan wrote an article published in *Commonweal* titled "The Bartlett Amendment: Abortions on Medicaid." The article could just as well have been written by the director of the National Abortion Rights Action league. The language and argumentation used is identical to that of the most forceful advocates of abortion on demand. Not once in the article did Congressman Drinan refer to the unborn child or to the God-given right to life; rather, it dealt with such matters as being less expensive to abort than to have to provide medical and financial assistance to a born child. Within eleven days of the Congressman's article appearing in *Commonweal*, it was included in the *Congressional Record* by Congressman John H. Dent (D-Pa.), who asked each member of Congress to read the article. Rep. Dent commented, "Our colleague makes a number of important and telling points in discussing abortion, not only administratively, but constitutionally and morally as well."

June 20, 1975—Congressman Don Edwards, Chairman of the House Judiciary Subcommittee on Civil and Constitutional Rights, who had refused to hold hearings on abortion since the January 22, 1973, Supreme Court decisions, told a pro-life colleague (requested anonymity) that Congressman Drinan had written him a confidential background memo arguing against hearings saying that they were not in the public interest, that pro-life people should work for the court to change its decision, and expressing opposition to a constitutional amendment.

June 23, 1975—A key staff member (requested anonymity) of the House Judiciary Subcommittee on Civil and Constitutional rights told me that Congressman Drinan was "the major opponent of hearings."

June 28, 1975—Congressman Tom Kindness told Father James Bramlage, Pro-Life Coordinator, Diocese of Cincinnati, that Congressman Drinan's opposition to hearings on abortion by the House Judiciary Subcommittee on Civil and Constitutional Rights was a key factor in their not being held to date.

August 1, 1975—Father Edward J. O'Connell, editor of the *St. Louis Review*, wrote "that as a member of the liberal leadership in America, if Drinan would raise his voice in opposition to abortion, it would have a telling effect on calling other liberals to reexamine the abortion question. But his voice has been silent and he has abrogated his responsibility in this area."

September 18, 1975—Senator Birch Bayh, leading opponent of a Human Life Amendment and candidate for President, told a Democratic gathering in Newton, Massachusetts, that he had consulted Congressman Drinan in making his decision on the abortion issue.

October 20, 1975—Mrs. Janet DesChenes, a leading Catholic laywoman in Massachusetts and a member of our Board, said that Catholics in Massachusetts were being confused on abortion because the most prominent Catholic priest in the state did not support legal protection for the unborn. Such confusion, she maintains, obviously hampers expanding the support for a Human Life Amendment.

November 1975—Writing in the *Democratic Review* magazine, Sue Tenebaum, of the Religious Coalition for Abortion Rights' legislative lobby, said she looks for the Jesuit legislator to help block any results in the upcoming hearings on the anti-abortion amendments. She praised Drinan as a "consistent" supporter "of individual decision on abortion as measured by House votes" and a good example "of men who are clearly able to separate personal beliefs from public policy."

December 8, 1975—Congressman Paul Simon, an opponent of a Human Life Amendment, asked Father Jack Quinn, Executive

Secretary, Illinois Catholic Conference, "Isn't Congressman Drinan's position a reasonable one, suggesting that we not pursue the constitutional amendment approach but rather try to have the Courts reconsider it."

December 8, 1975—Congressman Paul Findley, speaking to Father Jack Quinn, Executive Secretary, Illinois Catholic Conference, defended his pro-abortion voting record, saying "it was identical to Congressman Drinan's, whose position, incidentally, I espouse."

December 9, 1975—Congressman Edward Roybal, who opposes a Human Life Amendment, told me that he [held] essentially the same views of those of Congressman Drinan. An aide to Roybal (requested anonymity) told me that informally, just through conversations in the halls, Drinan was really hurting our effort.

January 3, 1976—Ed Doerr, President of Americans United for the Separation of Church and State, in a letter to the Editor to the *Washington Post*, referred to "Rep. Robert Drinan, a Catholic priest and member of Congress" to support his pro-abortion argument.

June 24, 1976—Voted in favor of federal funding of abortions.

July 21, 1976—Congressman Henry Nowak, in a constituent letter, referred to Congressman Drinan to help justify his voting for federal funding of abortions.

August 24, 1976—Father Laurent R. Laplante, Pro-Life Coordinator of the Diocese of Portland, Maine, said he had spoken to Senator Edmund Muskie, who opposes a Human Life Amendment, and Senator Muskie told him that he had discussed this matter with Congressman Drinan and that their positions were practically identical.

August 10, 1976—Voted for federal funding of abortions.

September 16, 1976—Voted against federal funding of abortions. Congressional analysts believe many legislators, who generally support federal funding of abortion, voted for the prohibition in order not to delay passage of the Labor-HEW Appropriations bill any longer.

I trust this information adequately responds to your inquiry.

My very best wishes and personal regards.

Sincerely yours,

Mark J. Gallagher
Congressional Liaison

P.S. Your understanding was correct. Congressman Drinan sponsored H.Con.Res. 268 on May 6, 1975, condemning the killing of
whales. And on October 30, 1975, he co-sponsored H.R. 10438, a
bill to amend the Federal Meat Inspection Act for the purpose of
requiring that meat inspected and approved under such Act be produced only from livestock slaughtered in accordance with humane
methods.

September 1996 Article on Drinan's Partial-Birth Abortion Essays and His Congressional Activity regarding Abortion

Our Sunday Visitor, September 8, 1996, page 9.

Father Robert Drinan under siege: New allegations dog the former congressman on his abortion views, both now and in the past

By Mary Meehan

"Father Drinan, you're dead wrong," thundered Cardinal John O'Connor of New York in his newspaper column. The cardinal was one of many Catholics who attacked Jesuit Father Robert Drinan over his June 4 column in *The New York Times*. The controversy still raged late last month.

In the column, Father Drinan said Congress should uphold President Clinton's veto of the bill banning partial-birth abortions.

The priest, a lawyer and former congressman who teaches at Georgetown University Law Center in Washington, complained that the bill "does not provide an exception for women whose health is at risk."

He also said it "would allow federal power to intrude into the practice of medicine in an unprecedented way."

Father Drinan's column appeared as the U.S. bishops urged Congress to override the Clinton veto.

Cardinal O'Connor, in a June 20 column in his archdiocesan paper, *Catholic New York*, took strong issue with the Jesuit.

"I am deeply sorry, Father Drinan, but you're wrong, dead wrong," Cardinal O'Connor declared, adding: "You could have raised your formidable voice for life; you have raised it for death. Hardly the role of a lawyer. Surely not the role of a priest."

Meanwhile, the Boston archdiocesan paper, *The Pilot*—circulating in the area Father Drinan represented as a Democrat from 1971–1981— also blasted the priest's column. A *Pilot* editorial called it "shocking, schizophrenic and even scandalous," adding that Father Drinan's "moral vision seems to be blind to the right to life."

In response, Father William McLaughlin, a pastor in Hyde Park, Mass., defended the Jesuit against what he called "character assassination." In a subsequent letter to *The Pilot*, he said that Father Drinan "was one of the most conscientious, courageous and honest" persons ever to serve in Congress.

Father Drinan declined an interview request from *Our Sunday Visitor* and did not respond to most of the *Visitor*'s written queries.

Meanwhile, members of the Georgetown Ignatian Society, a group critical of Georgetown University, petitioned Cardinal James Hickey to revoke Father Drinan's priestly faculties—including his authorization to preach and hear confessions—in the Washington archdiocese. In a June 21 letter to the cardinal, they cited a canon law provision calling for punishment of someone who harms public morals, and said Father Drinan had done so.

Auxiliary Bishop William Lori responded that Church officials had asked Father Drinan to publish—in *The New York Times* and "another publication"—a correction of his "indefensible" *Times* column.

The reference to "another publication" may have meant the *National Catholic Reporter*, which on May 31 published a column by Father Drinan supporting the Clinton position on partial-birth abortion. In that column, the priest said other kinds of late-term abortions are "statistically less safe" than partial-birth abortion.

After meeting with one or more staff of the U.S. bishops' pro-life secretariat, however, Father Drinan wrote a letter printed in the Aug. 9 issue of the *Reporter* acknowledging that he had "found reasons to doubt this assertion." But his letter did not withdraw his support of the Clinton veto. Georgetown Ignatian Society president Ann Sheridan described the letter as arrogant and in "absolute defiance" of what he was supposed to do.

But Father Drinan has had a defender in Jesuit Father Leo O'Donovan, president of Georgetown University. According to the Aug. 24 *Washington Times*, Father O'Donovan said his fellow Jesuit "is entitled to his own ideas and has a right to express them ... even when his opinions differ from those of other committed Christians and Catholics."

Father Drinan has been involved in the abortion issue for more than 30 years. In 1968, he warned that abortion, if legalized, might become "the birth control of the poor."

But as a congressman in the 1970s, after the *Roe vs. Wade* decision, he voted regularly for public funding of abortion. He claimed that equal-protection court rulings required public funding in order to avoid discrimination against the poor.

Father Drinan's congressional papers at Boston College show that he had cordial relations with Planned Parenthood and other abortion supporters. He assured them of his opposition to anti-abortion legislation (see enclosure below). Yet at the same time, while writing to opponents of abortion, he stressed his moral opposition to abortion.

Sometimes he urged pro-lifers to try to reverse the *Roe vs. Wade* decision through the courts, instead of pressing for a constitutional amendment against abortion. Writing to a fellow Jesuit on Nov. 13, 1974, he remarked that court reversal was "precisely the route taken during the past several decades by the leaders of the civil-rights movements. After some 50 years, the blacks of America finally got a decree in 1954 that vindicated total equality for that race."

Meanwhile, Drinan was working quietly behind the scenes to squelch pro-life initiatives.

In a Nov. 26, 1974, letter he wrote to a key Planned Parenthood lawyer, Father Drinan referred to a conference committee's decision to drop an anti-abortion amendment to a funding bill: "I can take at least a little credit for that minor victory over the powers of darkness," he wrote.

In the same letter, found in unprocessed material at the Rockefeller Archive Center in North Tarrytown, N.Y., Father Drinan remarked that "the so-called right-to-life movement attracts an extraordinarily large number of arrogant individuals."

He said that some pro-lifers who had met with him "became more than a little abusive, while others in the group made foolish claims about their alleged power at the polls."

Father Drinan's papers at Boston College contain similar comments. In a June 19, 1974, letter to a Harvard Divinity School professor, he said he had recommended the professor's articles to "so-called 'right-to-lifers'" he had met. Drinan added, "At least one of these individuals will in all probability be able to read them."

About two weeks earlier, one of Father Drinan's interns named Dawn had written the priest a memo about a woman who stopped by his congressional office to explain her devastating experience with abortion.

"She wanted you to know her personal history," Dawn wrote in a June 6, 1974, memo, since the woman felt that "Congress could learn from her experience." A handwritten note at the bottom of the memo was signed by "Abbot Robert," which Father Drinan has acknowledged was his nickname.

Addressed to "Dear Mother Dawn," the note said: "I hope that you heard her confession." Referring to the woman's personal history, the note asked, "Any more interesting details?"

But in a June 7 letter to the woman who had the abortion, Father Drinan said he shared her "deep concern" and praised her "activities on behalf of the inviolability of all human life."

A house divided: Drinan vs. Drinan?

IN 1974–75, THE ABORTION ISSUE deeply divided Congress, and Father Robert Drinan, then a Democratic congressman from Massachusetts, sent very different letters to activists on both sides of the issue.

- TO ABORTION SUPPORTERS, on Jan. 28, 1974, Father Drinan wrote: "I agree thoroughly with you that the proposal to amend the U.S. Constitution to forbid abortion is highly undesirable.... I will continue to resist this extraordinarily bad proposal."
- TO ABORTION OPPONENTS, on Jan. 29 1974, he wrote: "I appreciate your letter and thank you for your deep concern for the sanctity and inviolability of all human life, including fetal

life. You can be assured that I share the moral sentiments which you have spelled out in your letter."

- TO ABORTION SUPPORTERS, March 11, 1974: "I am happy to say that only a very few members of the House of Representatives have signed the discharge petition which would bring the matter [an anti-abortion constitutional amendment] to the floor.... It is not very pleasant to have to suggest that ... it appears that a certain small element within the Catholic Church is seeking to impose its views on the rest of the nation."

- TO OPPONENTS, Feb. 28, 1974: "Although the possibility or feasibility of amending the U.S. Constitution to provide against abortion remains in doubt at this time, I know that all of those individuals working for the protection of fetal life deepen within the mind of Americans that reverence which all of us should have for human life."

- TO SUPPORTERS, July 8, 1974: "I am very happy to have your letter and assure you that I have voted the correct way on all the foolish [anti-abortion] proposals made by Congressman Angelo Roncallo and Congressman Harold Froehlich of Wisconsin."

- TO OPPONENTS, June 19, 1974: "I do hope that everything that is feasible can be done to protect the sanctity and inviolability of unborn life."

- TO THE PRESIDENT OF THE PLANNED PARENTHOOD LEAGUE OF MASSACHUSETTS, Aug. 5, 1974: "I feel that hopefully we now have an impetus going in Congress which will never allow such a motion [an anti-abortion amendment] to become the law of the land. I have regularly received excellent information from your organization and will continue to rely upon you and your associates."

- TO OPPONENTS, Sept 11, 1975: "Contrary to what your letter states, I have not assumed a pro-abortion position. It is unfair and unjust for you to make that statement."

—From the Robert F. Drinan Papers,
Legislative Correspondence,
1974 and 1975 (Abortion)